The Modern Ayurvedic

C O O K B O O K ■ ■ ■ ■ ■ ■ ■ ■ ■

The Modern Ayurvedic
COOKBOOK

Healthful, Healing Recipes for Life

Amrita Sondhi

ARSENAL
PULP PRESS

VANCOUVER

THE MODERN AYURVEDIC COOKBOOK
Copyright © 2006 by Amrita Sondhi

Third printing: 2008

ARSENAL PULP PRESS
341 Water Street, Suite 200
Vancouver, BC
Canada V6B 1B8
arsenalpulp.com

The publisher gratefully acknowledges the Government of Canada through the Book Publishing Industry Development Program, and the Government of British Columbia through the Book Publishing Tax Credit Program for its publishing activities.

The author and publisher assert that the information contained in this book is true and complete to the best of their knowledge. All recommendations are made without guarantee on the part of the author and Arsenal Pulp Press. The author and publisher disclaim any liability in connection with the use of this information. For more information, contact the publisher.

TEXT AND COVER DESIGN by Diane Yee, Electra Design Group
CREATIVE DIRECTION by Lisa Eng-Lodge, Electra Design Group
EDITED by Bethanne Grabham and Nicole Marteinsson
COVER PHOTOGRAPHY by Nathalie Dulex, Heidi Priesnitz, and David Zielonka
YOGA PHOTOGRAPHY by Darren Alexander; CLOTHING courtesy of Movement (*movementglobal.com*); MODELS are James Nicholson (Pitta body type); Janet Wallden (Kapha body type), and Sonoka Ehara (Vata body type)

PRINTED AND BOUND IN CHINA

Library and Archives Canada Cataloguing in Publication

Sondhi, Amrita, 1959–
    The modern Ayurvedic cookbook : healthful, healing recipes for life / Amrita Sondhi.
Includes index.

ISBN 1-55152-204-7 (pbk.)

    1. Vegetarian cookery. 2. Medicine, Ayurvedic. I. Title.
TX837.S66 2006   641.5'636   C2006-903961-5

ISBN-13: 978-1-55152-204-3

Table of Contents

Dedication

I dedicate this book to all my invaluable comrades, students, and teachers, the "fringe dwellers" who keep pushing the edge on the "new normal" by practicing and regenerating the ancient healing arts; to those who pursue and create breakthroughs in health by being shining, living examples of vitality; and to the community of yogis and yoginis – locally and globally – who keep connecting to the source and transmitting the light.

Acknowledgments

I would like to thank my parents, family (all of you!), and friends who have always stood by me as I have gone off the beaten path. Joan and Nevenka, thanks for being shining examples of practicing what you preach, and having fun while doing it! Sandra Sammartino, thanks for synthesizing all your yoga knowledge, for being an invaluable teacher who appeared at the perfect time in my life, and for showing me how to transmit from my spirit, connect to the source, reconnect to my body, and how to pass on that learning. I would like to thank all who have hosted or helped me with cooking classes and fundraisers for the Pamoja Foundation. And to the residents of Bowen Island, among others, who constantly encouraged me to write this book and share my knowledge of Ayurveda, and who helped test recipes. Finally, I would like to express my deep gratitude for the wonderful team at Arsenal Pulp Press who worked tirelessly to help make this book a reality.

Introduction

Originating in India more than 5,000 years ago, Ayurveda is the oldest system of healing. The name derives from two root words in Sanskrit (the ancient Indian language): Ayus, which means life, and Veda, which means knowledge or science; therefore in English, Ayurveda is "life knowledge" or "life science."

At the heart of Ayurveda is our intimate connection to the elements in nature, and how they can help us to achieve a physical and spiritual balance in all aspects of our lives. For the sake of our health and well-being, this balance can be accomplished through a number of means, including diet and exercise. The ancient sages of India, who lived in the mountains practicing meditation and yoga, believed that all material forms, including our bodies, are made up of five essential elements – ether, air, fire, water, and earth – in varying degrees, maintaining a balance among these five elements is key to our physical, mental, and spiritual health.

Historically, the ideas and philosophies of Ayurveda were transmitted orally through the Vedas (ancient songs). The oldest song known is the "Rig Veda" ("in praise of knowledge"), which is almost as old as Ayurveda itself, and describes healing herbs and how they can be used. Later, by about 500 BCE, Ayurvedic knowledge began to be written down by the writers Charaka, Sushruta, and Vagbhata, which hastened its popularity. Two hundred years later, Ayurveda thrived with the advent of Buddhism, which was established in India under the rule of Ashoka the Great, and spread to China and Japan. But the Muslim invasion of India in the twelfth century CE led to Ayurveda being widely replaced by the Muslim system of healing, then further suppressed centuries later by the British, who feared the powers of the Ayurvedic doctors who were able to heal (or kill, if need be) in minutes by pressing specific *marma* (acupressure) points. With the return of Indian independence and the leadership of Mahatma Gandhi in the twentieth century, Ayurvedic schools and medical practices finally rose once again.

Today, this ancient and holistic healing science is arguably more popular than ever, and is a source of influences for many medical practitioners both east and west. Ayurvedic schools throughout India teach herbal medicine, massage, surgery, psychiatry, obstetrics, gynecology, astronomy, the use of mantra, meditation, and yoga – among many other healing practices – to improve every aspect of life, balancing body, mind, and spirit. And most importantly, because Ayurveda considers food an integral part of its healing system, it originated some of the oldest and most time-tested principles of nutrition. Indian women cooking in their homes know a lot about Ayurveda and regularly use its principles in their meal preparation both to maintain health and to cure a variety of illnesses, from the common cold to more serious ailments, with appropriate foods that balance the doshas. Currently, these ancient remedies are now being proven scientifically and practiced around the world, most notably by Dr Deepak Chopra, the medical doctor and well-known scholar of Ayurveda.

My journey to Ayurveda started during my mid-thirties, when I burnt out long before most people do. I was designing my clothing line in Europe, manufacturing it in Asia, and wholesaling it across Canada, as well as opening my own retail clothing store in Vancouver. I was on an emotional roller coaster driven by my passions and deadlines – I thought that taking breaks for exercise and making time to cook were self-indulgent – and inevitably, my health began to suffer. Luckily, I met a private trainer, Joan – now a good friend – and began my slow journey back to health. According to Joan's brochure, "A man spends his health to get his wealth and then he spends his wealth to get his health back again." This idea hit home for me. Exercise and healthy eating became an essential part of my daily life. Over time, I became aware of the effects of different activities and nutrients on my body. I started to track my changes according to the various seasons and times of day as well as what I was doing, and what I ate. I learned later that there was a science to it all: Ayurveda.

After my clothing store was robbed, I began practicing yoga to deal with stress, including the breathing exercises (*pranayama*); this transformed my life. Soon I trained to be a yoga teacher myself, and now have been teaching yoga for almost ten years. Yoga continues to have a deep impact on me, showing me that life can be an endless adventure. People who have not seen me for a while are amazed at my transformation, saying I have never looked better. More importantly, I feel better, both inside and out.

Embracing yoga naturally led me to study the Ayurvedic principles of cooking and nutrition. At the same time, this took me back to my Indian roots. Both my maternal and paternal grandparents emigrated from India to Africa in the early part of the twentieth century; I grew up eating delicious Indian cuisine at home, where food was always celebrated. My mother was a great cook who also taught Indian cooking to adults. I took part in her cooking classes by volunteering as the dishwasher, and by observation I learned a lot of the basics of food preparation and techniques I still use today.

Through my growing interest in health, fitness, and yoga, I met a great group of like-minded people who were energetic, fun-loving, and interested in improving themselves. We ate together regularly and talked about the latest trends in health, fitness, and diet. We discussed the positive effects of "super foods" and omega oils; debated over healthy carbohydrates, water consumption, cleanses, and sugars; and shared ideas about macrobiotic and raw food diets, and how to maintain a healthy digestive system.

I learned that to be fit and healthy, one has to cook regularly at home, in order to have more control over what goes into our bodies. Soon cooking became a new hobby for me. Because of this, searching for the finest and freshest (not necessarily the most expensive) ingredients has become one of my favorite activities; it allows me to indulge in daily treks to the local markets, in search of the most pleasing textures, colors, aromas, and flavors for my dishes.

This book is a culmination of my life, showcasing my love of cooking, cultures, health, and the principles of Ayurveda. I have discovered why traditional Ayurvedic recipes and methods of combining food have been around for centuries after watching how my guests feel satiated, peaceful, and joyful after eating.

According to Ayurveda, when we are feeling healthy and balanced, we start to extend that feeling to those around us, allowing us to contribute to our community and planet. After climbing Mount Kilimanjaro, the highest peak in Africa, on the morning of my fortieth birthday, I envisioned and co-founded the Pamoja Foundation (*www.pamoja.org*), which supports grassroots entrepreneurs in Kenya, where I was born.

It was through fundraising for Pamoja that I began organizing and teaching cooking classes to share my knowledge of Ayurveda. The participants always enjoyed the meals, and as a result wanted to know more about Ayurvedic cooking. Their curiosity and encouragement spurred me on to write this book.

Since knowing your own personal constitution, or dosha, is essential for knowing how to keep your life and health balanced, *The Modern Ayurvedic Cookbook* begins with an explanation of what doshas are, and a questionnaire so that readers can determine their own primary dosha. A section on the Six Essential Tastes of Ayurveda follows, which explains how food, specifically taste, affects people's personal constitutions. I then provide basic tips for herbs and spices, and staple recipes for ghee, paneer, and sprouting, which are traditional to Ayurvedic cooking.

Over 200 easy-to-follow vegetarian recipes make up the major portion of this book. (Please note that a few recipes include ingredients such as Worcestershire and oyster sauces, which are not strictly vegetarian.) Each recipe has symbols to indicate how it affects your dosha (see page 27). They also include variations for different doshas. Most recipes use whole grains and fresh foods rather than processed foods, which are considered toxic, or *tamasic*, in Ayurveda. Ayurveda stresses eating fresh foods, so I do not emphasize frozen, canned, or microwavable foods (although I make reference to a few recipes that freeze well if desired).

There also is an extensive appendix at the back of the book to introduce you to eating differently according to each season, various menu plans that emphasize the six tastes to get you started or to plan a party, and a simple twelve-day cleanse to help clear the digestive tract of toxins and improve the absorption rate of the nutrients you consume. And, since living an Ayurvedic lifestyle isn't just about the food, I also have included a section of yoga postures for your dosha, as well as alternative therapies (color and aroma therapy, and breathing and visualization techniques) that will help you to maintain a balanced sense of being in all regards.

Once you have learned the principles of Ayurvedic cooking, you will know how to balance out your unique constitution with food. For example, you will learn how to use spices to either increase your element of fire (Pitta), or decrease it; how to "ground" your element of air (Vata) by using good oils or fats and sweet tastes (which are not necessarily "sugary"; foods such as bread, rice, and cilantro are considered sweet in Ayurveda); and how to activate a lethargic state (Kapha) through increased movement and the consumption of more raw foods. Throughout,

I explain the basics of Indian cooking and how to get started if you have never tried it before. As a result, you will increase your repertoire of tasty, nutritious vegetarian cooking, and at the same time notice an increase in your sense of balance, well being, and energy.

Some of the ingredients used in these recipes may sound exotic, but most can be found at your local grocery store. But I suggest that you be a little adventurous in your shopping and explore ethnic neighborhoods wherever possible – like your city's Little India, Japantown, Chinatown, and Little Italy – for ingredients. Stores in these areas usually carry fresh produce, herbs and spices, whole grains, and a wide variety of beans, lentils, and vegetable protein often not found in conventional supermarkets.

I wish you well on your adventures in the world of Ayurveda! It's changed my life, and it can change yours.

Vata = Air   Pitta = Fire   Kapha = Earth

What are Doshas?

We are all born with three doshas that make up our body constitution. Most of us have a stronger primary dosha, a secondary dosha, and a third less prominent dosha; a few people are naturally balanced in all three. It is through Ayurveda that we try to bring all three doshas into balance. For example, a woman who is a Vata (meaning her primary dosha is Vata) would look to eat foods and engage in activities that are considered to have Kapha and Pitta qualities to bring herself into balance. Since our doshas reflect the elements of air, fire, and earth, it is not surprising that our food and environs affect each of these elements differently. For example, some people enjoy spicy food, while others cannot handle it; similarly, some may thrive in cool weather, and others may detest it. On page 16 there is the Dosha Questionnaire, which will help you to determine your primary and secondary dosha; you will then learn how to prepare meals appropriate for your body type by incorporating foods or ingredients that reduce (–) your primary dosha and increase (+) the other two doshas, thus bringing you into balance.

In general, if you feel out of balance, look for recipes that decrease (–) your primary dosha. For example, if you are a Pitta, look for recipes that have "– ." It is important to familiarize yourself with all three doshas so you can be more attuned to your body. Don't be afraid to experiment to find out what's right for you!

Our Dosha and Our Lifestyles

In our modern world, where we are always on the go and cell phones, laptops, and cars seem to be constant companions, it is easy for us to get a Vata imbalance. In general, if our Vata is over-stimulated, we need to calm it by eating warmer, heavier, moist foods with some "good oils" (see page 22), which include the salty, sour, and sweet tastes. Meditation and rest also helps Vata to cool down and unwind. Every time Vata goes into overdrive and we start to feel stressed, it is important to take a silent five-minute break and do nothing.

If our Pitta is aggravated, we feel fiery, aggressive, and confrontational. At these times, it is important to eat cooling foods like cucumbers (cool as a cucumber!), drink cool (but not cold) drinks, and include lots of raw fruits and vegetables in our meals. Avoid sour, fatty, and spicy foods as well as artificial stimulants. Eat meals in an atmosphere of serenity and order, go for walks in parks or on beaches as much as possible, and avoid strenuous physical exertion or overheating.

When Kapha is out of balance, we feel dull and lifeless, and can't get off the couch. It is important for us to get moving. Regular and varied exercise is extremely important when we have excess Kapha. We also need to reduce butter, oil, and sugar in our diet, increase consumption of foods with the pungent, bitter, and astringent tastes, incorporate stimulating, hot, and spicy ingredients, and avoid cold drinks. To balance Kapha, we should eat light, warm meals, avoid eating to pacify the emotions, and go for brisk walks after eating.

Vata

Element: Air

People born with Vata as their primary dosha are energetic, creative, and natural risk-takers who often initiate projects; however, when Vata is out of balance, they experience nervousness, anxiety, fear, fatigue, and depression. Other physical signs of Vata imbalance include constipation, dryness, flatulence, weight fluctuations, poor circulation, decreased sweating, and feeling easily exhausted.

Those with excess Vata or who have Vata as their primary dosha should concentrate on calming their anxiety and turning their fear into joy and fatigue into energy by following the Ayurvedic principles for reducing Vata.

Pitta

Element: Fire

People born with Pitta as their primary dosha are natural leaders and administrators, capable to take precise, decisive, and focused action; however, when Pitta is out of balance, they experience mood fluctuations, irritability, increased body temperature, restlessness, and impatience. Other physical signs of Pitta imbalance include broken capillaries, weight fluctuation, sweatiness, sleeplessness, and an over-active mind.

Those with excess Pitta or who have Pitta as their primary dosha should focus on turning irritability into focused, positive action, and balancing body temperature and moods, by following the Ayurvedic principles for reducing Pitta.

Kapha

Element: Earth

People born with Kapha as their primary dosha are the pillars of their communities. They have the ability to "follow-through," seeing projects to completion, and are affectionate and good-natured, experiencing the least mood fluctuations of the three doshas; however, when Kapha is out of balance, they experience sluggishness, feelings of being "stuck in a rut," strong attachments, addictions, possessiveness, over-sensitivity, and laziness. Other physical symptoms of Kapha imbalance include excess weight, cellulite, lack of motivation, and puffiness.

Those with excess Kapha or who have Kapha as a primary dosha should turn stagnant energy into activity, find freedom from attachments and addictions, and be creators of their own positive choices, by following the Ayurvedic principles for reducing Kapha.

Dosha Questionnaire

This test will help you determine your primary and secondary doshas. Take no more than 15 minutes to answer all the questions, as your first response that comes to mind is usually the best one. Circle the number that best pertains to you, and don't worry about being perfect. Once you have answered all questions, add up your Vata, Pitta, Kapha scores separately. The highest number is your primary dosha, the second highest will be your secondary dosha. Sometimes people have an equal score in all three doshas, although this is quite rare. Once you know your primary dosha, you will be able to choose foods and activities that keep you in balance and harmony; remember that we each possess a combination of all three doshas to varying degrees, and need to keep them all in balance.

It is a good idea to complete this questionnaire twice, the first time informed by your current lifestyle and environment (Vikruti) and the second by your experiences as a young child (Prakruti). In Ayurveda, knowing the difference between your Prakruti and Vikruti can give you new insight into your body, and how to restore it to optimal health. An important means of doing this is through diet, but remember that our health is also influenced by our lifestyle choices, environment, emotional state, the amount of exercise we do, and the people around us. (It is also beneficial to do this questionnaire every few years as our body constitution naturally changes over time.)

Vata	DOES NOT APPLY		SOMETIMES APPLIES		OFTEN APPLIES	
I perform activities very fast	1	2	3	4	5	6
I learn quickly and forget easily	1	2	3	4	5	6
I am enthusiastic and lively	1	2	3	4	5	6
I have a thin physique and don't gain weight easily	1	2	3	4	5	6
I am light and fast on my feet	1	2	3	4	5	6
I can be indecisive	1	2	3	4	5	6
I get bloated or constipated easily	1	2	3	4	5	6
My hands and feet tend to be cold	1	2	3	4	5	6
I worry and am anxious a lot	1	2	3	4	5	6
I don't like cold weather, food, or drinks	1	2	3	4	5	6
I speak quickly and my friends consider me a chatterbox	1	2	3	4	5	6
I am moody and emotional	1	2	3	4	5	6
I have difficulty falling asleep or I am a light sleeper	1	2	3	4	5	6
I have dry skin	1	2	3	4	5	6
I have an active imagination and my mind is often restless	1	2	3	4	5	6
My energy levels fluctuate	1	2	3	4	5	6
I get excited easily	1	2	3	4	5	6

Pitta	DOES NOT APPLY		SOMETIMES APPLIES		OFTEN APPLIES	
I am efficient	1	2	3	4	5	6
I am precise and orderly	1	2	3	4	5	6
I have a well-balanced body shape and a medium build	1	2	3	4	5	6
I am strong-willed, maybe forceful and am not easily influenced by others	1	2	3	4	5	6
I get tired easily and feel uncomfortable in hot weather	1	2	3	4	5	6
I perspire easily	1	2	3	4	5	6
I am impatient and quick to anger, though I may conceal it	1	2	3	4	5	6
I have a hard time skipping meals	1	2	3	4	5	6
I have a good appetite and can eat large amounts if I want to	1	2	3	4	5	6
I am determined, stubborn, and can be critical	1	2	3	4	5	6
I rarely get constipated	1	2	3	4	5	6
I can be a perfectionist	1	2	3	4	5	6
I prefer cool temperatures to hot	1	2	3	4	5	6
I enjoy cool foods and drinks	1	2	3	4	5	6
Overly spicy foods don't agree with me	1	2	3	4	5	6
I have difficulty with people disagreeing with me	1	2	3	4	5	6
I love good challenges and am focused in my efforts to achieve my goals	1	2	3	4	5	6

Kapha	DOES NOT APPLY		SOMETIMES APPLIES		OFTEN APPLIES	
My actions are slow and deliberate	1	2	3	4	5	6
I gain weight easily and lose it slowly	1	2	3	4	5	6
I am patient and even-tempered	1	2	3	4	5	6
I am not bothered if I skip a meal	1	2	3	4	5	6
I get congested easily and may have sinus problems	1	2	3	4	5	6
I sleep very deeply	1	2	3	4	5	6
I prefer eight or more hours sleep	1	2	3	4	5	6
I am a slow learner but have an excellent long-term memory	1	2	3	4	5	6
I don't get sick often	1	2	3	4	5	6
I don't like humidity or damp weather	1	2	3	4	5	6
I have smooth, soft skin	1	2	3	4	5	6
I have a large, solid body build	1	2	3	4	5	6
I have a slow metabolism	1	2	3	4	5	6
My energy levels are strong and I have good stamina and endurance	1	2	3	4	5	6
I am affectionate, caring, and sweet natured	1	2	3	4	5	6
I eat slowly	1	2	3	4	5	6
I make my decisions methodically	1	2	3	4	5	6

The Six Essential Tastes of Ayurveda

Ayurveda divides food into six tastes that influence the three doshas and thereby influence our overall sense of satiation and well-being. The six tastes are sweet, sour, salty, bitter, pungent, and astringent; each one affects our doshas differently. (Many foods have a combination of two or three tastes, such as oranges, which are considered both sweet and sour.) Ayurveda recommends that all six tastes be included in each meal; when they are, we will be left feeling harmonious, peaceful, and calm, as each dosha has been nourished. Note that only a little of each taste is necessary for it to satisfy and balance us; more is not necessarily better, and in fact, in certain situations it can be detrimental or toxic.

The guidelines offered here will teach you how to harmonize your doshas, and bring yourself back into balance when necessary. Although it is important to have the six tastes at every meal, don't become overly concerned with this, as it should be a goal, not a rule. As you learn to listen to your body, you will start to be attuned to how the various tastes affect you. Remember that as you get to know which tastes are good for your dosha, you may not be eating foods you typically would, but it is those familiar foods that may have been sending your dosha out of balance. Give your body the time it needs to get used to new tastes, and the subsequent feeling of balance that comes from changing your ingrained eating habits.

Here are the tastes that decrease, or pacify, each dosha:
Vata is pacified by sweet, sour, and salty tastes.
Pitta is pacified by sweet, bitter, and astringent tastes.
Kapha is pacified by pungent, bitter, and astringent tastes.

Sweet: Rice, bread, honey, milk, ghee, oils, all meats, and most "sweets" are considered sweet in Ayurveda. Most legumes, lentils, and beans are considered sweet as well as astringent, which increases Vata. An exception is urad dal (split black lentils), which are considered sweet and not astringent, so they calm Vata. Grains and vegetables, which contain carbohydrates, are considered sweet, and increase Kapha while decreasing Pitta and Vata. Foods with the sweet taste are considered heavy and therefore grounding.

Sour: Lemon, vinegar, yogurt, cheese, tomatoes, grapes, plums, and other sour fruits increase Pitta and Kapha and decrease Vata. These foods should be consumed in small amounts and not at all by those with excess Pitta or Kapha. Sour foods promote digestion, are good for the heart, and warm the body. But an excess of these foods can cause irritation, dizziness, or loss of vitality.

Salty: Salt, Kombu (and all other seaweeds), soy sauce, pickles, chutneys, bouillon, and salty condiments increase Kapha and Pitta and decrease Vata. Having at least a little salt in our diets is essential for our health; it also aids digestion. But consumed in excess, salty foods can cause bloating and water retention, or lead to inflammatory conditions. Too little may result in illness, thyroid problems, or leg cramps.

Pungent: Ginger, cumin, black pepper, cinnamon, cayenne, chilies, radishes, onions, and garlic decrease Kapha and increase Pitta and Vata (but a little of these foods are good for Vata due to their warming effect). Pungent tastes heat the body, stimulate digestion, and eliminate excessive fluids, thereby relieving colds and bronchitis. They also help to get our metabolisms moving if we are feeling sluggish. Consumed in excess, they can cause anger and aggression, as well as burning sensations, dizziness, dryness, and increased thirst.

Bitter: Green leafy vegetables (e.g., kale, spinach), bitter gourd, turmeric, fenugreek, lemon and orange rind, dark chocolate, and olives increase Vata and decrease Pitta and Kapha. They cool Pitta when out of balance and too fiery, and lighten Kapha when too heavy. Consumed in excess, bitter can produce envy, jealousy, and yes, bitterness.

Astringent: Beans, lentils, apples, pears, cabbage, broccoli, cauliflower, and potatoes increase Vata and decrease Pitta and Kapha. Consumed in excess, they produce flatulence, constipation, and a dryness of the body.

Getting Started: Tips and Basic Recipes

Basic Herbs and Spices for Ayurvedic Cooking

Herbs and spices are essential in Ayurveda; they stimulate the appetite and increase our ability to digest what we eat, increasing our overall health and well-being. Here is a list of basics herbs and spices you should keep on hand in your cabinet or refrigerator. See the Food Guidelines Chart in the Appendix (page 326) for information on what herbs and spices are appropriate for each dosha.

Dry: Bay leaves; black pepper; cardamom, ground and whole (pods); cayenne pepper; chilies, red; cinnamon sticks and cinnamon bark; cloves, whole; coriander, ground; cumin, ground and whole; curry leaves; fennel seeds; fenugreek; garam masala; mustard seeds, black; mustard seeds, crushed and whole; turmeric

Fresh: Cilantro; chilies, green; garlic; ginger

Fresh is Always Best

Just as freshly ground coffee has more aroma and flavor, the same goes for your ingredients. The fresher the spices, the more flavorful your food will be. I recommend keeping a coffee grinder on hand just for your spices. Whole dry spices can keep in the freezer for up to a year; grind them as you need them just as you would with coffee. Ground spices will keep for 4–6 months in a spice rack. To clean the coffee grinder, grind ½ slice of bread into breadcrumbs, then discard.

 + –

Garam Masala

Garam masala (which means "hot spices") is an Indian blend of dried spices that can be used in the same way as black pepper or other seasonings. It is a warming food which also stimulates digestion and circulation. For seasoning, only a little is needed, e.g., ¼–½ tsp.

Preheat oven to 200°F (95°C).

To break cinnamon sticks, place between a folded dishcloth and crush with a hammer or a rolling pin.

5 cinnamon sticks, broken (see note)	¼ cup black peppercorns
¼ cup cardamom pods with seeds	⅛ cup cloves

Sprinkle ingredients evenly on a baking sheet. Roast for 20–30 minutes, stirring from time to time to ensure they do not brown. Remove from oven and allow the mixture to cool. Break open each cardamom pod by squeezing between thumb and forefinger. Place cardamom seeds in mixture and discard pods. In a coffee grinder (not one usually used for coffee), grind ingredients until they become a fine powder. Store in an airtight container.

Good Oils and Good Fats

Oils are the main source of good, healthy fats in our diets. In general, choose oils that are expeller-pressed, which are those that have been extracted from seeds or nuts through a chemical-free mechanical process; or cold-pressed oils, which are expeller-pressed in a heat-controlled environment of less than 120°F (49°C). Unrefined oils – oils left in their virgin state after pressing – are very rich in nutrients, but when used for cooking, they have a lower smoke point (the temperature at which oil begins to decompose and give off fumes). Always store all types of oils in the refrigerator after they have been opened to extend their shelf life and maintain their nutritional value. Olive oil is the exception; it can be stored at room temperature.

Here are the "good oils" I recommend; use organic versions wherever possible:

• Coconut oil has a good flavor and is full of nutrients that are retained at high temperatures.

• Flax seed oil, like hemp oil, is full of essential omega-3 fatty acids. Use unheated, and add it to shakes, salad dressings, cereals, or toast. Refrigerate after opening and use within 6 weeks.

• Ghee (page 24) is butter that is free of impurities and cholesterol. Use sparingly if you are trying to lose weight. It is very calming to the nervous system. For great flavor and to calm Vata, use a little ghee mixed with olive oil when sautéing. Ghee can be stored at room temperature.

• Grapeseed oil maintains its healthy properties at high temperatures. Use sparingly if you are trying to lose weight.

• Hemp oil, like flax seed oil, is full of the essential omega-3 fatty acids and should be used unheated, such as in shakes and salad dressings. Refrigerate after opening and use within 6 weeks.

• Olive oil is an all-purpose oil as it is readily available, affordable, and cooks well at high heat without losing its nutritional value. Also use in salads, soups, and sauces.

• Sesame oil is another healthy oil. I recommend using only high quality versions that can be purchased at health food stores. Sesame oil is more expensive, but you only need to use a little for wonderful flavor.

"Good fats," an essential part of our diet, can be found in olives, avocados, almonds, walnuts, pistachios, pecans, and other nuts and seeds (including nut and seed butters). The key to health is to consume these good fats and oils in moderation. A diet too low in fat can lead to attention deficit disorder, heart disease, cancer, autoimmune disorders, skin and joint problems, premenstrual problems, and depression and other mood disorders. On the flipside, a diet too high in fat (particularly "bad" fats) can lead to obesity, cancer, and heart disease.

Trans fats are the worst of the "bad fats"; they clog up arteries and impair blood flow, which increases the risk of heart attacks and strokes. Trans fats are most often found in junk food, so it is best to avoid virtually almost all fast, fried, and processed foods, including packaged cookies, candy, crackers, non-dairy creamers, and instant and frozen foods. If you don't have enough time to cook, go to a health food store or local market and pick up something quick and healthy. Always read the package label so you know what you are putting in your body. Avoid trans fats as much as possible; this includes products that have hydrogenated or partially hydrogenated fats such as monoglycerides and diglycerides.

 - -

Ghee

Clarified butter, also known as ghee, is butter with the milk solids removed. Ghee is a digestive aid that improves the absorption of nutrients from food it's used with. It also is known to improve memory, lubricate the connective tissues, and act as a catalytic agent to carry the medicinal properties of herbs to the body. Ghee calms both Pitta and Vata, but should be used sparingly by Kapha and those who have high cholesterol or suffer from obesity, and should not be used when you want to detoxify (i.e. when you are on a cleanse). Ghee doesn't need to be refrigerated as the impurities have been removed.

To make ghee: In a pot on medium heat, melt 1 lb (500 g) unsalted butter completely (watch carefully to ensure it doesn't burn). Bring to a boil and skim off any foam, then reduce heat to low. Stir occasionally for 15–20 minutes. When the whitish curds turn light brown, it is ready. Skim off any additional foam, then pour through a sieve or cheesecloth into a glass container with a tight lid to store. Discard the curds at the bottom of the pan.

 - +

Paneer

Paneer is homemade cheese, similar in taste to Ricotta and cottage cheese, but better for you, as its souring process makes it easier to digest. Paneer is used in various Indian vegetable entrees such as Lata's Green Masala with Paneer (page 188) and appetizers like Aunty Zee's Paneer Samosas (page 64). You can also sauté paneer before adding to vegetable dishes, an easy way to add protein. Paneer is similar to tofu in texture as well as its ability to absorb flavors around it. In fact, you may substitute tofu in all the recipes that call for paneer, although it is worth trying paneer for its wonderful subtle flavor. If you are pressed for time, paneer is usually available packaged in Indian grocery stores, sold in cubes or large blocks.

To make paneer:
8 cups whole milk (see note)
6 tbsp plain yogurt

1 ½ tsp lemon juice, strained through a fine sieve

In a large heavy pot on high heat, bring milk to a boil (watch closely to ensure it does not burn) (see note). As soon as foam begins to rise, remove pot from heat. Add yogurt and lemon juice and mix well. The curds will start to solidify and separate from the liquid whey. Over a bowl, strain the mixture through a piece of cheesecloth, reserving the curds (paneer) in the cheesecloth. Wrap the cloth tightly around the curds, squeezing out the excess liquid.

Place the paneer, still wrapped in the cheesecloth, on a cutting board, and another board or baking sheet on top of it. Weight it down with about 15 lbs (7 kg) of heavy jars or cans and let sit at room temperature for 6–8 hours, until cheese is firm (i.e. consistency of firm tofu). Unwrap and cut into ¾-inch (2-cm) cubes. Cover and refrigerate until ready to use. The cheese can be frozen and used as needed. It will keep for up to 3 months in the freezer.

Makes 6–8 servings.

Sprouting Beans and Lentils

Sprouting beans and lentils increases their digestibility and significantly increases their nutritional value. This process breaks proteins and carbs into easily digestible amino acids, starches, and sugars. Sprouted beans are a rich source of protein, vitamins, and minerals, making them known as a super food. The yogis were said to have existed almost entirely on sprouted beans when they lived in the Himalayas. Here is a basic way to sprout beans and lentils to create a very nourishing and gentle food.

In a large bowl or pot of water, soak 2 cups beans or lentils overnight. In the morning, drain and rinse in a colander. Set colander over bowl or pot to aerate and cover with a clean damp dishcloth. Leave in indirect light. In the evening, rinse again, thoroughly. Once again, drain over bowl or pot and cover with damp dishcloth. Repeat the next morning and evening. By then, they will start to sprout little tails. When tails are about ¼-in (½-cm) long, store in an airtight container and refrigerate for up to 4 days or use immediately.

What the Symbols Mean

Each recipe includes the three dosha symbols:

 = Vata   = Pitta   = Kapha

as well as information on how the specific recipe affects each dosha:

[+] means that the recipe increases the qualities of the dosha and may aggravate you.

[slightly +] means that the recipe slightly increases the qualities of the dosha and may aggravate you if you have this in excess.

[Ø] means that the recipe has a neutral effect on the dosha.

[-] means that the recipe balances or decreases the qualities of the dosha.

Recipes may also include ingredient modifications to help calm specific doshas; e.g., a recipe such as Buckwheat Pancakes (page 33) slightly increases Kapha, but substituting the banana with grated apple will reduce Kapha and thus make the recipe better for those whose primary dosha is Kapha. (For more ideas on modifying recipes to suit your dosha, see the Food Guidelines Chart on page 326.)

 Some recipes have a tridoshic symbol, meaning they are appropriate and calming for all three doshas.

 Finally, some recipes have a vegan symbol (i.e. contain no animal products).

Remember, don't let the recipes intimidate you! Be open to experimenting, listen to your body, and discover how good you'll feel by cooking the Ayurvedic way.

Breakfast

Eating breakfast is important, given that we fast all night; it keeps the blood sugar level balanced. Try to use the best breakfast ingredients you can find (e.g., free range eggs, home-made almond milk, fresh breads right for your body type). I have included both lighter and heavier breakfasts, depending on your mood and appetite.

If you are a Vata, you will probably want to have something grounding and comforting with good carbs, such as Porridge with Stewed Berries (page 37). If you are a Kapha, you may want something like the Indian Omelet (page 50) or the Stove-top Granola (page 36). But Kaphas may not want to eat until mid-morning so make sure you take something healthy with you to eat then, like a fruit salad. If you are a Pitta, you may wake up so intent on your day's goals that you think you can skip breakfast, yet it will be the most important thing you do in your day; at least make a shake (pages 30–31) and take it with you. It is always important to listen to your body's needs. The health and well-being of your body will reflect in your day.

Breakfast Shake with Hemp Protein Powder & greens+™

This is a great way to start the day when you are not in the mood for a full meal, yet need to keep your wits about you. Notice how your energy level picks up after this.

greens+™ is a brand-name powdered whole food supplement rich in vitamins and antioxidants. It is available at health food stores.

½ cup blueberries
½ cup strawberries
½ cup bananas, sliced
 • *To reduce Kapha:
   use more berries instead*
½ cup plain yogurt
 • *To reduce Kapha: use a light version*
 • *To reduce Pitta: substitute another
   ½ cup milk*

½ cup milk
 • *To reduce Kapha: use goat's milk*
2 tbsp hemp oil
1 tbsp greens+™ (see note)
4 tbsp hemp protein powder
2 tsp maple syrup (optional)

In a blender, combine all ingredients and purée. If shake is too thick, add a bit more milk or water and purée again.

Makes 3–4 servings.

Hemp food is said to be the highest source of essential fatty acids in the plant kingdom. Essential fatty acids are responsible for the lustre in your skin, eyes, and hair. They are food for the brain, contribute to clear thinking, lubricate the arteries, and are vital to the immune system. Hemp foods contain no significant trace of THC and do not produce a psychoactive state.

I like Mum's Original hempseed oil and hemp protein powder because of their great taste and because they are 100% certified organic. Raw, uncooked hemp protein is a complete live protein, high in insoluble fiber, and a low-impact carb that the body can easily digest.

- -

Adrian's Breakfast Shake

My friend Adrian is a musician and a health practitioner, and uses this shake to help him wake up and energize his mornings. He keeps ripe bananas in the freezer so they are always available to throw in the blender. This shake is particularly good for Vata and Pitta.

Wolfberries (Goji berries) are available in Asian grocery stores. They are filled with nutrients and have high levels of antioxidants. If kept in a jar, these berries stay fresh for months.

30 wolfberries (see note)
1 cup hot water
2 bananas, sliced
  • *To reduce Kapha: use mixed berries*

3 heaping tbsp pineapple chunks
2 scoops hemp protein powder

In a bowl, soak wolfberries in hot water to soften, about 5 minutes. In a blender or food processor, combine wolfberries and water with all other ingredients. Blend until smooth. If shake is too thick, add more water, ¼ cup at a time.

Makes 2 servings.

  - +

Nevenka's Breakfast Shake

Nevenka, my long-time friend, fitness expert, and devoted holistic food eater, is always finding ways to make food healthier without forgoing taste. The applesauce is a great way to use natural sugars to sweeten this shake.

⅓ cup berries (any kind)
⅓ cup applesauce
⅓ cup plain yogurt
  • *To reduce Kapha: use a light version*

½ cup Almond Milk (see page 272)
  • *To reduce Kapha: use goat's milk*
2 scoops hemp protein powder
1 tbsp hemp oil (see note)

In a blender, combine all ingredients and blend until smooth and serve.

Makes 1–2 servings.

The green color of hemp oil comes from its high chlorophyll content. Chlorophyll is also one of the main ingredients in wheatgrass, one of the most healing foods.

slightly –

+ # Fresh Fruit Salad with

slightly + Yogurt & Flax Seeds

This fruit salad, a delicious and fresh way to start the day, includes essential omega oils to fuel the brain.

2 cups strawberries, sliced
2 cups blueberries
2 bananas, sliced
  • *To reduce Kapha: substitute 2 cups sliced apricots*
2 tbsp flax seeds, ground
  • *To reduce Pitta: use 2 tbsp hemp oil*

2 cups plain yogurt (may use vanilla-flavored yogurt)
Fresh mint leaves (for garnish)
1 strawberry (for garnish)

In a large bowl, combine fruit, flax seeds, and yogurt. Garnish with mint leaves and strawberry.

Makes 4 servings.

slightly

Buckwheat Pancakes

These nourishing and delicious pancakes digest well and make you feel just as good as they taste!

To make this recipe larger, simply multiply the amount of each ingredient by the number of desired servings.

½ cup buckwheat flour
½ tsp baking powder
½ a banana, mashed
  • To reduce Kapha: substitute with ¾ cup grated apple

½ cup soy milk (enough to mix batter)
1 tsp ghee (or coconut oil)
Maple syrup or apple sauce

In a large bowl, combine flour and baking powder and stir. Add banana and soy milk, and beat until mixture has become a smooth liquid. In a frying pan on medium-high heat, melt ghee and spread evenly over surface. Pour batter into rounds, about ⅓ cup of batter for each small pancake. When batter starts to bubble, flip to cook other side until golden brown. Serve with maple syrup or applesauce.

Makes 1 serving.

 ø |

Julia's Weekend Blueberry Pancakes

Julia is my little buddy and my friend Nevenka's ten-year-old daughter. These are great whole-grain pancakes packed with food value. Serve with pure maple syrup; Nevenka says that Quebec maple syrup is her favorite.

1 egg
1 cup brown rice flour
1 tsp baking powder

⅓ cup buttermilk
¾ cup fresh blueberries
1 tsp ghee

In a large bowl, beat egg. Add flour, baking powder, buttermilk, and blueberries and mix until well blended into a batter. In a frying pan on medium heat, melt ghee and spread evenly over surface. Pour batter into rounds, about ⅓ cup of mixture for each small pancake. As soon as they start to bubble, reduce heat, and flip to cook other side until golden brown.

Makes 2–4 servings.

Simply Delicious Crêpes

Breakfast never tasted so good! This is a basic recipe for crêpes; be creative with fillings. Try applesauce, baked bananas, cooked berries, or maple syrup.

½ cup brown rice flour
¼ tsp salt
1 egg

⅓ cup milk
⅓ cup water
1 tsp coconut oil

In a medium bowl, combine flour and salt. In a small bowl, beat egg. Add egg to flour mixture and stir until well mixed. Add milk and water gradually while continuing to mix until smooth. In a small frying pan on medium-high heat, melt coconut oil evenly over pan. Add ¼ cup of batter and tilt frying pan so that it spreads evenly. When crêpe bubbles and its underside is golden brown, flip and brown the other side. Remove and set aside on a plate. Repeat with remaining batter. If needed, melt additional coconut oil.

Makes 2 servings.

slightly +

slightly +

South Indian Dosas

vegan

Dosas are rice flour crêpes that are a South Asian breakfast specialty. They are sour and should be eaten with lentils or other savory fillings like the Delectable Curried Cauliflower with Ginger and Tomatoes (page 194). To reduce Kapha or Pitta, I recommend the Strengthening Tur Dal (page 152), or the Fit for a King Eggplant Bharta (page 189) to reduce Kapha even further. Serve in the traditional manner with Coconut Mint Chutney (page 262).

Making dosas takes practice, so please do not despair if they do not work the first time!

1 ½ cups rice flour
1 cup urad dal flour (see note)
½ tsp salt
¼ tsp fenugreek

2 cups water
6 tsp coconut oil
  (or other good oil, see page 22)

In a medium bowl, combine all ingredients except the oil. You may need to add an additional ¼ cup water to make a semi-thin paste (i.e. crêpe mixture). Refrigerate for at least ½–1½ days. (The longer this mixture soaks, the more tart it becomes.)

In a large frying pan on medium-high heat, melt ½ tsp of the oil evenly over surface. Add ¼ cup of the batter and tilt the pan so that it spreads evenly. Spread another ½ tsp oil at the edges and on top of dosa. When bottom is golden brown, flip and brown the other side. Roll dosa and place on a plate. Repeat with remaining batter.

Makes 6 servings.

Urad dal flour is available at Indian grocery stores and is sometimes called black mung, black lentil, or black gram flour. Urad dal are ¼-inch-long beans with black seed husks and pale yellow kernels, and are available dried, whole, split, and hulled. They are warm and heavy, and very beneficial and nourishing for Vata in small amounts.

+ + # Breakfast Rice

This instant and flavorful breakfast is great for using up extra rice and almonds left over from making almond milk (see pages 272–274). Vata, Kapha, and Pitta may use Basmati rice cooked al dente.

To make a savory version of this recipe, omit honey and ground cardamom and add salt and freshly ground pepper – my favorite.

2 cups organic short grain brown rice, cooked
1 cup plain yogurt

2 tbsp honey or maple syrup
Pinch of ground cardamom
¼ cup crushed almonds

In a medium bowl, combine rice and yogurt and stir. Add honey or maple syrup and cardamom and mix well. Sprinkle with crushed almonds and serve.

Makes 2 servings.

 - -
  # Stove-top Granola

This recipe is delicious and easy to make, as you do not have to turn on the oven. Serve with fresh fruit and non-dairy yogurt, or with applesauce to reduce Kapha.

1 cup rolled oats
⅓ cup walnuts, chopped
⅓ cup sunflower seeds
⅓ cup coconut, shredded
2 cardamom pods, slit at end

2 1-in (5-cm) long cinnamon sticks
⅓ cup raisins
⅓ cup flax seeds, ground
  • *To reduce Pitta: omit*

In a large heavy frying pan on medium-low heat, toast oats and walnuts, stirring constantly for 5 minutes. Add sunflower seeds, coconut, cardamom pods, and cinnamon sticks; continue to stir for another 10 minutes. Remove from heat and cool. Once cooled, remove cardamom pods and cinnamon sticks. Add raisins and flax seeds and mix well.

Makes 4 servings.

-
-
slightly +

Porridge with Stewed Berries

 This porridge is a great way to get both your fruit and grains. It's like eating dessert in the morning! It includes your essential omegas, too.

A non-vegan alternative: use organic low-fat milk intead of soy.

1 cup porridge oats
2 cups water
¼ tsp salt
¾ cup mixed berries, frozen
1 tbsp flax seeds
  • *To reduce Pitta: substitute with hemp oil or omit*

1 tsp Agave nectar
  (or your favorite sweetener)
1 cup soy milk

In a pot on medium heat, combine porridge oats, water, and salt. Bring to a boil then reduce to a simmer. Add berries and cook until done, about 7–10 minutes. Sprinkle with flax seeds, add Agave nectar and milk, and serve.

Makes 1–2 servings.

-
-
slightly +

Sona & Vijay's Breakfast

My brother Vijay and his wife Sona lived in Germany where they created this lighter version of Bavarian muesli, which is usually prepared with heavy cream. Tasty and full of fiber, this recipe is everything you need to start your day. Make it as soon as you get up and by the time you are ready for breakfast, it will be waiting for you.

1 cup 8-grain cereal
2 tbsp bran
1 tbsp flax seeds, ground
  • *To reduce Pitta: omit and add 1 tbsp hemp oil just before serving*

1 tbsp sunflower seeds
1 tbsp walnuts, roughly crushed
2 cups milk
  • *To reduce Kapha: use goat's milk*
½ cup fresh berries

In a medium bowl, combine all ingredients except berries and let sit for 20–30 minutes. Just before serving, add berries.

Makes 1–2 servings.

-
+
- # Breakfast Stir Fry

Do you ever wake up in the morning and not want eggs but still want something savory, energizing, and filling, with some protein to carry you through the day? I felt like that one morning and created this. It hit the spot and now it has become a staple for me.

I recommend using tofu that has been marinated in something tasty – you can buy it this way or flavor your own.

1 tsp olive oil
1 tsp toasted sesame oil
½ cup broccoli florets and stems, chopped
½ cup celery, chopped
¼ cup yellow bell peppers, chopped
¼ cup red bell peppers, chopped
¼ cup cashew nuts
  • To reduce Kapha and Pitta: omit

Dash of Bragg all-purpose seasoning (or other soy sauce)
Dash of your favorite chili sauce
  • To reduce Pitta: omit
Dash of oyster sauce
1 cup medium tofu, cubed (see note)

In a wok or frying pan on medium-high, heat oils. Add all vegetables and cashew nuts, and sauté for a few minutes. Add dashes of all three sauces. Cover with lid to let veggies steam for about 2 minutes. Add tofu and stir to mix well. Cook for another minute. Serve immediately.

Makes 2 servings.

Tofu Scramble

 This is a wonderful substitute for scrambled eggs; the tofu absorbs all the flavors, so it's very tasty. If possible, use frozen, leftover tofu as it easily crumbles. I like to serve this with a glass of almond milk for extra protein and natural oils.

1 tsp ghee
1 tbsp onions, chopped (optional)
1 tbsp fresh cilantro leaves, chopped
  (or fresh parsley)
¼ cup tomatoes, diced
¼ tsp fresh green chilies, minced

¼ tsp turmeric
Salt to taste
2 cups medium tofu, frozen, thawed
  and crumbled
1 tsp water

In a medium frying pan on medium heat, melt ghee. Add all ingredients except tofu and water and sauté for 2 minutes. Add tofu and water and sauté for another 2–3 minutes, until most liquid has been absorbed.

Makes 2–4 servings.

-
-
-

Tofu Veggie Breakfast Wrap

 A great egg-free vegetarian breakfast that can be easily packed to eat on the go.

1 tbsp extra-virgin olive oil
½ onion, sliced finely lengthwise
¾ cup red bell peppers, sliced finely
   lengthwise
½ cup broccoli florets and stems,
   chopped
⅓ cup tofu, cubed or crumbled
Salt and freshly ground pepper to taste

¼ tsp turmeric
Chili sauce to taste
   • *To reduce Pitta: omit*
2 tortillas
4 slices mozzarella cheese
   • *To reduce Kapha: omit*
¼ cup fresh cilantro leaves, chopped

In a large frying pan on medium-high, heat the oil. Add onions, peppers, and broccoli and sauté for 2 minutes, stirring frequently. Cover with lid and reduce heat to medium-low allowing veggies to cook in their own steam for 2–3 minutes. Add tofu, salt, pepper, and chili sauce and sauté on medium heat for another 2 minutes until tofu has absorbed most of the liquid. Remove pan from heat.

Set oven to broil. On a baking sheet, arrange the tortillas. Place two mozzarella slices down the center of each tortilla. Melt cheese on tortillas under the broiler. As soon as cheese is melted, remove tortillas from oven and set each on a plate. Place ½ tofu filling down the center of each tortilla, leaving at least 1½ in (4 cm) at the bottom empty. Sprinkle cilantro on top of filling. Fold bottom up to form an envelope base and roll tortilla sides up.

Makes 2 servings.

-
+
+

Breakfast Pasta

If you love pasta, this is a good way to get your breakfast grains and protein. It's also great for a midnight snack.

Pasta:
2 cups pasta spirals (whole wheat or
    brown rice pasta)
1 tsp salt

Sauce:
1 tbsp ghee or butter
½ cup onion, chopped
½ cup mushrooms, sliced
1 tsp Italian seasoning (dried or fresh)
Dash of hot sauce or chilies
  • *To reduce Pitta: omit*
Dash of Worcestershire sauce
Salt and freshly ground pepper to taste

Custard:
2 eggs
  • *To reduce Pitta and Kapha:*
    use 1 egg and 2 egg whites
½ cup milk
¼ cup vegetable stock
¼ cup Parmesan cheese, grated
  (for garnish)

Bring a large pot of water to a boil, then add pasta and salt. Cook according to package directions until pasta is al dente (do not overcook or you will increase the sugar content). While pasta is cooking, in a large frying pan on medium, heat ghee or butter. Add onions and mushrooms and sauté until mushrooms are soft, 4–5 minutes. Stir in Italian seasoning, chilies, Worcestershire sauce, salt, and pepper. In a medium bowl, beat eggs, milk, and vegetable stock until well mixed and set aside. When pasta is done, drain and add to frying pan, stirring until well mixed. Reduce heat to medium-low and pour in egg mixture, stirring constantly to ensure eggs are still saucy and not scrambled, about 3–4 minutes. Stir in Parmesan cheese and more freshly ground pepper, then serve.

Makes 2–4 servings.

-
+
ø # Sweet French Toast

 A sweet yet filling breakfast, and the strawberries and mint make it a special treat.

5 eggs
  • *To reduce Pitta and Kapha: use 2 eggs
    and 5 egg whites*
Pinch of salt
1 tbsp water
4 slices bread, your choice
  • *To reduce Kapha: use rye
    or millet bread*

4 tsp ghee (or good oil, see page 22)
8 fresh strawberries, quartered
4 tbsp maple syrup
Sprigs of fresh mint (for garnish)

In a large bowl, combine eggs, salt, and water and beat until frothy. Dip a slice of bread in the bowl, letting it soak up ¼ of the egg mixture, covering evenly. In a frying pan on medium-high heat, melt 1 tsp of ghee. Fry bread until lightly brown on each side, 1–2 minutes. Repeat until all 4 slices are done. Serve with strawberries and honey or maple syrup. Garnish with mint.

Makes 2–4 servings.

-
+
+ # Savory French Toast

This is a family favorite.

5 eggs
- *To reduce Pitta and Kapha: use 3 eggs and 4 egg whites*

Salt and freshly ground pepper to taste

1 tbsp water

Dash of Worcestershire sauce

4 slices bread, your choice
- *To reduce Kapha: use rye or millet*

4 tsp ghee (or good oil, see page 22)

In a large bowl, combine eggs, salt, pepper, water, and Worcestershire sauce and beat until frothy. Place a slice of bread in the bowl, letting it soak up ¼ of the egg mixture, covering evenly. In a frying pan on medium-high heat, melt 1 tsp of ghee. Fry bread until lightly brown on each side, 1–2 minutes. Repeat until all 4 slices are done. Serve with extra Worcestershire sauce to taste.

Makes 2–4 servings.

-
+

slightly + # Tomato Swiss Emmentaler Scramble

Emmentaler cheese makes this egg recipe egg-tra special.

Use cherry tomatoes when they are in season as they are packed with flavor.

8 eggs
- *To reduce Pitta and Kapha: use 4 eggs and 8 egg whites*

1 tbsp oil

½ cup onions, minced

1 tsp fresh green chilies, or to taste
- *To reduce Pitta: omit*

½ cup tomatoes, diced (see note)

1 tbsp fresh cilantro leaves

Salt and freshly ground pepper to taste

½ cup Swiss Emmentaler cheese, grated
- *To reduce Pitta and Kapha: omit*

1 tbsp fresh cilantro leaves (for garnish)

In a medium bowl, beat eggs and set aside. In a large frying pan on medium-high, heat oil. Sauté onions and green chilies for 1 minute. Add tomatoes and 1 tbsp cilantro and sauté until onions begin to caramelize and tomatoes soften. Reduce heat to medium and pour in egg mixture. Using a spatula, keep folding mixture so eggs are cooked through, about 1–2 minutes. Add cheese, remove from heat, and mix cheese through until it melts. Garnish with cilantro and serve.

Makes 4–6 servings.

Tomato, Mint & Parmesan Scramble

The mint adds a refreshing and cooling note to this dish.

4 eggs
  • *To reduce Pitta and Kapha:*
    use 2 eggs and 4 egg whites
1 tsp olive oil
¼ cup onions, minced
½ cup tomatoes, diced

½ cup zucchini, diced
Salt and freshly ground pepper to taste
¼ cup mint, dried or fresh
¼ cup Parmesan cheese, grated
  • *To reduce Kapha: omit*

In a medium bowl, beat eggs and set aside. In a frying pan on medium high, heat oil. Add all vegetables, salt, pepper, and mint, and sauté for 3–4 minutes, until onions have softened. Add eggs and sauté until eggs are cooked through, about 1 minute. Sprinkle with Parmesan and serve immediately.

Makes 2–4 servings.

Cumin Scrambled Eggs

The cumin adds a delicate flavor to these eggs. This is also great for a light supper.

Since ancient times, cumin has been used medicinally to stimulate digestion and calm the stomach.

4 eggs
  • *To reduce Kapha and Pitta:*
    use 2 eggs and 4 egg whites
2 tsp water

2 tsp oil (or 1 tsp butter or ghee
  and 1 tsp olive oil)
½ tsp whole cumin seeds
¼ tsp turmeric
½ tsp salt (or to taste)

In a medium bowl, combine eggs and water and beat, then set aside. In a frying pan on medium-high, heat oil. Add cumin seeds and sizzle for 30 seconds. Add eggs while stirring constantly. Stir in turmeric and salt and cook for an additional 1–2 minutes, until eggs are no longer runny. Serve immediately.

Makes 2–4 servings.

–
 slightly +

 ø

Eggs with Turmeric & Parsley

Another tasty, nutritious way to eat your eggs. The ghee calms Vata while the turmeric acts as a natural antibiotic and blood cleanser. The cayenne speeds up the metabolism, which is excellent for reducing Kapha. Parsley is cooling for Pitta and an excellent source of iron.

When making this recipe, make sure to watch your heat settings. Reduce heat if it gets too hot as this dish can easily burn.

4 eggs
  • *To reduce Pitta and Kapha: use 2 eggs and 4 egg whites*
1 tbsp water
1 tbsp ghee (or good oil, see page 22)
¼ cup onions, minced

½ cup tomatoes, chopped
2 tbsp fresh parsley, chopped
¼ tsp turmeric
Salt and freshly ground pepper to taste
Pinch of cayenne pepepr
  • *To reduce Pitta: omit*

In a bowl, combine eggs and water and beat, then set aside. In a frying pan on medium-high, heat ghee. Stir in onions and sauté for 1 minute; add tomatoes and sauté for another minute. Stir in parsley and sauté for another 30 seconds, mixing well. Pour in eggs and add turmeric, salt, pepper, and cayenne. Gently lift eggs when the bottom sets so eggs are cooked through. Cook for an additional 2 minutes until eggs no longer runny. Serve immediately.

Makes 2–4 servings.

-
+
+ # Immi's Scrambled Eggs

My cousin Immi is presently studying at the University of St Andrews in Scotland. He claims that this recipe cures hangovers, and that it has been tried and tested on college students. He says the chilies are the key. (This makes sense in Ayurveda, as the Pitta-increasing chilies help to reduce the Kapha state.) He recommends two eggs per person.

You can use your favorite cheese in this recipe.

4 eggs
2 tsp tomato purée
Salt and freshly ground pepper to taste
1–2 tsp red chili flakes
2 tbsp milk

½ circle Boursin full fat cheese, garlic and herb flavor, crumbled (see note)
2 tbsp ghee (or butter)

In a large bowl, beat eggs. Add all other ingredients except ghee, and whisk with a fork until well mixed. Set aside. In a frying pan on medium heat, melt ghee evenly over the pan. Pour in egg mixture, constantly stirring and folding until the eggs are cooked through. (Immi recommends that you leave these eggs slightly soft and runny.) Serve immediately.

Makes 2 servings.

Spicy Scrambled Eggs

Very tasty; beware, these could get addictive.

Turmeric is a natural antibiotic and blood cleanser. Cumin aids the digestion, ginger warms the body, cilantro pacifies all the doshas, and chilies add kick to your metabolism.

6 eggs
  • *To reduce Kapha and Pitta: use 3 eggs and 6 egg whites*
3 tbsp milk or water
½ tsp salt
¼ tsp freshly ground pepper
1 tbsp oil
1 tbsp onions, minced

1 tsp fresh ginger, minced
2 tbsp fresh cilantro leaves, chopped
¼ tsp turmeric
1½ tsp fresh green chilies, minced
  • *To reduce Pitta: omit*
½ tsp ground cumin

In a medium bowl, beat eggs. Add milk, salt, and pepper and whisk with a fork until well mixed. Set aside. In a frying pan on medium-high, heat oil. Add onions and ginger and sauté for 1 minute. Add cilantro, turmeric, green chilies, and cumin. Mix well. Reduce heat to low and pour in egg mixture. Cook for 3–4 minutes, until eggs are cooked through. Serve immediately.

Makes 3–4 servings.

     Variation: Substitute 5 cups tofu for the eggs and use water instead of milk.

-
+
ø # Indian Omelet

An Indian breakfast favorite on weekends. Save leftovers to cut into triangles for snacks or a late lunch. Serve with chapatis or your favorite toast, and a pickle.

6 eggs
  - *To reduce Pitta and Kapha: use 3 eggs and 6 egg whites*

2 tbsp water

Salt and freshly ground pepper to taste

1 tbsp ghee (or good oil, see page 22)
  - *To reduce Kapha: use a light oil*

½ cup red onions, chopped

2 tsp fresh green chilies
  - *To reduce Pitta: use ½ tsp*

½ cup fresh cilantro leaves, chopped (or 4 tsp green chutney, see page 259 or 260)

In a large bowl, combine eggs and water and beat until frothy. Add salt and pepper to taste. In a large frying pan on medium-high, melt ghee evenly over pan. Add onions, chilies, and cilantro and sauté until onions are softened. Pour in egg mixture, spreading evenly over the frying pan. Reduce heat to medium. Lift eggs gently with a spatula to ensure that eggs are cooked through. Cover with a lid and gently steam for a minute or two, checking to make sure it does not burn. If bottom is done and top is still runny, place frying pan under the broiler for a few minutes (make sure you are using an ovenproof frying pan).

Makes 3–4 servings.

+

+

- # Mexican Brunch

I love this for weekend brunches as it's packed with taste and fiber. You can make it richer by adding Soothing Guacamole (page 54), but not if you want to reduce Kapha. To reduce Vata, omit the beans; and to reduce Pitta, use a mild salsa.

1 cup refried beans
  (use canned, if desired)
  • *To reduce Vata: omit*
4 tsp ghee or butter (or good oil,
  see page 22)
4 eggs

4 corn tortillas
½ cup salsa
4 heaping tbsp plain yogurt
4 tsp fresh cilantro leaves, chopped
  (or parsley) (for garnish)

Preheat oven to 300°F (150°C).

In a small pot on low, heat refried beans. In a large frying pan on medium heat, melt ghee evenly over pan. Add eggs one at a time and fry sunnyside up or over easy. While eggs are cooking, heat corn tortillas under broiler for 2 minutes, then place on individual serving plates. Spread each one with ¼ of the refried beans. Top each with an egg, followed with a dollop of salsa and a tablespoon of yogurt. Garnish with cilantro and serve.

Makes 4 servings.

Appetizers & Snacks

Two key principles of an Ayurvedic diet are a) eat balanced meals, and b) avoid snacking. Snacks, however, are a great way to avoid blood sugar highs and lows, which can tamper with our metabolisms and make us feel exhausted. In this chapter I have included some tasty, nutrient-filled snacks that will stop you from reaching for that next cup of coffee or donut in a desperate attempt to get through the day. Many are portable, like the Vegatable Samosas (page 62) or the Endvo Savory Squares (page 68). The Spiced Pecans (page 76) and Spiced Almonds (page 77) are easy to keep on hand for those sudden low-energy moments. There are also a number of fabulous and healthy appetizers that are great openings to any meal.

–

slightly +

+ # Soothing Guacamole

 This is a quick, delicious, and nutritious appetizer or snack, filled with the essential fatty acids and protein of the avocado. It is a calming dish that reduces Vata. The garlic adds a nice punch to the recipe. Serve this dip with baked tortilla chips or veggie sticks.

Avocados are a cholesterol-free food. For every 1 oz (30 g) of avocado, there are 5 g of fat, but it is monounsaturated, often called the "good fat." Avocados are rich in B vitamins, folic acid, and antioxidants that aid our bodies in the elimination of "free radicals," or disease-causing toxins known as ama in Ayurveda.

¼ tsp fresh green chilies, or to taste
  • *To reduce Pitta: omit*
1 clove garlic
  • *To reduce Pitta: omit*
2 tbsp fresh cilantro leaves

½ cup tomatoes, chopped
  • *To reduce Pitta: omit*
1 cup avocado, chopped
  (see note)
Juice of ½ a lemon or lime
Salt to taste

In a blender or food processor, combine chilies, garlic, and cilantro and blend until finely chopped. Add tomatoes, avocado, lemon or lime juice, and salt and blend until the mixture is quite smooth, but still has some chunks of tomato.

Makes 1 ½ cups.

Don't rinse out the delectable remainders in your blender; instead, use them to make this Yogurt Guacamole Lassi. Once you have transferred your guacamole to a bowl, add 1 tbsp plain yogurt and 8 oz water to the blender or food processor and blend again. Pour in a glass and enjoy!

Black Bean Dip
with Sun-dried Tomatoes

I love the taste of sun-dried tomatoes, but they can increase Kapha if they are stored in oil. If your body feels heavy and you want to reduce Kapha, use sun-dried tomatoes that are sold dry and reconstitute them in hot water. If you want to calm Vata, use the tomatoes in oil. Serve this dip with baked tortilla chips, crackers, pita bread, or veggies.

If you soak the beans for a few hours beforehand, the cooking time and amount of water you need will be reduced. See Cooking Beans on page 137 for more information.

1 tsp salt
1 cup black beans, dried (see note)
1 tbsp balsamic vinegar

¼ cup sun-dried tomatoes in oil (see note above)
Chili sauce to taste (optional)

In a medium pot of water on high heat, bring salt and beans to a boil, then reduce heat to low and simmer until beans are cooked, approximately 2 hours. Check occasionally, as you may need to add some more water. Drain beans and then, in a blender or food processor, combine beans, vinegar, sun-dried tomatoes, and chili sauce and purée until smooth. Add a little water if dip is too thick.

Makes 1 ¼ cups.

+

-

slightly + # Four-Layer Bean Dip

My friend Kathy often makes this for potluck dinners where it is always a hit. Serve with tortilla chips, pita bread, or your favorite crackers.

2 cups avocados, mashed
1 tbsp lemon juice
½ tsp salt
¼ tsp freshly ground pepper
1 cup sour cream
  • *To reduce Kapha: use a light version*
½ cup mayonnaise
½ cup green onions, chopped
  (about 1 bunch)

2 cups tomatoes, chopped
  • *To reduce Pitta: omit*
½ cup black olives, pitted and chopped
2 cups cheddar cheese, grated
  • *To reduce Pitta and Kapha:*
    use Mozzarella
1½ cups refried beans
  (use canned, if desired)

In a bowl, combine avocados, lemon juice, salt, and pepper and mix well, then set aside. In another bowl, combine sour cream and mayonnaise and mix well, then set aside. In a third bowl, combine green onions, tomatoes, olives, and cheese. Stir together, then set aside. In a 9-inch pie pan, spread beans evenly over the bottom. Then spread avocado mixture over beans, and follow with sour cream mixture, and cheese mixture.

Makes 8 cups.

+

slightly +

- # Indian-Style Hummus

 Adding a few spices creates an Indian variation on traditional hummus. To reduce Kapha, serve with veggies and baked tortilla chips.

To make your own ground cumin from whole cumin seeds, lightly toast them for a few minutes in a dry skillet before grinding them in a coffee grinder (not one regularly used for coffee beans).

3 cloves garlic
  • *To reduce Pitta: only use 2 cloves*
¼ green Serrano chili pepper, or more to taste
  (or your choice of chili sauce)
  • *To reduce Pitta: omit*
1 tbsp fresh cilantro leaves
2 cups chickpeas (garbanzo beans), cooked or canned (see Cooking Beans, page 137)

2 tbsp tahini
Juice of 1 lemon
1 tbsp olive oil
¼ tsp ground cumin (see note)
1 tsp salt, or to taste

In a blender or food processor, pulse garlic until chopped. Add the green chili and cilantro and pulse. Add all remaining ingredients and blend until smooth.

Makes 2 cups.

slightly +

slightly +

+ # Eggplant Dip

The secret to this recipe is ensuring that the eggplant is well cooked before you mash and blend it with the other ingredients. It is hard to believe how simple and delicious this dish is!

To reduce Kapha and Vata, add ½ tsp green chutney (page 259 or 260); to reduce Pitta, add 1 tbsp freshly chopped mint leaves.

2 large eggplants
1 tbsp olive oil
  • *To reduce Vata: add extra tbsp oil*
1 clove garlic

4 tbsp lemon juice
¾ tsp salt, or to taste
1 tbsp tahini

Set oven to broil.

Rub both eggplants with olive oil until they are shiny. With a fork, pierce holes all over eggplants. Broil for at least 40 minutes, turning each once, until eggplants are soft and wrinkled. Remove from oven and let cool. Peel off skin and discard. In a medium bowl, mash eggplant flesh until it is pulpy. In a blender or food processor, pulse garlic until minced. Add eggplant and all remaining ingredients, pulsing until smooth.

Makes 6 servings.

slightly +

+ # Sun-dried Tomatoes & Pine Nut Cream Cheese Dip

Serve as a dip for veggies or as a spread for your favorite whole grain crackers. It also makes a great addition to sandwiches or wraps. For variety, try substituting fresh dill for mint leaves.

Non-vegetarians can omit the pine nuts and add 1 cup cooked tuna or salmon.

Persian or Middle Eastern grocery stores usually carry the freshest mint and nuts, as these are staples in their dishes.

¼ cup onions, roughly chopped
¼ cup fresh mint leaves
2 tbsp sun-dried tomatoes in oil
 • *To reduce Kapha: use dry and reconstitute in hot water*

Salt to taste
1 cup cream cheese
 • *To reduce Kapha: use a light version*
¼ cup pine nuts, toasted (see notes)

In a blender or food processor, mince onions. Add mint leaves and pulse until leaves are finely chopped. Add sun-dried tomatoes, salt, and cream cheese and blend until smooth. Add pine nuts and pulse until just mixed.

Makes 1 ½ cups.

Toasting pine nuts really brings out their flavor. While they are toasting, watch them carefully as they will not take more than a few minutes to brown. Here are 2 different methods for toasting:

In the oven: Set oven to broil. Spread one single layer of nuts over a baking sheet. Toast until golden brown.

In a frying pan: In a dry frying pan on medium heat, place a single layer of nuts and toast until golden brown, stirring constantly.

-
-
slightly +

Spinach Dip

This dip is a delectable way to get some of your daily intake of greens. I've always loved spinach dip, but I find many versions are too heavy. Serve with baked tortilla chips or fresh veggies, especially to reduce Kapha.

Spinach – which is healing for the lungs and liver – is good for all doshas. It also helps to reduce Kapha.

1 bunch spinach, roughly chopped (about 5 cups) (see note)
2 cloves garlic
2 tbsp green onions, chopped (about 2 stalks)
½ fresh green chili, or to taste
  • *To reduce Pitta: omit*
¼ cup fresh parsley

¼ cup fresh cilantro leaves
1 tbsp lemon juice
Salt and freshly ground pepper to taste
2 cups light sour cream
  • *To reduce Vata: use a full-fat version*
¼ cup light mayonnaise
  • *To reduce Vata: use a full-fat version*

In a medium pot of water on high heat, bring to a boil and add spinach. Cover with lid and blanch for 2–3 minutes, until spinach is wilted. Drain and set aside.

In a blender or food processor, pulse garlic, green onions, and chili until minced. Add parsley and cilantro and pulse for a few seconds. Add spinach, then pulse again. Add all remaining ingredients and blend until just mixed.

Makes 2½ cups.

slightly +

slightly +

- # Baked Pakoras (Bhajias)

Pakoras, also known as bhajias, are tasty vegetable bites coated in a gram flour batter. Traditionally they are deep-fried, but this is a baked version that can be eaten guilt-free. Pakoras are an Indian favorite often served at tea time or as an appetizer with drinks.

I think pakoras are best served with Taramind Chutney, but they can also be served with a variety of condiments including hot chili sauce, Coconut Mint Chutney (page 262), or green chutney (page 259 or 260). See page 257 for more on condiments.

Gram flour, made from ground chickpeas, is also known as chana, besan, or chickpea flour. It is often used in Indian cuisine.

1½ cups gram flour (see note)
¾ tsp ground cumin
½ tsp fresh ginger, grated or minced
½ tsp garlic, crushed or minced
1 tsp fresh green chilies, minced
1 tsp salt, or to taste
1 cup plain yogurt

1 bunch spinach, chopped
(about 4–5 cups)
½ tsp baking powder
Olive oil spray
½ cup Tamarind Chutney (page 261)
(see note)

Preheat oven to 350°F (180°C).

In a large bowl, combine flour, cumin, ginger, garlic, chilies, salt, and yogurt and beat with a wooden spoon until well mixed. Stir in spinach and baking powder. Pour mixture into a lightly-oiled 9-inch loaf pan. Cover with foil and bake for about 70 minutes. Test with a toothpick; if it comes out clean, it's done. Cut into slices, lightly cover with olive oil spray, and place on a baking sheet. Increase oven heat to broil and place in oven for 4 minutes, flipping once, until slightly crisp and brown. (Watch carefully to ensure they do not burn.)

Makes 10 servings (2 per person).

Vegetable Samosas

Samosas are tasty with tea or as an appetizer served with Tamarind and/or Cilantro Mint Chutneys (page 261 and 259) and lemon wedges. It is customary to squeeze the lemon into the samosa with each bite. My friend Nevenka eats the samosa filling on its own for an easy, tasty snack. The filling is fairly spicy, so those with sensitive palates may want to increase the vegetables by adding another ½ cup each of peas, carrots, and potatoes.

To make this recipe tridoshic, omit onions, cayenne, and fresh green chilies.

Curry leaves are available in Indian grocery stores.

Non-vegetarians can substitute beef for the potatoes and adjust seasoning to taste.

Filling:
1 ½ tbsp olive oil
2 tsp black mustard seeds
1 cup onions, chopped
  • *To reduce Pitta: reduce to ½ cup or omit*
½ tsp turmeric
8 curry leaves (optional) (see note)
3 cups potatoes, parboiled and cubed
1 ½ cups peas, parboiled
1 ½ cups carrots, parboiled
Juice of ½ a lemon
½ tsp cayenne pepper
  • *To reduce Pitta: omit*

½ tsp garam masala
2 tsp salt
¼ cup fresh cilantro leaves (packed), finely chopped
½ fresh green chili, minced
  • *To reduce Pitta: omit*

Paste:
1 tbsp flour
1 tbsp water

1 pkg samosa pastry (see note)
Olive oil spray

You can buy ready-made samosa pastries in Indian grocery stores. If you prefer, you can use your favorite pastry recipe instead of the pre-made samosa pastries. Roll out the dough until it is $^1/_8$ th-in thick. Cut into 6-in (10-cm) wide circles. Place your filling in the center and fold over, pinching edges. Baste with egg whites, and bake until golden brown on all sides.

For filling:

In a large saucepan on high, heat oil, then add black mustard seeds and cover with lid until they pop, about 30 seconds. Stir in onions, then reduce heat to medium-high, and sauté for about 4 minutes, until onions start to brown. Add turmeric and curry leaves, and continue to sauté for 1 minute. Stir in potatoes, peas, carrots, lemon juice, cayenne, garam masala, and salt. Mix well and cook for about 3 minutes. Turn off heat, add cilantro and green chilies, and mix well. Let cool completely. Remove curry leaves.

For paste:

In a small bowl, combine flour and water and mix well. Set aside.

For samosas:

Preheat oven to 350°F (180°C).

Follow package directions for defrosting samosa pastry. Use 1 tbsp of filling per samosa wrapper and follow package directions for folding. Use paste to seal edges (make sure they are well sealed). Place samosas on a baking sheet and lightly cover with olive oil spray. Bake for 30 minutes, or until they start to brown (watch carefully to ensure they do not burn). Flip over, spray with olive oil, and bake for another 20–30 minutes until brown.

Makes 6–8 servings (2 per person).

Frozen food is usually frowned upon in Ayurveda, but these samosas freeze really well for up to 10 days without losing their flavor. They are easy to defrost by re-heating them in the oven for about 10 minutes at 350°F (180°C), or for 1 minute (2 samosas at a time) in the microwave on high.

−

 +

 −

Aunty Zee's Paneer Samosas

My Aunty Zarina likes to make these samosas really hot and spicy! But if you're not used to chilies, use only 1 or 2 instead of 4. Chilies add lots of flavor and are scrumptious with the lime juice, mint, cilantro, and ginger. I sometimes substitute the paneer (Indian cottage cheese) with extra-firm tofu to create a protein-filled snack. These are best served with Tamarind Chutney (page 261).

This recipe can be made tridoshic if you eliminate green chilies and cashews and use 14 oz (400 g) of extra-firm tofu or paneer made from goat's milk.

Filling:
5 cups paneer, grated (see page 24)
1 bunch fresh cilantro leaves, chopped (about 3 cups)
1 bunch fresh mint leaves, chopped (about 3 cups)
10 green onions, sliced, white parts only
¼ cup cashew nuts, chopped
4 fresh green chilies, minced, or to taste
   • To reduce Pitta: use 2 or omit

1 tsp fresh ginger, minced
Juice of 1 lime
1 tsp salt, or to taste
Freshly ground pepper to taste

Paste:
¼ cup flour
2 tbsp water

1 pkg samosa pastry (see note)
Olive oil spray

You can buy ready-made samosa pastries in Indian grocery stores. If you prefer, you can use your favorite pastry recipe instead of the pre-made samosa pastries. Roll out the dough until it is $\frac{1}{8}$th-in thick. Cut into 6-in (10-cm) wide circles. Place your filling in the center and fold over, pinching edges. Baste with egg whites, and bake until golden brown on all sides.

For filling:

Grate paneer onto a large platter so that it remains loose and doesn't become one sticky ball. Set aside. In a medium bowl, combine all other filling ingredients and mix well. Add paneer and mix lightly with fingers; continue to keep the paneer from clumping together. Set aside.

For paste:

In a small bowl, combine water and flour and mix well. Set aside.

For samosas:

Preheat oven to 300°F (150°C).

Follow package directions for defrosting samosa pastry. Use 1 tbsp of filling per samosa wrapper and follow package directions for folding. Use paste to seal edges (make sure they are well sealed). Place samosas on a baking sheet and lightly cover with olive oil spray. Bake for 30 minutes, or until they start to brown (watch carefully to ensure they do not burn). Flip over, spray with olive oil, and bake for another 20–30 minutes until brown.

Makes 6–7 servings (2 per person).

+

slightly +

- # Stuffed Mushroom Caps

I have been serving this recipe as a warm appetizer for years. These mushrooms are simple to make and pleasing to the palate.

12 large mushrooms
1 tsp ghee (or butter)
1 tsp olive oil
2 dry red chilies
  • *To reduce Pitta: omit*

¼ cup onions, minced
2 cloves garlic, minced
⅓ cup fresh parsley, minced
¼ cup Parmesan cheese, grated

Preheat oven to 350°F (180°C).

Remove stems from mushrooms and lay mushroom caps on a baking sheet, tops down. Finely chop stems and set aside. In a frying pan on medium-high, heat the ghee and oil. Add dry red chilies and sauté for about 1 minute, until chilies begin to blacken. Add onions and garlic and sauté for 1 minute. Add mushroom stems and sauté for an additional 2 minutes. Cover with lid and continue to cook for another 3 minutes. Add parsley and cook for another 2 minutes, uncovered. Remove pan from heat. Stuff mushroom caps evenly with the cooked mixture and discard chilies. Sprinkle each stuffed mushroom cap with Parmesan cheese and bake for 10 minutes until cheese has melted and starts to brown.

Makes 6 servings (2 per person).

+

slightly −

− # Khandvi Rolls

My friend Renu, who lives in Mombasa, Kenya, offered me this special treat while I was visiting her. It is a great afternoon pick-me-up and gets Kapha moving. Try it instead of a donut!

3 tbsp plain yogurt
1 cup water
1 cup gram flour
Salt to taste
¼ tsp turmeric
½ tsp cayenne pepper (or paprika)
3 tbsp lemon juice
2 cups water (for boiling)
3 tbsp olive oil

½ tsp black mustard seeds
½ tsp cumin seeds
1 tbsp sesame seeds
2 tbsp fresh green chilies,
  finely chopped (for garnish)
  • *To reduce Pitta: use only 1 chili or omit*
¼ cup fresh cilantro leaves, chopped
  (for garnish)

In a bowl, whisk together yogurt and 1 cup water until smooth. In a separate bowl, combine flour, salt, turmeric, cayenne pepper and lemon juice. Add yogurt mixture to this bowl and mix until smooth.

In a large pot on high heat, bring 2 cups water to a boil. Reduce heat to medium to simmer and add gram flour mixture. Stir frequently to ensure it does not stick to the bottom of the pan. Cook until mixture becomes a thick sauce. Remove from heat and spread onto a greased baking sheet (do this while the mixture is very hot). Leave to cool and dry out, about 15 minutes. Once cooled, cut into 3-in (4½-cm) wide strips and roll lengthwise. Cut the rolls into 1-in (2 ½-cm) wide pieces and place on serving platter.

In a small pot on medium-high, heat oil. Add mustard seeds and cover with lid until they pop, about 30 seconds. Add cumin seeds and heat for about 10 seconds, then add sesame seeds. With a spoon, sprinkle seeds over rolls. Garnish with chopped green chilies and cilantro.

Makes 8–12 rolls.

Endvo Savory Squares

My mother makes these regularly and they never last long! I love this dish as it is filled not only with protein but lots of veggies, and it's easy to take to work or on a picnic.

If the dish browns before the suggested baking time, cover with a sheet of foil or greaseproof paper for remaining time.

Vagar is a group of spices sautéed together to bring out their flavors. It is often used in Indian cooking to spice up various dishes.

Vegetable mixture:
2 cups cream of wheat
¾ cups gram flour
1½ tsp salt
Chili powder to taste
¼ tsp turmeric
2 tsp fresh ginger, grated
½ tsp fresh green chilies, finely chopped (optional)
 • *To reduce Pitta: omit*
2 tsp ground cumin
3½ cups cabbage, grated
2 cups carrots, grated (can use frozen packets of carrot and pea mix)
2 tsp curry leaves, chopped
1 tbsp lemon juice

Vagar: (see note)
½ tsp mustard seeds
1 tsp cumin seeds
2 tsp sesame seeds
2 tsp curry leaves, chopped
3 dry red chilies

2 cups buttermilk
1 cup water
¼ cup olive oil
2 tsp baking powder
1 tbsp sesame seeds

Preheat oven to 400°F (200°C).

Lightly oil an oblong 12-in (30-cm) cake pan and set aside. In a large bowl, combine all vegetable mixture ingredients and stir. Stir in buttermilk and water and mix until it has consistency of a loose batter (add more water if necessary). Set aside. In a small bowl, combine all vagar ingredients except dry red chilies and mix well. Set aside.

In a small frying pan on medium-high, heat oil. Add dry red chilies and sauté until they are almost black, then add rest of the vagar ingredients from bowl. As the seeds start to pop, add to vegetable mixture. Mix well, then add baking powder and mix well again. Pour into the greased baking dish. Sprinkle sesame seeds evenly over top of mixture. Bake for 20 minutes, then reduce temperature to 350°F (180°C) and bake for another 50 minutes, or until golden brown. Test with a toothpick; if it comes out clean, it's done. Cut into squares and serve.

Makes 16–24 squares.

slightly +

slightly +

- # Potato Tikis

These potato tikis are another all-time favorite of mine. They are easy to make for impromptu guests or as a quick snack. Serve with Tamarind Chutney (page 261) or a green chutney (see note), and lemon wedges.

You can use either of the two green chutneys as a condiment with this recipe (see page 259 and 260).

3 cups potatoes, cooked, well drained, and mashed
1 tsp olive oil
4 tbsp lemon juice (about 1 lemon)
¼ cup onions, minced
1 tsp fresh green chilies, finely chopped, or to taste
  • *To reduce Pitta: omit*

2 tbsp fresh cilantro leaves, chopped, or to taste
1 tsp salt, or to taste
2 eggs
1 cup breadcrumbs

Olive oil spray

Preheat oven to 300°F (150°C).

In a large bowl, combine all ingredients except eggs and breadcrumbs and mix well. Form dough into 12–14 balls (2 in/5 cm in diameter) with hands and then flatten into 1-in/2½-cm thick patties and set aside.

In a medium bowl, beat eggs and set aside. In a separate bowl, place breadcrumbs.

Lightly cover baking sheet with olive oil spray. Dip each patty in egg batter, then coat in breadcrumbs. Place patties on sheet and lightly cover with olive oil spray. Bake for 5 minutes, then turn patties over and bake for 5 additional minutes, or until browned.

Makes 6–8 servings.

-
-
slightly +

Savory Dokra Squares

Someone discovered this fast and easy way to make an age-old Indian snack. I like to avoid the microwave as much as possible, but with this recipe it is hard to resist. Serve with Tomato Chutney (page 258), green chutney (page 259 or 260), or chili sauce.

You may add a chopped green chili to batter, or sprinkle a little cayenne pepper on top once in baking dish to add flavor and color. Pitta should omit.

1 cup cream of wheat
Salt to taste
1 tsp canola oil (can add 2 tsp to make it moister and reduce Vata)
¼ tsp turmeric
½ tsp whole cumin seeds, crushed
1–2 tbsp fresh cilantro leaves, chopped

1½ tsp lemon juice
1 cup plain yogurt
¼ cup water
1 heaping tsp Eno Fruit Salt (see note)

In a large bowl, combine all ingredients except Eno and mix well. Pour batter into a shallow microwavable dish. Quickly stir in the Eno, which will start to activate immediately. Cut through batter with a knife or fork (as if baking pastry), immediately cover tightly with plastic wrap, and place in microwave on high for 8 minutes. Allow to sit for at least 4 minutes after cooking, then cut into diamond-shaped squares.

Makes 12–16 squares.

Eno Fruit Salt is made up of bicarbonate soda, tartaric acid, and Rochelle salt. It was invented by Jonathan Eno, a London chemist, and was a remedy for upset stomachs. It can be found in the pharmacy section of your grocery store.

Bhel Puris

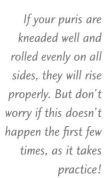

Puris are deep-fried pastry chips that are served either with a meal or as an appetizer. They also appear as part of the Bhel Indian Tea Time Snack (page 73) and Puris & Chat (page 74). Kaphas should eat in moderation, no more than four per meal.

If your puris are kneaded well and rolled evenly on all sides, they will rise properly. But don't worry if this doesn't happen the first few times, as it takes practice!

⅔ cup rice flour
⅔ cup spelt flour
1 tsp salt

3–9 tbsp cold water
Vegetable oil (for deep frying)

In a medium bowl, combine both flours and salt. Add 3 tbsp water and knead until dough can be gathered into a ball. If the dough is not yet sticky, add more water 1 tbsp at a time, until it is able to form a ball; be careful not to add more water than is needed. Knead dough for about 5 minutes until it is smooth and elastic. (This can be done in the food processor in 1 or 2 minutes with a pastry blade.) Again, gather dough into a ball, cover it with a sheet of wax paper, and let it sit for at least 30 minutes before rolling it out.

On a lightly floured surface with a rolling pin, roll dough into a paper-thin sheet. Cut into 2-in (5-cm) rounds with a cookie cutter or the rim of a glass. Transfer rounds onto a lightly floured clean, flat surface. Lay a damp tea towel over them to keep them from drying out. Gather leftover dough into a ball and roll out again, repeating the process until there is no more dough left.

In a deep frying pan or wok, heat 2–3 inches of oil until a drop of dough comes instantly to the surface. Deep-fry 8–10 puris at a time for 1–2 minutes, turning over frequently until they are golden brown on both sides. Remove with a slotted spoon onto a plate lined with paper towels.

Makes 75–80 puris.

slightly +

Bhel Indian Tea Time Snack

 Bhel is a favorite "street food" in India and a special treat for guests. It looks festive and colorful when ingredients are served in individual bowls for guests to combine themselves on puris, much like tacos. Half the fun is putting them together to suit your personal taste.

Another way to serve this snack is to add all ingredients except lime wedges and chutneys to a large bowl, toss, and serve with lime wedges and chutney on the side so guests can add their own.

3 cups puffed rice
  (may use cereal instead)
1 onion, chopped
  • *To reduce Pitta: omit*
2 tomatoes, diced
  • *To reduce Pitta: omit*
2 cups potatoes, boiled and diced
  • *To reduce Vata: use only a small amount or omit*
3 tbsp fresh cilantro leaves, chopped
½ cup fine sev (see note)
2 cups mung bean sprouts, parboiled
  (see Sprouting, page 25)

¼ cup almonds, crushed
  • *To reduce Kapha: omit*
1 lime, sliced into wedges
4 tbsp green chutney
  (page 259 or 260)
  • *To reduce Pitta: use version without chilies*
4 tbsp Tamarind Chutney (page 261)
  • *To reduce Pitta and Kapha: omit*
Salt to taste
10–12 Bhel Puris (page 72)

Serve each ingredient (except puris) in separate bowls so guests can make their own combinations on a puri.

Makes 5–6 servings (2 puris per person).

Fine sev is a snack that is made of thin strands of dough (made from gram flour) and deep-fried until crispy. It looks like golden angel hair pasta that has been broken into small pieces. Salt and spices are added as flavoring. Fine sev can be found at Indian grocery stores.

- ø +
slightly

Puris & Chat

This is another favorite savory street food snack. If you can't find puris at your local Indian grocery stores, or make them yourself (page 72), use circular tortilla chips.

1 cup potatoes, boiled and cubed
½ cup Tamarind Chutney (page 261)
4 tsp whole cumin seeds, toasted
3 fresh green chilies, finely chopped
  • To reduce Pitta: omit

½ cup plain yogurt, whipped up and runny
3 tsp cayenne pepper
12 Bhel Puris (page 72)

Serve each ingredient (except puris) in separate bowls. You or your guests can pop a hole in a puri and stuff with 1 tsp diced potato, 1 tsp tamarind chutney, and a pinch each of cumin seeds and green chilies. Add 1 tsp yogurt sprinkled with a pinch of cayenne.

Makes 4–6 servings (2 or 3 puris per person).

- + -

Deviled Eggs with Green Chutney

My spicy version of the old favorite! A tasty way to get your daily protein.

4 hard-boiled eggs, peeled
2 tsp mayonnaise
  • To decrease Kapha: use light mayonnaise
Salt to taste

2 tsp green chutney (page 259 or 260)
  • To reduce Pitta: use version without chilies
A few fresh cilantro leaves, chopped (for garnish)
¼ tsp cayenne pepper (for garnish)

Cut eggs in half vertically and scoop out yolks, and place in a separate bowl. Add mayonnaise, salt, and chutney to yolks and mash with a fork. Fill egg white cavities with yolk mixture. Garnish with cilantro and sprinkle with cayenne.

Makes 4 servings (2 halves per person).

-
-
+ # Green Chutney Cheese Toast

Nanistya, a friend from high school, became so addicted to this dish that once she moved to Montreal, my mother would make jars of chutney and send them to her!

4–6 slices of bread of your choice

Per slice:

1–2 tsp green chutney
  (page 259 or 260)
  • *To reduce Pitta: use Cilantro Mint Chutney (page 259)*

1 thin slice Mozzarella
  • *To reduce Vata: use cheddar*

Set oven to broil.

Spread each slice of bread with chutney. Cover with slices of cheese. Place on a baking sheet and broil until cheese bubbles and starts to brown. (Watch carefully to ensure that they
do not burn.)

Serve immediately, or for canapés, cut into squares and serve.

Makes 4–6 servings (1 slice per person).

-

slightly +

+ # Spiced Pecans

 Whenever we go on weekend getaways, my friend Nevenka brings these pecans, which give us the extra energy we need on our action-packed itineraries. Eat in small quantities.

Coconut oil is available at most health food stores.

¼ cup coconut oil (see note)
⅓ cup tamari or soy sauce
2 tsp ground ginger

¼ tsp cayenne pepper, or to taste
Olive oil spray
4 cups pecans

Preheat oven to 300°F (150°C).

In a small pot over low heat, melt coconut oil. While oil is melting, in a small bowl, combine tamari, ginger, and cayenne and set aside. Lightly cover a baking sheet with olive oil spray or line with parchment paper. Spread pecans out on baking sheet in a single layer. Pour coconut oil over pecans and mix to coat. Bake for about 15 minutes. Remove from oven and immediately toss with tamari mixture. Return to oven and bake for 10 additional minutes. Remove from oven and cool at room temperature. Store in a sealed container.

Makes 4 cups.

-

-

+ # Spiced Almonds

Careful – these are addictive! A great snack with tea or as an energizing pick-me-up anytime. Almonds are known to be "brain food." Remember, a ¼ cup serving is all you need!

Tree nuts – i.e. almonds, pecans, and walnuts – contain no cholesterol. Most of their calories come from unsaturated fats, or the essential fatty acids that our bodies need in small amounts.

1 ½ tsp ground cumin
1 ½ tsp salt
¼ tsp cayenne pepper, or more
  to taste
  • To reduce Pitta: omit

1 large egg, white only
2 ½ cups almonds, blanched (see note)
Olive oil spray

Preheat oven to 300°F (150°C).

In a small bowl, combine cumin, salt, and cayenne and set aside. In a medium bowl, beat egg white until frothy. Add spice mixture and almonds, and toss to mix well. Lightly cover a baking sheet with olive oil spray or line with parchment paper. Spread almonds out on baking sheet in a single layer. Bake for 25–30 minutes, stirring once or twice during the baking process. Make sure almonds stay in a single layer. Remove from oven and cool at room temperature. Store in a sealed container for up to 1 week.

Makes 2½ cups.

Although almonds generally increase Pitta, blanched almonds to not. To blanch almonds, soak them overnight in a pot of water in the refrigerator. In the morning, drain them and return to pot. Pour boiling water over them, then allow water to cool enough for you to pop skins off by squeezing them between your thumb and forefinger.

Salads

In Ayurveda, it is important to have at least some raw food like salad at every meal, as it aids digestion; the French have also known this for centuries, often referring to salad as "the broom." But raw food eaten alone can in fact be difficult to digest, especially for Vatas who should include some seasonal raw foods in their diet, but not as full meals, which are fine for Pittas and Kaphas.

Since summer is a Pitta season – hot and fiery – it is natural that all doshas enjoy more raw salads at this time to cool down. Leafy greens and herbs provide a bitter taste that brings out the sweetness and other contrasting flavors of the salad ingredients. In this chapter, I have included salads with cooked ingredients as well as an array of raw salads, which can be served as accompaniments to any dish, or as complete, balanced meals.

At the end of this chapter are great salad dressings that add flavor to raw greens and vegetables and are a great source for good oils (e.g., flax or hemp oil) (see page 22), which are important to our diet and digestive health – Pitta and Kapha benefit from oils in small amounts. Dressings also provide a sour taste that is beneficial to all constitutions, but calms Vata the most.

Can't Beet It Salad

I love the textures and flavors in this salad. The beets are warming and are a good contrast to the fennel, which is cooling. Beets also fortify the blood, while fennel cleanses the liver. The walnuts add a nice crunch and are a stimulating food for the brain. This salad can be made with or without the goat's cheese, depending on how heavy or light you want it.

Beets are rich in folic acid, which benefits the female reproductive system. They are also good for alleviating hemorrhoids, uterine disorders, and constipation.

Salad:
2 cups beets, steamed until just soft, cooled, and sliced (see note)
2 cups fennel bulbs, thinly sliced
⅓ cup walnuts, halved
½ cup softened goat's cheese, crumbled (optional)

Dressing:
2 tbsp extra-virgin olive oil
¼ cup rice vinegar
1 tsp honey (for Kapha) or maple syrup (for Pitta) (optional)
1 tsp fresh ginger, minced
½ tsp salt, or to taste

In a large bowl, combine all salad ingredients and gently toss. In a jar, combine all dressing ingredients and shake well. Pour over salad, toss again, and serve.

Makes 4–6 servings.

slightly +

slightly +

Grated Beet, Carrot

- **& Broccoli Salad**

This raw salad is rich in nutrients, textures, colors, and flavors. Pumpkin seeds are full of fiber, good oil, zinc, and iron, and are beneficial to all constitutions, but Vatas can eat more of these than Pittas and Kaphas. Pittas should reduce the amount of carrots and beets as they can be healing if consumed in excess.

Salad:

Mixed greens, enough for one medium-sized salad bowl (I love the organic ready-made mixes)

1 cup sunflower seed sprouts, loosely packed (may substitute other sprouts)

¾ cup carrots, grated
  • *To reduce Pitta: decrease to ½ cup*

¼ cup beets, grated
  • *To reduce Vata: increase to ½ cup*

¼ cup broccoli florets, chopped into bite-sized pieces

1 heaping tbsp dried cranberries
  • *To reduce Vata: omit or substitute raisins*

1 tbsp raw pumpkin seeds
  • *To reduce Vata: increase to 2 tbsp*

¼ cup fresh mint leaves, chopped
  • *To reduce Pitta: increase to ½ cup*

Dressing:

Juice of 1 lemon

4 tbsp hemp seed oil or olive oil

1 clove garlic, crushed
  • *To reduce Pitta: omit*

1 tsp Dijon mustard
  • *To reduce Pitta: omit*

Salt and freshly ground pepper to taste

In a medium bowl, combine all salad ingredients and toss. In a jar, combine all dressing ingredients and shake well. Pour over salad, toss again, and serve.

Makes 4–6 servings.

+

- # Refreshing Apple Walnut
- # Celery Salad

This is a crisp, light salad; the red apples make a lovely contrast with the green celery and red leaf lettuce. I often make this without the olive oil when I want to reduce Kapha. The lemon juice helps to bring out the sweetness of the apples.

Salad:
6 cups red leaf lettuce, shredded
2 unpeeled red apples, diced (with peel showing decoratively)
2 stalks celery, sliced
½ cup walnuts, chopped
  • *To reduce Kapha: use sunflower seeds*

Dressing:
6 tbsp lemon juice
4 tbsp olive oil
  • *To reduce Kapha: omit*

In a medium bowl, combine all salad ingredients and toss. Drizzle with lemon juice and olive oil, toss again, and serve.

Makes 4–6 servings.

The Essential Green Salad

I love getting my fiber from crisp greens and my essential fatty acids and protein from avocados. A good quality balsamic vinegar and olive oil define this salad.

Add sunflower or pumpkin seeds or throw in some raisins or grapes to add more color and texture to this salad.

Salad:

4 cups mixed greens

1 avocado, sliced
  • *To reduce Kapha: use snow peas*

1 cup cucumbers, sliced
  • *To reduce Kapha: substitute celery*

1 cup broccoli florets, chopped

1 cup alfalfa sprouts

Dressing:

⅓ cup balsamic vinegar

¼ cup extra-virgin olive oil

Salt and freshly ground pepper to taste

In a large bowl, combine all salad ingredients and toss. Drizzle with balsamic vinegar and olive oil. Season with salt and pepper, toss again, and serve.

Makes 6 servings.

Pear & Pecorino

Mixed Green Salad

My friend Gayle shared this simple and heavenly salad recipe with me. The saltiness of the cheese brings out the sweetness of the pears and the rich taste of the balsamic honey dressing. High quality ingredients are key to making this recipe as tasty as possible.

Bartlett red pears work best in this recipe.

Using a vegetable peeler is a handy way to make cheese shavings.

2 tbsp balsamic vinegar
1 tsp Agave nectar (or honey)
3 ripe pears, sliced (see note)
3 cups mixed greens
3 tbsp olive oil

½ cup Pecorino Romano cheese
　shavings (see note)
¼ tsp freshly ground pepper
¼ cup fresh basil leaves, torn into
　small pieces (for garnish)

In a medium bowl, combine balsamic vinegar and Agave nectar and mix until smooth. Add pears to bowl and toss until coated on all sides with mixture. On individual serving plates, divide mixed greens evenly. Arrange pear slices on each bed of greens. Drizzle oil over each salad and scatter cheese shavings. Season with pepper and garnish with basil.

Makes 2–4 servings.

+

-

- # Crunchy Broccoli Slaw

I love this crunchy alternative to regular coleslaw. Broccoli is sustaining and rich in vitamins A and C. The raisins add a nice sweetness. Include this in your summer meals or lunches to go.

Raisins balance out all the doshas if they are pre-soaked in water. They are prized in Ayurveda for their nourishing and healing properties. It is best to buy organic raisins to avoid toxic chemicals.

For a non-vegan alternative, use regular mayonnaise instead of vegan.

Salad:

2 cups broccoli stems, julienned and tough bits discarded

1 cup carrots, grated

1 cup purple (red) cabbage, finely chopped into fronds

¼ cup raisins (optional) (see note)

Dressing:

½ cup vegan mayonnaise (see note)
  • *To reduce Kapha: substitute yogurt*

4 tbsp apple cider vinegar

½ tsp salt

In a medium bowl, combine all salad ingredients and toss. In a jar, combine all dressing ingredients and shake well. Pour over salad and toss again. Cover and refrigerate for 30 minutes to enhance the flavors.

Makes 4 servings.

Broccoli & Almond Armor Salad

The almonds, red onions, and currants in this salad are a nice mixture of pungent and sweet tastes. Broccoli is a super cancer-fighting food. This is another good way to get your daily greens and fiber.

This salad tastes wonderful after being chilled for a few hours, or overnight for the next day.

Salad:
3 cups broccoli florets
½ cup red onions, chopped
  • *To reduce Pitta: use ¼ cup or omit*
¼ cup almonds, chopped
½ cup currants

Dressing:
½ cup plain light yogurt
¼ cup light mayonnaise
2 tbsp honey
1 tbsp vinegar
Salt and freshly ground pepper to taste

In a medium bowl, combine all salad ingredients and toss. In a separate bowl, combine all dressing ingredients and mix well. Pour over salad and toss again. Adjust seasoning to taste, then serve (see note).

Makes 4 servings.

Tomato, Parsley & Yellow Bell Pepper Salad

Enjoy this colorful, crunchy medley! I love dishes like this that are quick, tasty, good-looking, and nutritious.

Salad:
1 cup tomatoes, cubed
2 cups fresh parsley, chopped
1 cup yellow bell peppers, cubed

Dressing:
2 tbsp balsamic vinegar or 3 tbsp
  lemon juice
2 tbsp olive oil (or flax or hemp oil)
Salt and freshly ground pepper to taste

In a medium bowl, combine all salad ingredients and toss. Drizzle with balsamic vinegar and oil. Season with salt and pepper, toss again, and serve.

Makes 4 servings.

Mediterranean Breeze Salad

This salad is fabulously healthy as the mint is cooling and the tomatoes are packed with vitamin C.

1 cup tomatoes, chopped
1 cup avocado, chopped
¼ cup packed fresh mint leaves, chopped
1 tbsp green onions, minced

2 tbsp lemon juice
2 tbsp olive oil (or flax or hemp oil)
1 tsp salt
¼ tsp cayenne pepper (optional)

In a large bowl, combine tomatoes, avocado, mint, and green onions and toss. Drizzle with lemon juice and oil. Sprinkle with salt and cayenne, toss again, and serve.

Makes 2 servings.

slightly

Tomato, Feta & Mint Salad

A Greek twist on the classic tomato and bocconcini salad.

8 vine-ripened tomatoes, sliced
1 cup feta cheese
  • *To reduce Kapha: use goat's feta*
1 bunch fresh mint leaves
¾ cup small black olives, pitted
  • *To reduce Kapha: use ¼ cup, sliced*

Juice of 3 lemons
¼ cup olive oil
  • *To reduce Kapha: use a light version*
Salt and freshly ground pepper to taste

On a platter, arrange tomato slices. Crumble feta evenly over tomatoes. Arrange mint leaves over and under tomato slices. Scatter olives over salad, then drizzle with lemon juice, then olive oil. Season with salt and pepper. Cover and refrigerate for at least 30 minutes to enhance the flavors.

Makes 4–6 servings.

slightly +

Fresh Daikon & Endive Salad

This recipe includes mint or dill and endive, which are bitter, aiding digestion and cleansing the liver. Arrange artfully on a platter.

As it is important to have some raw vegetables to accompany every meal to cleanse and balance the doshas, feel free to experiment! Select a variety of vegetables, sprinkling them with salt, lemon juice, or rice vinegar.

1 daikon, cut into 2-in/5-cm-long sticks
  • *To reduce Pitta: use half a daikon*
A few sprigs fresh dill (or mint leaves)
1½ cups cucumbers, cut into 2-in/5-cm-long sticks
2 cups carrots, cut into 2-in/5-cm-long sticks

1 bunch watercress leaves
2 heads of endive leaves, separated
Salt to taste
Juice of 1 lemon
  (or 4–6 tbsp rice vinegar)

On a platter, arrange all ingredients except salt and lemon juice. Sprinkle with salt and lemon juice and serve.

Makes 6–8 servings.

+ -

The Dainty Cachumber

This is one of my favorite Indian salads or condiments that gives depth to any meal. Vatas and Pittas only need a small portion whereas Kaphas can indulge.

Tomatoes are a rich source of vitamins A and C.

Ideally, refrigerate the salad for ½ hour to enhance the flavors.

1 onion, sliced (see note)
2 large tomatoes, cubed (see note)
3 tbsp apple cider or rice vinegar
¼ tsp salt

¼ tsp cayenne pepper or fresh green chilies, chopped (optional)
¼ cup fresh cilantro leaves, minced (optional)

In a large bowl, combine all ingredients, toss, and serve (see note).

Makes 4–6 servings.

 + -

slightly

The Great White Salad

This salad is simple and a delectable way to add raw foods to your diet, an essential of Ayurveda.

Daikon, known to be a great blood cleanser, looks like a giant white carrot. It is available in Asian markets and most produce departments.

1½ cup cucumbers, chopped
1½ cup daikon, thinly sliced (see note)
1 tsp salt

6 tbsp rice vinegar
2 tbsp sweetener
(Agave nectar is recommended)

In a colander, place cucumber and daikon and sprinkle with salt, then set over a sink or bowl to drain for 5–10 minutes. Rinse and gently squeeze excess water out of vegetables. In a jar, combine rice vinegar and sweetener, mixing well until sweetener dissolves. In a serving bowl, combine vegetables and dressing and toss. Let sit for 15–30 minutes before serving.

Makes 4–6 servings.

- + -

slightly

The Bittersweet Salad

I love the sweetness of the carrots with the bitter punch of the daikon in this salad. It adds fiber and vitamins to a meal and cleanses the digestive system.

1 cup carrots, thinly sliced
1 ½ cups daikon, thinly sliced
1 tsp salt

¼ cup rice vinegar
2 tbsp sweetener
  (Agave nectar is recommended)

In a colander, place carrots and daikon and sprinkle with salt, then set over a sink or bowl to drain for 5–10 minutes. Rinse and gently squeeze excess water out of vegetables. In a jar, combine vinegar and sweetener and mix well until sweetener dissolves. In a serving bowl, combine vegetables and dressing and toss. Let sit for 15–30 minutes before serving.

Makes 4 servings.

ø - -

The Cleansing Bitter Greens

Just as the title suggests, this salad is good and good for you.

As a variation, sprinkle with rice vinegar and omit the oil. This is a good way to reduce Kapha.

Salad:
6 cups dark green leaf lettuce, torn
2 cups arugula, torn
1 cup radicchio, torn into small pieces

Dressing:
¼ cup walnut or olive oil
  • *To reduce Kapha: omit*
¼ cup balsamic vinegar
Salt and freshly ground pepper to taste

In a large bowl, combine all salad ingredients and toss. Drizzle with oil and balsamic vinegar. Season with salt and pepper, toss again, and serve.

Makes 6–8 servings.

The Perfect Pomegranate & Spinach Salad

Pomegranates are an excellent source of antioxidants and strengthen the digestive tract. The pomegranate seeds add sweetness and color, and are a delectable flavor combination with the spinach.

When purchasing pomegranates, choose fruit that are blemish-free, brightly colored, and heavy. Store them in a cool, dry place.

Salad:

5–6 cups spinach leaves, chopped (about 1 bunch)

⅓ cup fresh cilantro leaves, chopped (may use parsley)

1 cup pomegranate seeds (the seeds from 1 pomegranate) (see notes)

⅓ cup pine nuts, toasted

¼ cup red onions, sliced (optional)

• To reduce Pitta: omit

Dressing:

4 tbsp olive oil

4 tbsp apple cider vinegar

2 tsp honey

Salt and freshly ground pepper to taste

In a large bowl, combine all salad ingredients and toss. In a jar, combine dressing ingredients and shake well. Pour dressing over salad, toss again, and serve.

Makes 4–5 servings.

Pomegranates were known as "the Crown Jewels" in the ancient Mediterranean region as they were the fruit of choice for kings and nobles. They date back to 3000 BCE and were one of the first domesticated crops in Mesopotamia, now a region of modern Iraq. They are also known for their medicinal powers – the Babylonians believed that chewing the seeds made them invincible in battle.

+

slightly +

− # Crunchy Spinach Salad

This is a delicious salad with lots of crunchy textures, colors, and flavors. Spinach is cooling, soothing, nourishing, and full of iron. It has the pungent taste essential in Ayurveda.

Before adding dried herbs to salads, crush them between the palms of your hands to bring out the flavor.

Salad:
5–6 cups spinach leaves, chopped (about 1 bunch)
½ cup red bell peppers, diced
½ cup yellow bell peppers, diced
1 cup carrots, grated
1–2 tbsp raisins or dried cranberries
2 tbsp walnuts, chopped
2 tbsp feta cheese, crumbled (optional)
 • *To reduce Kapha: omit or use goat's feta*

Dressing:
⅓ cup olive oil
¼ cup balsamic vinegar
1 tbsp honey
 • *To reduce Pitta: use Agave nectar or maple syrup*
1 tsp Dijon mustard
 • *To reduce Pitta: omit*
Salt and freshly ground pepper to taste
1 tsp dried basil or oregano (see note)
1 clove garlic, minced (optional)
 • *To reduce Pitta: omit*

In a large bowl, combine all salad ingredients and toss. In a jar, combine all dressing ingredients and shake well. Pour over salad, toss again, and serve.

Makes 4–6 servings.

+ +

slightly

Warm Spinach & Walnut Salad

A lovely, warm salad packed with iron, essential oils, and protein. Very simple and satisfying.

5–6 cups spinach, chopped
 (about 1 bunch)
½ cup walnuts

2 tbsp Bragg all purpose seasoning, or your favorite brand of tamari or soy sauce

In a pot of boiling water, blanch spinach for a few seconds until just wilted and bright green. Drain and gently squeeze excess water out. In a blender or a food processor, purée walnuts. In a large bowl, combine spinach, walnuts, and seasoning, toss gently and serve.

Makes 4–6 servings.

ø ø -

Thai Godot Salad

I love all the flavors and textures in this colorful dish. It's a feast for the eyes and nourishing to the body.

6 cups baby spinach leaves
1 cup red bell peppers, chopped
1 cup yellow bell peppers, chopped
½ cup red onions, sliced
 • *To reduce Pitta: omit, or use ¼ cup*
1 cup bean sprouts
1 cup sugar snap peas, ends chopped
 and strings removed

½ cup pecans or cashews, crushed
 • *To reduce Kapha: use sunflower seeds*
¾ cup fresh cilantro leaves, chopped
¾ cup Thai basil, chopped
1 cup Chinese curly cabbage, shredded
Thai Salad Dressing (page 108)

In a large bowl, combine all ingredients except dressing. Toss with Thai Salad Dressing and serve.

Makes 6–8 servings.

Cooling Couscous Salad

 This is a grounding comfort food that looks great and is easy to make. The mint adds a wonderful flavor and is cooling for Pita.

2 tsp vegetable bouillon powder
5 cups water
3½ cups couscous, uncooked
(I prefer whole wheat organic
   couscous)
1 cup tomatoes, diced
   • *To reduce Pitta: use red bell peppers*
1 cup cucumbers, diced
   • *To reduce Vata: use zucchini*
¼ cup fresh mint leaves, chopped
¼ cup fresh parsley, chopped

¼ cup green onions, chopped
⅓ cup sun-dried tomatoes, chopped
   • *To reduce Kapha: use the dry tomatoes*
   reconstituted in water rather than the
   ready-made oil version
½ cup crumbled feta cheese
   • *To reduce Kapha: use goat's feta*
Juice of 1 lemon or lime
1 tbsp olive oil
Salt and freshly ground pepper to taste

In a large pot, bring water and bouillon powder to a boil, stirring until bouillon is dissolved. Remove pot from heat and stir in couscous; let sit covered for 5 minutes. In a large bowl, combine all remaining ingredients. Add couscous and mix well, adjust seasoning for taste. Chill and serve.

Makes 6 servings.

Tabbouleh Twist
with Olives & Walnuts

I love this refreshing favorite with a twist: the addition of olives and nuts. The essential oils and the protein make this tabbouleh a yummy and complete meal for lunch.

1 ½ cups cracked wheat (also called bulgur wheat)
3 cups boiling water
½ cup fresh parsley, chopped
⅓ cup green onions, chopped
½ cup fresh mint leaves, chopped
1 cup tomatoes, diced
• *To reduce Pitta: use red bell peppers instead*

½ cup black olives, sliced
• *To reduce Kapha: use ¼ cup*
⅓ cup walnuts, toasted
• *To reduce Kapha: use ¼ cup*
2 tbsp extra-virgin olive oil
• *To reduce Kapha: use a light version*
4 tbsp lemon juice
1 clove garlic, minced
• *To reduce Pitta: omit*

In a large bowl, combine cracked wheat and boiling water and set aside to allow cracked wheat to soak. In another bowl, combine all remaining ingredients and mix well. Once cracked wheat has absorbed the water, about 10 minutes, add to other ingredients and toss. The flavors get stronger if you let this sit for a while before serving.

Makes 6 servings.

slightly +

+

- # Millet with Sautéed Vegetables

I made this salad for a picnic with some friends at an oceanside park. It satisfied our ravenous appetites and was a hit amidst the crashing waves and salty air. You can serve this dish warm or cold.

1 cup millet
  • *To reduce Vata: use couscous*
2 cups water
2 tbsp olive oil
½ cup onions, chopped
1 cup zucchini, finely sliced and
  quartered

1½ cups tomatoes, diced
¾ cup mushrooms, chopped
1 tbsp tamari or soy sauce
1 tbsp rice vinegar or lemon juice
1 tsp dried basil or 2 tbsp fresh basil,
  chopped

In a large pot, bring millet and water to a boil. Immediately reduce heat to a simmer and cook until done, about 15 minutes. While millet is cooking, in a large frying pan on medium-high heat, sauté onions in oil. When onions start to brown, add other vegetables, and reduce to low and cook for about 10 minutes, stirring from time to time. (If mixture starts to get dry, cover it with a lid so that it can cook in its own steam.) Add tamari, rice vinegar, and basil and cook for another 5 minutes. Add vegetable mixture to millet and mix well. Season to taste and serve.

Makes 6 servings.

slightly +
-

Geeta's Buckwheat Noodle, Mango & Bell Pepper Salad

My sister Geeta is a film producer and often pressed for time. She shared with me her favorite potluck dish that is always a hit. It is fast and easy to prepare, yet does not compromise on style, nutrition, or flavor.

Buckwheat noodles are sold dry, and are available in health food stores and Japanese markets.

1 red bell pepper, diced
1 mango, peeled and diced
3 tbsp red onions, diced
½ tsp fresh ginger, minced
2 tbsp extra-virgin olive oil
Dash of sesame oil
2 tbsp tamari or soy sauce

2–3 tbsp rice vinegar
2 bunches buckwheat noodles
  (see note)
Juice of ½ a lime
3 tbsp fresh cilantro leaves, chopped
Black sesame seeds (for garnish)

In a large bowl, combine peppers, mangoes, onions, ginger, oils, tamari, and rice vinegar. Toss well and set aside. In a large pot of boiling water, cook noodles according to package directions. Drain and set aside to cool. (Noodles may get sticky, but when you add the oil, the strands will separate.) Once cooled, add noodles to bowl and toss well. Refrigerate for a few hours. Just before serving, add lime juice, cilantro, and sesame seeds and toss well.

Makes 6 servings.

Rainbow Wild Rice Salad

I used to buy various versions of this salad in take-out delis, but now I prefer to make my own. This makes a great lunch to take with you. If you want to make it heartier, add some goat's cheese, or serve with the Light Lentil Salad (page 99).

Salad:
2 cups wild rice, cooked
½ cup red bell peppers, diced
½ cup yellow bell peppers, diced
¼ cup pecans
2 tbsp currants or cranberries
¼ cup pineapple, chopped
  • *To reduce Kapha: omit*
½ cup water chestnuts, sliced

2 tbsp green onions, white parts
  only, chopped
1 tsp fresh green chilies, minced
  (optional)
  • *To reduce Pitta: omit*

Dressing:
¼ cup rice vinegar
¼ cup olive oil

In a medium bowl, combine all salad ingredients and toss. In a jar, combine all dressing ingredients and shake well. Pour over salad, toss again, and serve.

Makes 4–6 servings.

+

-

- # Light Lentil Salad

vegan

This dish is wonderful to eat at home or to take out for lunch, providing you with both protein and veggies. Green lentils do not need soaking and cook quickly. I always have some on hand as they keep well in a jar. If you need to reduce Vata, try it with split mung or sprouted mung beans (see Sprouting, page 25); they will both cook in the same amount of time. For a heartier meal, serve with the Rainbow Wild Salad (page 98).

1 cup green or brown lentils
1 cup celery, diced
½ cup carrots, diced
1½ cups vegetable stock

¼ cup lemon juice
½ tsp salt, or to taste
½ cup fresh parsley, chopped

In a large pot, combine lentils, celery, carrots, and vegetable stock. Bring to a boil, then reduce heat to a simmer and cook until lentils are soft, about 20 minutes. Keep an eye on the pot; if liquid starts to dry out, add additional water. Remove pot from heat, transfer mixture to a bowl, and stir in lemon juice. Allow to cool, then add salt and parsley. Toss and serve.

Makes 4–6 servings.

+

-

- Mixed Bean Salad

This recipe is another great take-out lunch, also nice for potlucks or a buffet. It can be paired with a rice salad.

1 ½ cups chickpeas (garbanzo beans), cooked or canned
1 ½ cups black beans, cooked or canned
1 ½ cups red kidney beans, cooked or canned
1–2 tsp garlic, minced
  • *To reduce Pitta: omit*
1–2 tbsp olive oil
  • *To reduce Kapha: use 1 tbsp*

2 tbsp green onions, chopped
3 tbsp fresh cilantro leaves, chopped
2 tsp fresh green chilies, minced
  • *To reduce Pitta: omit, or use just enough to add flavor*
¼ tsp ground cumin
½ tsp salt
Freshly ground pepper to taste
4 tbsp lemon juice or vinegar (your choice of vinegar)

In a large bowl, combine all ingredients and mix well. Refrigerate for at least 2 hours, adjust seasoning if necessary, and serve.

Makes 6 servings.

Sprouted Mixed Bean Salad

I like to make this early in the morning when my beans have sprouted tails of just the right length (¼-in/5-mm). While the beans cook, I prepare the other ingredients; once the salad is put together, I refrigerate it until lunch or dinner. This is always a hit at my yoga retreats and makes another great take-out lunch dish.

For a non-vegan alternative, substitute 1 tsp honey for the maple syrup.

Salad:
2 cups mixed beans, sprouted and
    cooked (see Sprouting, page 25)
1 cup red bell peppers, chopped
1 cup celery, chopped
¼–½ cup red onions, minced

Dressing:
⅓ cup rice vinegar
⅓ cup olive oil
1 tsp Dijon mustard
1 tsp garlic, minced
1 tsp dry Italian herbs
1 tsp maple syrup (see note)
Salt and freshly ground pepper to taste

In a medium bowl, combine all salad ingredients and toss. In a jar, combine all dressing ingredients and shake well. Pour over salad and toss again. Refrigerate for at least ½ hour before serving, giving the beans time to fully absorb the flavors.

Makes 4–5 servings.

You can experiment with your own combination of beans for this recipe. I buy a mix from a fab Persian grocery store nearby, which includes black beans, kidney beans, adzuki beans, black-eyed peas, red lentils, and brown masoor lentils.

+

-

- # Picnic Medley Salad

 This is a delicious protein and vegetable combination that is rich in fiber, texture, color, and flavor. Make it to bring on picnics.

Salad:
1½ cups black beans, cooked
  or canned
1½ cups sweet corn niblets,
  cooked or canned
1 cup red bell peppers, diced
1 cup fresh parsley, chopped
  (or fresh cilantro leaves)

Dressing:
¼ cup apple cider vinegar (or other
  vinegar or lemon juice)
¼ cup olive oil
  • *To reduce Kapha: use a light version*
½ tsp fresh green chilies, finely
  chopped
  • *To reduce Pitta: omit*
Salt and freshly ground pepper to taste

In a large bowl, combine all salad ingredients and toss. In a jar, combine all dressing ingredients and shake well. Pour over salad, toss again, and serve.

Makes 4 servings.

New Potato Salad

This is my favorite salad for summer picnics and barbecues when new potatoes are in season. Although this recipe is tridoshic, Kaphas should eat this salad in moderation.

To create a distinctly Indian flavor, use cilantro instead of parsley, and add ½ tsp of minced green chili instead of chili flakes.

10–12 new potatoes (skins on)
2 stalks celery, thinly sliced
1 shallot, minced
1 hard-boiled egg, diced (optional)
Salt and freshly ground pepper
  to taste

Dash of chili flakes (optional)
½ cup fresh parsley, chopped
2 tbsp mayonnaise
  • *To reduce Kapha: use a light version*
1 tsp olive oil
  • *To reduce Vata: increase to 1 tbsp*

In a large pot of salted water, bring potatoes to a boil. Reduce heat to a simmer and cook until done, 15–20 minutes. While potatoes are cooking, in a large bowl, combine celery, shallots, egg, salt, pepper, chili flakes, and parsley and mix well. Drain potatoes and cut in halves or quarters. In a bowl, toss potatoes with olive oil and mayo while still warm, then add to other mixture and mix well. Serve slightly warm or chilled.

Makes 2–4 servings.

-
 -
 -

Calming Wakame Seaweed Salad

As a child growing up in Kenya, I ate frequently at the home of our Japanese neighbors and developed a taste for – actually, almost an addiction to – seaweed. Once the Hirasawas, our neighbors, went back to Japan, my mother would go to Japanese markets when she traveled abroad to buy it for me since it was not available in Kenya. Seaweed is filled with nutrients and rich in minerals. This is a simple, dosha-calming salad with nice subtle flavors. Apart for the soaking time, it is quick to prepare.

Wakame seaweed is sold dry, and is available in health food or Japanese grocery stores.

Small cucumbers are good in this recipe. They are available in Japanese or ethnic markets; I find mine in Persian grocery stores.

¼ lb Wakame seaweed (see note)
Water at room temperature, enough
  to cover seaweed
1 ½ cups cucumbers, thinly sliced
  (see note)

½ tsp salt
¼ cup rice vinegar
1 tbsp sweetener
3 tbsp tamari or soy sauce

In a large bowl, cover seaweed with water and set aside to soak until soft, about 15 minutes (or longer if you prefer it softer). In a colander, place cucumbers and sprinkle with salt, then set over a sink or bowl to drain for 30 minutes. In a jar, combine vinegar, sweetener, and soy sauce and shake well to mix, ensuring sweetener dissolves. When seaweed is soft, cut into bite-size-pieces. Gently squeeze excess water out of cucumbers and add to a serving bowl with seaweed. Add dressing and toss. Let sit for 5–10 minutes before serving.

Makes 4–6 servings.

+ + # Everyday Salad Dressing

This dressing is rich in omega-3s and flavor. The oils calm the nervous system and Vata.

Instead of olive oil, flax seed oil is a good option for Kapha, and hemp oil is good for Pitta.

For a non-vegan alternative (or to reduce Kapha), substitute 1 tsp honey for the maple syrup.

¼ cup extra virgin olive oil (see note)
  • *To reduce Kapha: use 2 tbsp extra lemon juice instead*
¼ cup lemon juice or rice vinegar
1 tsp garlic, minced
  • *To reduce Pitta: omit*

1 tsp maple syrup, or to taste (see note)
1 tsp Dijon mustard
  • *To reduce Pitta: omit*
Salt and freshly ground pepper to taste

In a jar, combine all ingredients and shake well. Let dressing sit for 30 minutes or longer before using to enhance the flavors. If you store this in the refrigerator, let sit at room temperature before using so the oil becomes less thick.

Makes ½ cup.

 + + # Spicy French Dressing
slightly

This recipe is based on a dressing that is a mainstay in my family. It adds a rich, tangy flavor to any fresh salad. Try pairing it with one garnished with onions or fresh cilantro, or drizzle it over fresh sliced tomatoes.

½ cup olive oil (or flax seed or hemp oil)
½ cup apple cider vinegar (or vinegar of your choice)
Salt and freshly ground pepper to taste

¼ tsp cayenne pepper
½ tsp dry English mustard (or Dijon)
1 tsp Worcestershire sauce
2 tsp honey or Agave nectar (optional)

In a jar, combine all ingredients and mix well, ensuring honey dissolves and mustard does not clump.

Makes 1 cup.

- + - # Fortifying Lemon & Garlic Dressing

This dressing is for garlic lovers. It is very effective for cleansing the system and fending off colds (garlic is a natural antibiotic). This is a light, refreshing dressing, especially if you reduce or omit the oil.

4–6 tbsp lemon juice
4 tbsp flax seed or hemp oil
  • *To reduce Kapha: use 2 tbsp or omit and add 2 tbsp more lemon juice*

1–2 tsp garlic, minced (1 or 2 cloves)
Salt and freshly ground pepper to taste
1 tbsp fresh herbs (or ½ tsp dry) (optional)

In a jar, combine all ingredients and shake well. For a stronger flavor, refrigerate for a minimum of 10 minutes before using.

Makes ½ cup.

- ø ø # Tridoshic Salad Dressing

Rice vinegar is gentle on all constitutions and has a nice light flavor. Try this dressing over daikon sticks, carrot sticks, and bitter greens like endive or watercress.

1 tbsp light olive oil
¼ cup rice vinegar

Salt and freshly ground pepper to taste

In a jar, combine all ingredients and shake well.

Makes ¼ cup.

+ +

slightly

Cleansing Lemon & Cumin Dressing

This is a light, refreshing dressing that enhances the flavor of raw salad ingredients. Both lemon and cumin are cleansing as they help break down fat and eliminate toxins.

Juice of 1 lemon
4 tbsp light olive oil
• *To reduce Vata: use a full-fat version*

¼ tsp ground cumin
¼ tsp salt, or to taste

In a jar, combine all ingredients and shake well.

Makes ½ cup.

 + +

Simple Olive Oil & Balsamic Vinegar Dressing

This is one of my favorite dressings; I use it almost daily. The key is to use a high-quality extra-virgin olive oil and balsamic vinegar, which you can find at Italian grocers or specialty shops.

½ cup olive oil
⅓ cup balsamic vinegar

Salt and freshly ground pepper
  to taste

In a jar, combine all ingredients and shake well.

Makes about 1 cup.

–
slightly +

 –

Thai Salad Dressing

I love this dressing's mixture of the sweet and sour flavors. Sesame oil is full of healing and detoxifying properties that benefit the brain and nervous system. This is a wonderful pick-me-up if you are feeling sedentary (for Kapha states) and has the sweet and sour tastes to calm Vata. To give the dressing more kick, add the suggested garnishes to your favorite salad.

For a non-vegan alternative (or to reduce Kapha), substitute 1 tbsp honey for the maple syrup.

Dressing:
1 tbsp fresh ginger, grated or finely chopped
1 tsp garlic, minced (about 1 clove)
 • *To reduce Pitta: omit*
4 tbsp lime juice (about one lime)
4 tbsp olive oil
 • *To reduce Kapha: use a light version*
Dash of sesame oil
1 tbsp tamari or Bragg all-purpose seasoning (or soy sauce)
1 tbsp maple syrup (see note)

Salad garnishes:
½ tsp fresh green chilies, minced, or to taste
 • *To reduce Pitta: omit*
¼ cup fresh cilantro leaves, chopped
¼ cup fresh basil leaves, chopped

In a jar, combine all dressing ingredients and shake well. Add garnishes to salad and toss. Pour dressing over salad, toss again, and serve.

Makes ½ cup dressing.

+ -
slightly

Creamy Cilantro Dressing

This lovely and light dressing is delicious on your favorite salads and on sliced cucumbers, and its combination of spices makes it good for all doshas.

To reduce Pitta, use Homemade Yogurt (page 266). To reduce Kapha, use a light version.

½ cup plain yogurt (see note)
  • *To reduce Kapha: use light yogurt*
¼ tsp turmeric
2 tbsp lemon juice
¼ tsp ground coriander
⅛ tsp ground cardamom
½ tsp maple syrup
  • *To reduce Kapha: use honey*

½ tsp fresh ginger, minced
1 clove garlic, crushed or minced
Salt and freshly ground pepper to taste
¼ tsp fresh green chilies, minced
  • *To reduce Pitta: omit*
¼ cup fresh cilantro leaves, finely chopped

In a bowl, combine all ingredients and mix together well.

Makes ½ cup.

 + +
slightly

Miso Dressing

Rich with flavor, vitamins, and protein, this miso dressing is almost oil-free. I love it over wilted spinach or steamed veggies sprinkled with sesame seeds.

¾ cup miso paste (see note)
3 tbsp honey
3 tbsp rice vinegar
2 tbsp hot water

2 tbsp Bragg all-purpose seasoning or tamari (or soy sauce)
¼ tsp organic sesame oil

In a bowl, combine all ingredients and stir until smooth.

Makes about 1 cup.

Miso is a thick paste made by fermenting soybeans with sea salt and often rice or barley. Miso tastes salty and, depending on the grains used and fermentation time, may also be sweet. It is used in soups or sauces and is rich in nutrients. Miso should be cooked for only a few minutes and only on simmer, as high heat can decrease its nutritional value.

Soups

Soups are comfort food; they also make nourishing appetizers and snacks, and some are hearty enough to be complete meals in themselves. Soups replenish us when we are tired or run down, quickly and efficiently filling our need for essential nutrients without taxing the digestive system. In particular, clear soups calm the nervous system, while other light soups cleanse our digestive tracts if we have consumed too many heavy foods. Soups also are a great way to use any odds and ends in the refrigerator and pantry for a delicious, spur-of-the-moment meal. (Having said that, keep in mind that the fresher your ingredients, the better the soup!) Adding beans, lentils,

tofu, or miso gives soups the protein content we all need.

This chapter includes both lighter and heartier recipes. The Clear Vegetable Soup (page 112) can be nourishing either on its own or as a base for other soups. The Sprouted Mung Bean Soup (page 126) is filled with protein, vitamins, minerals, and essential amino acids – the building blocks to good health which benefit all constitutions. The Beat the Cold Soup (page 117) really works when you are feeling under the weather. And the chickpea and lentil soups are substantial meals when paired with your favorite bread.

-
slightly +

- # Clear Vegetable Soup

 This is a fragrant consommé that can be enjoyed on its own or as a stock for your favorite soup recipe.

1 cup onions, roughly chopped
1 ¼ cups carrots, roughly chopped
1 ¼ cups celery, roughly chopped
⅓ cup fresh cilantro leaves
  (or parsley), roughly chopped
1 ¼ cup apples, roughly chopped
3 slices fresh ginger (optional)
2 bay leaves
10 whole peppercorns
  • *To reduce Pitta: use 4*

1 cinnamon stick
  (about 2-in/5-cm long)
2 cloves
  • *To reduce Pitta: omit*
Salt to taste
¼ tsp turmeric
¼ cup fresh herbs, roughly chopped
  (e.g., thyme, sage, mint)
10 cups water

In a large pot on high heat, combine all ingredients and bring to a boil. Immediately reduce heat to a simmer, cover with lid, and cook for 45 minutes. Strain before serving or using.

Makes 8–10 cups.

Here are three options to suit a variety of recipes calling for stock. The simpler the stock, the more suitable it is for subtle ingredients.

- + -
 Variation 1: **For a more nourishing and pungent stock:** Add 3 whole garlic cloves; juice of ½ a lemon (To reduce Kapha: omit); and 1 cup fresh parsley, roughly chopped.

- - -
 Variation 2: **For a stock with a French country flavor:** Add 1 fennel bulb, roughly chopped; substitute onions with 2 leeks, sliced; and omit cloves, turmeric, cinnamon stick, ginger, and cilantro.

- ø -
 Variation 3: **For a simpler stock:** Omit cinnamon stick, ginger, and cilantro.

-
-
+ # Acorn Squash Soup

This is a delicious soup for cool nights. It is a good source of vitamin A and is easy and quick to make.

I like to purée my soups right in the pot with a hand blender, but you can also use a food processor or traditional blender.

1 acorn squash
1 tsp good oil (see page 22)
1 tsp fresh ginger, finely chopped
¼ tsp turmeric
½ tsp ground cumin
1 fresh green chili, halved, or cayenne pepper to taste
  • To reduce Pitta: omit
1 cinnamon stick
  (about 2-in/5-cm long)

½ tsp salt, or to taste
1 tsp vegetable bouillon powder
4 cups water
1 tsp Agave nectar or maple syrup
¼ cup fresh parsley, chopped
  (for garnish)
¼ cup plain light yogurt (for garnish)

Preheat oven to 350°F (180°C).

Cut acorn squash in half and bake for 30–40 minutes. Remove from oven and cool. When squash is cool enough to handle, peel skin and dice. Set aside. In a medium pot on medium-high, heat oil, then add ginger and sauté for 30 seconds. Stir in turmeric, cumin, and green chili and sauté for another 30 seconds. Add squash, cinnamon stick, salt, bouillon, and water. Cover with lid and cook until squash starts to soften. Add nectar or maple syrup, mix well, and continue to cook until squash is soft. Remove cinnamon stick and green chili. In a blender or food processor, purée until smooth. (Be careful when blending hot liquids.) Garnish with parsley and a dollop of yogurt and serve.

Makes 2–4 servings.

Carrot Ginger Soup

I love this soup's sweet taste from the caramelized onions and carrots combined with warm spices. Carrots are a rich source of vitamin A and ginger is good for the circulation and digestion.

Whole pepper-corns add flavor without a lot of heat. If you don't purée them, be sure to remove them before serving to avoid biting into one.

1 ½ tbsp olive oil
2 cups onions, chopped
4 tsp fresh ginger, minced
  • *To reduce Pitta: use 1 tsp ginger*
7 cups carrots, chopped
  • *To reduce Pitta: use 5 cups carrots and 2 cups celery*
5 cups water

2 tsp salt
1 cinnamon stick
  (about 2-in/5-cm long)
10 whole peppercorns (see note)
  • *To reduce Pitta: use 5 whole peppercorns*
2 tbsp fresh parsley, chopped
  (for garnish)

In a medium pot on medium-low, heat oil. Add onions and ginger and sauté until onions are caramelized, about 5–8 minutes. Stir in carrots, water, salt, cinnamon stick, and peppercorns. Bring to a boil, cover, then reduce heat to simmer until done, about 15–20 minutes. Remove cinnamon stick and peppercorns. In a blender or food processor, purée until smooth. (Be careful when blending hot liquids.) Garnish with parsley and serve.

Makes 6–8 servings.

Variation: For a thinner soup, add 1–2 cups water and 1–2 tsp vegetable bouillon powder.

–

slightly +

slightly + # Spiced Pumpkin Soup

 This warm and nourishing soup is great anytime of the year, not just Halloween!

2 tsp good oil (see page 22)
1 medium onion, chopped
1 clove garlic, minced
½ tsp fresh ginger, grated
½ tsp ground cumin
1 fresh green chili, slit at end (optional)
  • To reduce Pitta: use ¼ green chili, slit

4 cups vegetable stock (page 112)
4 cups pumpkin, cubed
1 tsp maple syrup (optional)
¼ tsp ground nutmeg (for garnish)
2 tbsp fresh cilantro leaves, chopped
  (or parsley) (for garnish)

In a large pot on medium-low, heat oil. Add onions and sauté for about 4 minutes. Stir in garlic, ginger, cumin, and green chili and continue to sauté until onions are caramelized, about 4 minutes. Add vegetable stock and pumpkin. Cook until pumpkin is soft, about 10–15 minutes, then stir in maple syrup. In a blender or food processor, purée until smooth. (Be careful when blending hot liquids.) Garnish with nutmeg and cilantro and serve.

Makes 4–6 servings.

slightly

Sona's Zucchini Soup

My sister-in-law Sona introduced this soup to our family. Her simple recipe quickly became a favorite and has been circulated around the world to family and friends.

*You can substitute
3 cups of the
vegetable stock
(page 112) for the
bouillon and
3 cups of water.*

1 tbsp good oil (see page 22)
1 cup onions, sliced
2 cups zucchini, sliced
3 cups water
2 tsp vegetable bouillon powder
  (see note)

¼ tsp cayenne pepper (optional)
  • To reduce Pitta: omit
Salt and freshly ground pepper
  to taste
4 tbsp plain yogurt
  (for garnish)

In a large pot on medium-low, heat oil. Add onions and sauté until caramelized, about 7–8 minutes. Add zucchini, cover with lid, and cook for 3–4 minutes. Add water, bouillon, and cayenne, increase heat, and bring to a boil. Reduce heat to low and simmer until zucchini has softened, about 5–6 minutes. In a blender or in a food processor, purée until smooth. (Be careful when blending hot liquids.) Season with salt and pepper, garnish with yogurt, and serve.

Makes 4–6 servings.

Spinach Vegetable Soup

This recipe offers a tasty, easy way to get a hearty serving of vegetables and nutrients. Serve with your favorite bread.

*You can substitute
2 cups of vegetable
stock (page 112)
for the bouillon and
2 cups water.*

1 tbsp olive oil
1 cup onions, sliced
½ tsp fresh ginger, minced
½ tsp ground cumin
2 cups water
2 tsp vegetable bouillon powder
  (see note)

1 cup sweet potatoes, cubed
½ cup carrots, sliced
5–6 cups spinach, chopped
  (about 1 bunch)
Salt and freshly ground pepper
  to taste

In a large pot on medium-high, heat oil. Add onions and ginger and sauté until onions start to caramelize, about 5 minutes. Stir in cumin and sauté for another minute. Add water, bouillon, and all vegetables. Cook until sweet potatoes are softened, about 15 minutes. Stir in salt and pepper, then serve.

Makes 4–6 servings.

Beat the Cold Soup

I live in rainy Vancouver where residents seem to suffer from colds at least twice a year. I usually manage to avoid them, unless I forget to follow the Ayurvedic principles and start to skip meals, or eat out too much. The last time I started to feel a cold setting in, I created this soup to "beat" it!

1 tbsp good oil (see page 22)
½ cup onions, chopped
3 tsp fresh ginger, minced
2 tsp fresh green chilies, minced
  • To reduce Pitta: omit
2 tsp garlic, minced
½ cup celery, diced
½ cup carrots, diced
¼ tsp cayenne pepper
½ tsp turmeric
½ tsp garam masala
½ cup mushrooms, chopped

¾ cup zucchini, chopped
¼ cup tomatoes, diced
2 cups vegetable stock (page 112)
4 whole peppercorns
2 cloves
1 cup broccoli and cauliflower florets
  (mixed),
Juice of 1 lemon
Salt to taste
¼ cup fresh cilantro leaves, chopped
  (for garnish)

In a large pot on medium-high, heat oil. Add onions, ginger, and green chilies and sauté until onions start to soften, about 4 minutes. Stir in garlic and celery and continue to sauté for a few minutes. Add carrots, cayenne, turmeric, and garam masala and sauté for a few more minutes. Add mushrooms and zucchini and sauté for another minute. Stir in tomatoes and sauté for an additional minute. Add vegetable stock, peppercorns, and cloves, then reduce heat and simmer for 10 minutes. Add broccoli and cauliflower florets and cook for another 7 minutes until softened. Just before soup is done, stir in lemon juice and salt to taste. Remove peppercorns, garnish with cilantro and serve.

Make 4–6 servings.

-
-
+ # Yummy Yam Soup

Yams are a rich source of beta carotene and vitamin A. This easy, nutritious dish calms Vata and Pitta.

1 tsp ghee (or butter)
1 tsp olive oil
¾ cup onions, sliced
2 cloves garlic, sliced
6 cups yams, cubed
1 tbsp vegetable bouillon powder
1 tsp salt
1 cinnamon stick
   (about 2-in/5-cm long)

1 clove
2 whole peppercorns
¼ tsp turmeric
6 cups water
4 tbsp plain yogurt (for garnish)
4 tsp fresh parsley, chopped
   (for garnish)

In a large pot on medium-low, heat ghee and oil. Add onions and sauté until they start to soften, about 4 minutes. Add garlic and continue to sauté until onions are caramelized, about 4 minutes. Add remaining ingredients except for garnishes. Bring to a boil, then reduce heat to low and simmer until done, about 20 minutes. Check seasoning and consistency. If the soup is too thick, add a little more water. Remove cinnamon stick. In a blender or food processor, purée until smooth. (Be careful when blending hot liquids.) Garnish with yogurt and parsley and serve.

Makes 4–6 servings.

+ Spinach & Sweet Potato Soup

This simple and filling soup is one of my favorite ways to get my iron, carbo-hydrates, and fiber. The sweet potatoes balance the spinach, making this a beneficial combination for Pitta.

1 tbsp olive oil
1 cup onions, chopped
1 tsp fresh ginger, minced
1 tsp garlic, minced
3½ cups sweet potatoes, cubed
5–6 cups fresh spinach, chopped
  (about 1 bunch)

1½ cups water
1 tsp salt, or to taste
Freshly ground pepper to taste
¼ tsp garam masala, or to taste

In a large pot on medium-high, heat oil. Add onions, ginger, and garlic and sauté until onions start to caramelize, about 5 minutes. Add sweet potatoes, spinach, water, and salt, cover with lid, and cook until sweet potatoes are softened, about 15–20 minutes. In a blender or food processor, purée until fairly smooth, but leave a bit chunky. (Be careful when blending hot liquids.) Stir in pepper and garam masala, then serve.

Makes 4 servings.

slightly +

Immune-Boosting Shiitake Mushroom & Vegetable Soup

This is a restorative soup that's rich with flavor from the shiitake mushrooms. Their meatiness combined with the texture of the cabbage, carrots, and sweet potatoes make this quite a hearty soup. I enjoy this for breakfast, lunch, or dinner, depending on my mood!

Dried shiitake mushrooms are easy to keep on hand. They enhance the immune system and are beneficial to all doshas, especially Kapha.

Sesame oil calms the nervous system and Vata.

Sometimes I add more water to the mushroom broth because the shiitakes can absorb a lot of liquid.

12 dried shiitake mushrooms
  (see note)
6 cups water (for soaking mushrooms)
1–2 tbsp good oil (see page 22)
  • *To reduce Vata: use 2 tbsp oil; to reduce Kapha: use 1 tbsp oil*
1 tbsp sesame oil (see note)
¾ cup onions, chopped
1 cup carrots, chopped
2 cups sweet potatoes, cubed
1 cup Chinese cabbage, chopped
  (or any cabbage)

1 clove garlic, minced
2 tsp fresh ginger, minced
½ cup spinach leaves, chopped
  (optional)
⅓ cup Bragg all-purpose seasoning
  or tamari or soy sauce
¼ cup miso paste (optional)
Freshly ground pepper to taste
¼ cup green onions, sliced
  (for garnish)

In a bowl, soak mushrooms in water for half an hour. Remove mushrooms, but reserve broth. Thinly slice mushrooms and set aside. In a large pot on medium-high, heat oil. Add mushrooms and sauté for a few minutes. Stir in sesame oil and onions, and continue to sauté until onions start to brown, 2–3 minutes. Add carrots and sweet potatoes and sauté for 2–3 minutes. Add cabbage, garlic, and ginger and stir. Cover with a lid and cook for 2 minutes. Add reserved broth (see note) and cook until vegetables are soft, about 20–25 minutes. Add spinach leaves (if using), Bragg, miso (if using), and pepper, and cook until spinach is wilted. Garnish with green onions and serve.

Makes 6–8 servings.

 Asparagus Miso Soup

 This soup is great for your body – miso is a good source of protein that is smooth and easy to digest, and asparagus calms the nervous system.

1 tsp olive oil
¼ cup onions, chopped
1 tsp fresh ginger, minced
2 tbsp vegetable bouillon powder
3 cups hot water
2 cups sweet potatoes, diced
  • To reduce Kapha: use regular potatoes
2 cups asparagus, chopped

Freshly ground pepper to taste
A pinch of cayenne pepper (optional)
Squeeze of lemon juice
1 tbsp miso paste
Salt or soy sauce to taste
1 tbsp plain yogurt (or sour cream)
  (for garnish)

In a large pot on medium-high, heat oil. Add onions and ginger and sauté until onions start to soften, about 4 minutes. In a bowl, dissolve bouillon in hot water, then add to pot. Add sweet potatoes and bring to a boil. Reduce heat and simmer for 10 minutes. Add asparagus and cook for an additional 5–10 minutes, until vegetables are just softened. Add pepper, cayenne, lemon juice, and miso, and stir continually until miso dissolves completely. Check for seasoning. Add salt or soy sauce, if necessary; if soup is too salty, add a little water. Remove from heat and lightly mash soup, leaving it somewhat chunky; if you prefer a thinner soup, add a bit more water. Garnish with yogurt (or sour cream) and serve.

Makes 4 servings.

slightly +

slightly +

-

Warming Cauliflower, Broccoli & Miso Soup

This is another of my favorite vegetable soups. Cauliflower and broccoli are filling, tasty, and a good source of fiber, and both are known to be cancer fighters. Broccoli is also a good source of vitamin A and C.

You can vary this recipe by using only cauliflower and omitting the broccoli.

2 tsp vegetable bouillon powder
1 cup hot water
1 tbsp olive oil
2 cups onions, chopped
½ tsp fresh green chilies, minced, or to taste
  • *To reduce Pitta: omit*
1 clove garlic, minced

5 cups cauliflower florets
4 cups broccoli florets
3½ cups water
3 cloves
1 cinnamon stick
  (about 2-in/5-cm long)
¼ cup miso paste
Salt and freshly ground pepper to taste

In a small bowl, dissolve bouillon in hot water and set aside. In a medium pot on medium-low, heat oil. Add onions and sauté until they start to soften, about 4 minutes. Add chilies and garlic and sauté until onions are caramelized, about 4 minutes. Add cauliflower, broccoli, and water. Increase heat and bring to a boil. Add cloves and cinnamon stick, reduce heat to low, and simmer until broccoli and cauliflower have softened, 15–20 minutes. Remove cinnamon stick and cloves. In a blender or food processor, purée until fairly smooth, but leave a bit chunky. (Be careful when blending hot liquids.) Add miso and stir until it dissolves completely. Add hot water if you desire a thinner consistency. Season with salt and pepper and serve.

Makes 4–6 servings.

slightly +

Miso Soup with Tofu, Green Onions & Seaweed

 This is a great energy booster to serve as a starter, snack, or meal; as easy to make as a cup of tea!

4½ cups water
1 tbsp thin black seaweed (see note)
4 tbsp miso paste
¼ cup medium tofu, cubed

2 green onions, white parts only, chopped
A dash of cayenne pepper

In a large pot on high heat, combine water and seaweed. Bring to a boil, then turn off heat. Add miso and stir until dissolved completely. Stir in tofu, onions, and cayenne and serve.

Makes 4 servings.

I recommend using Hijiki or Arame seaweed for this recipe, available dried in Asian markets and health food stores. You can also presoak the seaweed in cold water for 15 minutes before adding it to the soup, but I prefer simply boiling it with the water and watching it come to life! It should double in size when ready.

 ø - Variation: Add more water and a dash of Bragg all-purpose seasoning to make this tridoshic.

-
slightly +
-

Hearty Red Lentil, Barley & Vegetable Soup

A wonderful one-dish meal, packed with nutrients and protein.

If you are pressed for time, omit the barley, add lentils with the water, and cook for another 20 minutes until lentils are soft.

2 tsp olive oil
½ cup onions, chopped
1½ tsp garlic, minced
1 tsp fresh ginger, minced
 • *To reduce Pitta: omit*
½ cup celery (including some leaves), diced
½ tsp ground coriander
½ tsp ground cumin
¼ tsp cayenne pepper
½ tsp turmeric

1 cup carrots, sliced
¾ cup tomatoes (including liquid), chopped
¼ cup fresh parsley, chopped
2 bay leaves
1 tsp salt, or to taste
4 whole peppercorns
3 cloves
4 cups water
¼ cup barley
½ cup red lentils

In a large pot on medium-high, heat oil. Add onions, garlic, ginger, and celery and sauté for a minute. Stir in coriander, cumin, cayenne, and turmeric and sauté for another 2 minutes. Add carrots and sauté for 2–3 minutes. When liquid in mixture starts to evaporate, add tomatoes and their juice. Cook for another few minutes. Add parsley, bay leaves, salt, peppercorns, cloves, water, and barley, reduce heat to medium, and cook for 20 minutes. Stir in lentils, reduce heat to simmer, and cook for 25 minutes until lentils are soft. Remove bay leaves and peppercorns, and serve.

Makes 4–6 servings.

slightly +

 # Red Lentil Soup

 Quick and replenishing, this is one of my favorite meals after a run. I prepare this soup before I shower, and by the time I am dressed, it is ready.

1 tbsp olive oil
½ cup onions, finely chopped
1 tsp garlic, minced
1 tsp fresh ginger, minced
½ cup celery, finely chopped
½ cup carrots, finely chopped
⅔ cup red lentils
6 cups water

2 tsp vegetable bouillon powder
2 cloves
3 whole peppercorns
1 cinnamon stick
  (about 2-in/5-cm long)
Salt and freshly ground pepper to taste
1 tbsp fresh cilantro leaves, chopped
  (for garnish)

In a large pot on medium-high, heat oil. Add onions, garlic, and ginger and sauté for 1 minute. Add celery and carrots and cook for 3–4 minutes. Add lentils, water, and all other ingredients except salt, pepper, and cilantro and bring to a boil. Reduce heat to simmer, cover with lid, and cook for 20–25 minutes, until lentils are soft. Remove cinnamon stick and peppercorns. Add salt and pepper to taste, garnish with cilantro, and serve.

Makes 4–6 servings.

Sprouted Mung Bean Soup

 Sprouted mung beans are filled with protein and amino acids, which are the building blocks to good health. This soup is balancing and restorative for all the doshas, and easy to digest.

If you use cooked mung beans instead of sprouted, your soup will be ready after only 5 minutes of simmering.

1 tbsp olive oil
  • *To reduce Kapha: use a light version*
¼ cup onions, chopped
1 tsp fresh ginger, minced
1 tsp fresh green chilies, minced
  • *To reduce Pitta: only use half the amount or omit*

¼ cup celery, chopped
4 cups vegetable stock (page 112)
3 cups sprouted mung beans (see page 25) (see note)
Juice of ½ a lime

In a large pot on medium, heat oil. Add onions, ginger, and green chilies and sauté for 1 minute. Add celery and continue to sauté for 5–6 minutes, until onions are caramelized. Add vegetable stock and sprouted mung beans. Bring to a boil, then immediately reduce heat to low and simmer until done, 20–30 minutes. Stir in lime juice and serve.

Makes 4–6 servings.

 + –
slightly

Variation 1: Add these ingredients just before serving:
6 tbsp plain yogurt (*to reduce Kapha: use a light version*) 6 tsp Tamarind Chutney (see page 261); ¼ cup fresh cilantro leaves, chopped.

 + –

Variation 2: Add 6 tsp Cilantro Garlic Chutney (page 260) just before serving.

+

-

slightly +

Spicy Chickpea Soup
with Coconut, Cilantro & Yogurt

I took this dish to my friend Shelley's house for supper recently to see if she liked it. Not only did she like it, she couldn't wait to buy the book! Serve this filling soup with fresh bread for a complete meal..

Curry leaves are available in Indian grocery stores. They are used in soups for their distinct flavor and healing properties. In Ayurveda, curry leaves are known to be detoxifying, cooling, and bitter. Personally, I like to leave them in the soup as they continue to add flavor, but if you do, warn your guests not to eat them!

1 ½ tbsp good oil (see page 22)
   (for onions)
¾ cup onions, chopped
1 ½ tbsp good oil (see page 22)
   (for mustard seeds)
1 tsp black mustard seeds
1 tsp garlic, minced
   • To reduce Pitta: omit
1 tsp fresh ginger, minced
1 tsp turmeric
2 tsp ground coriander (or cumin)

2 cups chickpeas (garbanzo beans),
   cooked or canned
3 cups vegetable stock (page 112)
6 curry leaves (see note)
½ cup coconut milk
2 tbsp Tamarind Chutney (page 261)
   (or 2 tbsp lemon juice and 1 tsp
   maple syrup)
½ cup fresh cilantro leaves, chopped
   (for garnish)
½ cup plain yogurt (for garnish)

In a large pot on medium-low, heat 1 ½ tbsp oil. Add onions and sauté until caramelized, about 6–8 minutes. Push onions to one side of pot and heat another 1 ½ tbsp oil. Add mustard seeds, cover with lid, and let pop for 30 seconds, then stir together with onions. Add garlic, ginger, turmeric, coriander (or cumin), and sauté for another 3–4 minutes. Add chickpeas and stir for another few minutes. Add vegetable stock and curry leaves and simmer for 15–20 minutes.

Pour half the mixture from pot into a blender or food processor. (Make sure curry leaves stay in pot.) Add coconut milk and purée until smooth, then return to the pot. (Be careful when blending hot liquids.) Add tamarind chutney and stir well. Discard curry leaves (see note). In a separate bowl, combine cilantro and yogurt. Garnish soup with a dollop of cilantro-yogurt mixture, and serve.

Makes 4–6 servings.

+

-

-

Deb's Hearty Chickpea Soup

I live on Bowen Island off the coast of British Columbia and love Deb's soups at the Snug Café. She shared with me her recipe for one of my favorites. The chickpeas add protein and the grated cabbage adds texture, making it a hearty one-meal dish.

2 tbsp good oil (see page 22)
3 cups onions, chopped
4 tsp garlic, minced
  • *To reduce Pitta: omit*
1 cup water
4 cups tomatoes, diced
8 cups cabbage, grated
3 potatoes, diced
4 cups vegetable stock (page 112)
2 cups chickpeas (garbanzo beans), cooked or canned

4 cups vegetable stock (page 112) (for purée)
2 cups chickpeas (garbanzo beans), cooked or canned (for purée)
Juice of 1 lemon
2 tbsp sweet paprika
2 cups fresh parsley, chopped
Salt to taste (optional)

In a large pot on medium-high, heat oil. Add onions and garlic and sauté for a few minutes. Add water and continue to cook until onions are soft. Add tomatoes, cabbage, potatoes, and 4 cups vegetable stock, reduce heat, and simmer for 15–20 minutes, until vegetables are soft. Stir in 2 cups chickpeas and continue to cook. In a blender or food processor, combine another 4 cups vegetable stock and another 2 cups chickpeas and purée until smooth. (If using hot stock, be careful when blending hot liquids.) Pour mixture into soup. If too thick, add a little more vegetable stock. Stir in lemon juice, paprika, parsley, and salt (if necessary), and serve.

Makes 8–12 servings.

-
-
+ # Chilled Cucumber & Coconut Soup

This is a refreshing, cooling soup with a perfect mixture of warming spices.

2 cups cucumbers, chopped
½ tsp salt, or to taste
2 cloves garlic
  • *To reduce Pitta: omit*
1 tsp fresh ginger, minced
¼ cup fresh mint leaves, chopped
½ cup fresh cilantro leaves, chopped
1 tsp fresh green chilies, minced
  • *To reduce Pitta: omit*

Juice of 1 lime
¼ tsp ground cumin
1 cup coconut, grated
2 cups plain yogurt
¼ cup fresh cilantro leaves, chopped
  (for garnish)
¼ tsp cayenne pepper (for garnish)

In a bowl, combine cucumbers, salt, garlic, ginger, mint, cilantro, chilies, lime juice, and cumin and mix well. Cover and refrigerate for 3–4 hours. Once chilled, in a food processor or a blender, purée mixture and coconut. Pour into a serving dish, and stir in yogurt until smooth. If too thick, add ¼ cup of water. Garnish with cilantro, sprinkle with cayenne, and serve.

Makes 4 servings.

+

+

− Kathy's Gazpacho

Kathy was one of my first friends I made when my family moved to Canada from Kenya. It was through visits to her family's summer home that I first discovered Bowen Island, where I now reside in a wonderful community where cooking and sharing meals is celebrated. Every summer, when Kathy spends time on Bowen Island, her refrigerator is never without this soup. It is refreshing and light and has all the nourishment needed on hot sunny days.

Non-vegetarians can add 1 lb of cooked shrimp to this recipe.

To reduce Vata, add 2 cups of fresh breadcrumbs and an extra 2 cups of tomato juice.

2 cloves garlic
1 large jalapeño pepper
2 cups cucumbers, roughly chopped
2 celery stalks with leaves, sliced
1 red bell pepper, roughly chopped
1 small red onion, sliced
4 tomatoes, sliced
1 avocado, roughly chopped
1 cup fresh parsley, roughly chopped

1 cup tomato juice or V8 juice
½ cup fresh lime juice
¼ cup flax seed or hemp oil
1 tsp ground cumin, or more to taste
Salt and freshly ground pepper to taste
A few parsley sprigs (for garnish)
1 cup plain yogurt (for garnish)
  • *To reduce Kapha: omit or use a light version*

In a blender or food processor, mince garlic and jalapeño. Add cucumbers, celery, red bell peppers, onions, and tomatoes and pulse. Add remaining ingredients except garnishes, and pulse until quite smooth. Refrigerate until chilled. Garnish with a dollop of yogurt and a sprig of parsley, then serve.

Makes 6–8 servings.

 Chilled Mixed Fruit Soup

My friend Kathy has wonderful dinner parties in the summer and often serves this as the starter, making it a great conversation piece.

Fresh fruit is always best eaten on its own, or 15 minutes before another course – it's good for the digestion.

3 cups strawberries, quartered
3 nectarines, pitted and diced
3 plums, pitted and chopped
2½ cups blueberries
1 cup raspberries
1 cup blackberries
1½ cups peach nectar
   • *To reduce Vata: use fresh orange juice*

3 cups water
6 tbsp Agave nectar (or sweetener)
½ tsp cinnamon
1½ cups plain yogurt (for garnish)
   • *To reduce Pitta and Kapha: use a light version*
Sprigs of fresh mint (for garnish)

In a large bowl, combine ½ cup of strawberries, 1 nectarine, 1 cup of blueberries, and all the raspberries and blackberries and set aside. In a large pot, combine all remaining ingredients except garnishes and bring to a boil. Reduce heat to low and simmer until fruit is soft, about 15 minutes. In a blender or food processor, purée until smooth. (Be careful when blending hot liquids.) Return to pot, add reserved fruit while soup is still hot. Let cool, then cover with lid and refrigerate until chilled, about 30 minutes. Garnish with a dollop of yogurt and some mint leaves, then serve.

Makes 10 servings.

Entrées

In Indian cooking, a meal rarely consists of a single dish; traditionally, several dishes are served in combination. A complete "entrée" includes a protein (e.g., beans or tofu), a grain (e.g., rice or chapatis), vegetables (e.g., vegetable bajis or curries), condiments (e.g., raita and pickles), and something raw to aid digestion (e.g., salad or Dainty Cachumber [page 89]). An ideal meal includes all six tastes – sweet, sour, salty, pungent, bitter, and astringent – to balance out the doshas (see page 20).

If you are not sure how to set up a balanced Ayurvedic menu, refer to the suggested Menu Plans (page 293) until you feel comfortable creating your own. Also, I have included some one-pot dishes that only need a grain dish or a few condiments to create a balanced meal.

It is important to eat meals that suit your constitution and state of *agni* or digestive fire. If your agni is low – you feel heavy or lethargic after eating – choose meals that will gently restore it (e.g., the kitcharis or mung dal with simple spices). Eating meals that are too heavy

for an overtaxed digestive system can be compared to putting too much wood on a small fire: it will be smothered and and go out. If your agni is treated correctly with proper food choices and portions, its fire should easily consume or "digest" the food, giving you constant energy and a balanced feeling, sustaining you until your next meal.

In this chapter, you will find both traditional Indian recipes as well as some with a modern fusion bent. Our bodies are most familiar with foods we eat in our own particular "culture," so when you introduce new foods into your diet, start slowly to allow your body to assimilate them. Remember, your body speaks to you, telling you what it needs; listen to it.

There are many simple, easy recipes here that can be prepared in under 30 minutes with a minimum of ingredients, as long as you are equipped with the basic Indian spices (see page 21).This chapter begins with the essential three elements of a nutritious and balanced Ayurvedic meal. First are bean, lentil, and tofu dishes that I call "the meat" of the book. I have included tips on how to cook beans and lentils for readers who may be new to cooking them. The rice dishes follow because when combined with legumes, they create a complete protein. Next are the vegetable dishes, filled with flavor and nutrients, then a few pasta and egg dishes, as well as a Traditional "Buttermilk" Curry (page 214). You can mix-and-match protein, rice, and vegetable dishes to create a nutritionally-balanced meal that suits your own particular dosha.

Beans, Lentils & Tofu

Pulses (also known as legumes, and comprised of peas, beans, and lentils) mixed with grains are a staple of many diets all over of the world and are an essential component of eating the Ayurvedic way to maintain health and vitality. The combination of pulses with grains (usually rice), which add the essential amino acids that pulses lack, forms a complete protein. The most beneficial serving ratio of rice to pulses for optimal complete protein content is about 2:1; e.g., 1 cup of rice to ½ cup of lentils.

In India, beans and lentils are known as *gram* (the larger, whole pulse) and *dal* (the smaller, split pulse), respectively. The chickpea, which is also known as the garbanzo bean in the West, is *channa* in India, so when you are shopping at Indian or specialty markets and see a package labeled "channa dal," you'll know it is split chickpeas!

Incorporating more beans and lentils (along with rice or other grains) into your meals is a great way to improve your health as they are known to decrease blood fats and hardening of the arteries, lower cholesterol levels, and promote a healthy heart. Pulses are a good source of iron and B vitamins and are high in fiber and low in fat; they are also inexpensive and can be stored for a long period of time without refrigeration. Some people find beans and lentils difficult to digest; those who do, or those who do not already eat them regularly, should introduce them into their diet slowly (about once or twice a week) to give the digestive tract time to adapt.

Before cooking, it is best to soak dried beans and lentils overnight as it helps to break down the starches and their notorious gassy properties – some pulses do not require soaking, see chart on page 137 for details. Plus, soaking shortens the cooking time while increasing their protein and vitamin C content. Pre-soaking, or "sprouting," pulses also increases their nutritional value (up to an amazing forty times!) as it is brings the seed that was dormant back to life. For more information on sprouting, see page 25.

After soaking, beans and lentils must be cooked thoroughly to ensure easy digestion. You'll know they are done when they are tender in the middle without being mushy – with the exception of the split yellow mung bean and red (also known as Masoor or Egyptian) lentil, which inevitably turn mushy and somewhat soupy.

Mung beans are among the easiest to digest, making them beneficial for all the doshas. They are considered cooling and restorative, giving strength and vitality. The cooling qualities of mung beans are best balanced by warm spices – like ginger, green chilies, cumin, and mustard seeds – to aid digestion. Additionally, the sour tastes of lemon or Tamarind Chutney (page 261) will further help to stimulate agni. Kidney beans and chickpeas are more difficult to digest and should only be eaten when agni is high, a common attribute of Pitta. If you want to calm excess Vata, look for recipes with urad dal (black lentils). Kaphas will benefit from the dishes Channa Dal (page 157), Quick & Easy Red Masoor Dal (page 156), and Strengthening Tur Dal (page 152).

Cooking Beans and Lentils

Here is a general recipe for cooking most beans and lentils. Note that you should use about 1 cup beans or lentils for every 3–4 cups of water for cooking. You may need to add more water depending on the altitude you live in and the stove and pots you use. Keep in mind that the longer you soak the beans and lentils, the less cooking time they require.

TYPE OF BEAN OR LENTIL	AMOUNT OF DRIED BEAN OR LENTIL	AMOUNT OF WATER FOR SOAKING	SOAKING TIME	AMOUNT OF WATER FOR COOKING	COOKING TIME	YIELDS AMOUNT OF COOKED BEANS AND LENTILS
All beans and lentils, except ones listed below	1 cup	2–3 cups	6–8 hours	3–4 cups	40–60 minutes (dependent on soaking time)	2 cups
Azuki beans	"	"	"	"	"	3 cups
Black beans	"	"	"	"	"	2¼ cups
Kidney beans	"	"	"	"	"	2¼ cups
Red, brown, and green lentils	"	Not required	Not required	"	20 minutes	2½ cups
Split yellow mung beans	"	Not required	Not required	"	20 minutes	2 cups
Tur dal	"	2–3 cups	1–2 hours	"	40–60 minutes (dependent on soaking time)	2 cups

Continued on next page

1 cup dry beans or lentils
2–3 cups water (for soaking)
3–4 cups water (for cooking)
¼ tsp turmeric
1 tsp salt
2 slices fresh ginger
1 6-in (15-cm) stick kombu

1 fresh green chili, slit at end
(optional)
  • *To reduce Pitta: omit*
1 tsp good oil (see page 22)
  • *To reduce Kapha and Pitta: omit*
⅛ tsp hing (optional)

In a large pot or bowl, soak beans or lentils overnight in water for no more than 12 hours; lentils require a minimum of 4 hours (see chart on page 137 for exceptions). Drain soaked beans or lentils. In a large pot, combine water and beans or lentils and bring to a boil. A froth may rise to the surface; skim off as much as possible with a slotted spoon. Add all remaining ingredients. Reduce heat to simmer; make sure there is always enough water to prevent drying or burning. Beans or lentils are done when the center is tender, but not mushy. Discard kombu, ginger, and chili (if using) before serving.

Additional Tips for Cooking Beans and Lentils:

• Make sure you start with dried pulses that are fresh. Old pulses take a long time to cook and may have lost some of their nutrients. Dried pulses keep for up to a year when stored in a cool dark place. Also, always rinse them before cooking and pick out stones and debris.

• Don't soak split mung and red lentils, as they become too mushy.

- Once pulses have been soaked, drain them and cook in fresh water.

- Bean and lentil dishes are often prepared in two stages. First, the pulses are cooked, and then the *vagar* (a blend of spices) is sautéed and added to the cooked beans and lentils before serving. The vagar not only enhances the flavor of the mild-flavored pulses, but it also aids digestion.

- Pulses cook slower when salt or anything acidic is added during their cooking process so some people add the salt at the end. I prefer to have the pulses absorb the salt, so I add it earlier.

- Cooking pulses with fresh ginger aids their digestibility, as does adding kombu and hing.

- Kombu is a dried, black seaweed available at health food stores and Japanese grocers. Indians traditionally use ginger and hing when preparing beans and lentils. Using kombu instead is a contemporary, cross-cultural touch that is also full of minerals and nutrients. Kombu should not be eaten, so ensure you discard before serving.

- Hing (asafoetida) is spice made from dried resin that comes ground or in rock form and is available in Indian markets. A small jar will last a long time as you only need ⅛ tsp in your beans.

- Simmering means liquid continues to bubble occasionally. This usually requires medium or medium-low heat, however you should always adjust the heat to ensure bubbling is at its lowest point.

- Removing the froth that appears on the surface helps to prevent flatulence.

-
-
slightly +

Kala Channa in Coconut Sauce

Black chickpeas (kala channa, also known as Bengal gram) are smaller in size than white or yellow chickpeas. They have an earthy taste and a robust, nutty flavor, and the combination of spices, caramelized onions, and coconut sauce gives this dish its rich flavor. I took this Kala Channa to a picnic and the hostess served it with tortillas she had on hand. It is also good served with rice.

To make your own "light" coconut milk, simply add water to it, i.e. half regular coconut milk to half water.

1 cup dried black chickpeas

1 tbsp good oil (see page 22)
1 tsp mustard seeds
2 cups tomatoes, diced
1 tsp fresh ginger
1 clove garlic, minced
½ tsp ground cumin
½ tsp ground coriander
¼ tsp cayenne pepper
¼ tsp turmeric

Salt to taste
¾ cup coconut milk
  • *To reduce Kapha: use a light version (see note)*
4–5 curry leaves
Juice of 1 lemon
  (or Tamarind Chutney, page 261)
1 cup onions, thinly sliced
1 tsp ghee (or butter)
1 tsp olive oil

Soak and cook chickpeas (see page 137).

In a large pot on medium-high, heat oil. Add mustard seeds, cover with lid, and let pop for 30 seconds. Immediately add tomatoes, ginger, garlic, cumin, coriander, cayenne, turmeric, and salt. Reduce heat to medium and sauté until tomatoes have softened and spices are cooked, about 8–10 minutes. Add cooked chickpeas, coconut milk, and curry leaves. Cook for another 10–15 minutes. Add lemon juice, stir, and remove from heat. (If dish is too thick or too salty, add more water.) In a frying pan on medium, heat ghee and olive oil. Add onions and sauté until caramelized, about 8–10 minutes. Add to chickpea mixture, remove curry leaves, and serve.

Makes 4 servings.

Chickpea Curry

 Chickpea curry is best served with rice or chapatis and a Yogurt Raita (page 265); add green vegetables and the Dainty Cachumber (page 89), and you have a complete meal!

Save 1½ cups of water that the chickpeas were cooked in to add to this recipe.

1⅔ cups dried chickpeas (garbanzo beans)
1½ cups reserved water (see note)
2 tbsp good oil (see page 22)
¼ cup onions, minced
1 tbsp fresh ginger, minced
¼ tsp turmeric

½ tsp ground cumin
½ tsp ground coriander
½ tsp garam masala
¼ cayenne pepper, or to taste
Juice of 1 lemon
¼ cup fresh cilantro leaves, chopped
 (for garnish)

Soak and cook chickpeas until they are ⅔ done (see page 137).

In a medium pot on medium, heat oil. Add onions and sauté until they start to brown, 3–4 minutes. Add ginger, turmeric, cumin, coriander, garam masala, and cayenne, and sauté for another minute. Add chickpeas and reserved water. Bring liquid to a boil, then reduce heat to medium and simmer for about 20 minutes. When chickpeas are tender but not mushy, add lemon juice and adjust for salt. Serve garnished with cilantro.

Makes 4–6 servings.

slightly +

slightly +

\-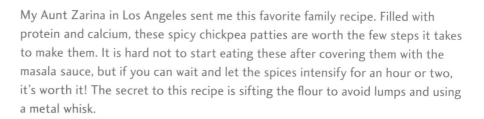

Aunty Zee's Masala Patties (or Dokri Nu Shak)

My Aunt Zarina in Los Angeles sent me this favorite family recipe. Filled with protein and calcium, these spicy chickpea patties are worth the few steps it takes to make them. It is hard not to start eating these after covering them with the masala sauce, but if you can wait and let the spices intensify for an hour or two, it's worth it! The secret to this recipe is sifting the flour to avoid lumps and using a metal whisk.

Dhanna jeera is simply an equal mixture of ground coriander (dhanna) and ground cumin (jeera). You can purchase it at Indian grocery stores, or just make it yourself, mixing equal parts coriander and cumin powders.

Patties:
2 cups gram flour
¾ cup onions, chopped
2–3 fresh green chilies, chopped
  • To reduce Pitta: use less or omit
1½ tsp dhanna jeera (see note)
1½ tsp salt
Juice of 1 lemon or lime

Masala:
¼ cup grapeseed oil (or good oil, see page 22)
1 tsp black mustard seeds
½ tsp whole cumin seeds
2 dried red chilies
  • To reduce Pitta: use 1

6–8 curry leaves (optional)
2 cups tomatoes, diced
1 tsp fresh ginger, minced
1 clove garlic, minced
  • To reduce Pitta: omit
¾ tsp ground cumin
¾ tsp ground coriander
¼ tsp turmeric
1½ tsp salt
Juice of 1 lemon or lime
1 tbsp tomato paste
2 cups plain yogurt
½ cup water
1 tbsp gram flour
¼ cup fresh cilantro leaves, chopped (for garnish)

For the patties:

(This can be done a day earlier and refrigerated.) In a medium bowl, sift flour, then add all remaining patty ingredients, mix well, and set aside. In a large pot, bring 4 cups of water to a boil. Add patty mixture then reduce heat to low. Stir continuously with a whisk to avoid lumps, and cook for 10–15 minutes until it begins to bubble. On a lightly greased baking sheet, spread the cooked mixture with a spatula to make a 12 × 12-in (30 × 30-cm) square and let it cool. When it has completely cooled, cut into 1 1/2-in (4-cm) squares and separate.

For the masala:

In a large frying pan on medium-high, heat oil. Add mustard seeds, cumin seeds, chilies, and curry leaves. Cover with lid for 30 seconds while the mustard seeds pop. Stir in remaining masala ingredients except yogurt, water, flour, and cilantro. Reduce heat to medium-low and cook for 15–20 minutes, until oil appears on the surface. Gently add the square patties to the masala and cover them with sauce. Turn off heat. Serve immediately or let sit for 1–2 hours for flavors to intensify.

Just before serving, in a bowl, beat together yogurt, water, and flour, ensuring there are no lumps. Add to the masala and patties and heat on low for about 5 minutes until heated through. (Do not overcook as the patties will absorb too much liquid.) Garnish with fresh cilantro and serve.

Makes 4–6 servings.

+

-

- # Tea Party Channa Bateta

Indians love having tea parties, where this is often served to guests along with Tamarind Chutney (page 261) and savory snacks such as Savory Dokra Squares (page 71), or Baked Pakoras (page 61). Channa Bateta can also be served as part of a main course.

1 tsp good oil (see page 22)	¼ cup fresh cilantro leaves, chopped
½ tsp black mustard seeds	1 tsp salt, or to taste
1 ½ cups potatoes, boiled and cubed	1 ½ cups chickpeas (garbanzo beans),
½ tsp turmeric	cooked or canned (see page 137)
1 tsp fresh green chilies, minced	2 tbsp lemon juice
½ tsp cayenne pepper, or to taste	1 tsp sweetener

In a large pot on medium-high, heat oil. Add mustard seeds, cover with lid, and let pop for 30 seconds. Immediately add potatoes, turmeric, green chilies, cayenne, cilantro, and salt and stir and sauté for 2–3 minutes. Add chickpeas, stir, and cook for 2 minutes. Add lemon juice and sweetener and mix well. For a thicker consistency, mash ¼ cup of the bean and potato mixture separately and return to pot.

Makes 2 servings.

+

-

- # Quick Black Beans

I like making this when I'm hungry and want a tasty, satisfying meal. The leftovers are great for lunch the next day. Serve with rice or your favorite bread.

1 tbsp good oil (see page 22)
1 tsp sesame oil
¾ cup onions, chopped
½ tsp fresh ginger, minced
1 tsp garlic, minced (about 1 clove)
   • To reduce Pitta: omit
½ tsp fresh green chilies, chopped
   • To reduce Pitta: omit
1 cup zucchini, quartered and sliced
1 cup yellow bell peppers, diced

1 cup red bell peppers, diced
2 cups spinach
Tamari (or salt) to taste
Chili sauce to taste
   • To reduce Pitta: omit
2 cups black beans, cooked
   (see page 137)
½ cup plain yogurt (for garnish)
¼ cup fresh cilantro leaves, chopped
   (for garnish)

In a pot on medium-high, heat oils. Add onions, ginger, garlic, and chilies, and sauté for 1–2 minutes. Add zucchini, peppers, spinach, tamari (or salt), and chili sauce. Cover with lid, reduce heat to medium, and cook for 4–5 minutes. Add beans and mix until heated through. Serve in individual bowls with a dollop of yogurt and a sprinkling of cilantro.

Makes 2 servings.

slightly +

\-

ø # Small Red Bean Curry

I took this to a potluck dinner and it was polished off with rave reviews! The cilantro balances all the doshas. Serve this with rice or chapatis, Cumin Raita (page 267), and a vegetable dish for a complete, balanced meal.

Small red beans are smaller, slightly rounder, and darker versions of red kidney beans. They are sometimes called Mexican red beans, or simply red beans. They should be available at any market, but pinto, red kidney, or Azuki beans are good substitutes.

2 cups dried small red beans (see note)

2 tbsp good oil (see page 22)
1 cup onions, minced
2 tbsp fresh ginger, minced
2 tsp garlic, minced
2 tsp ground coriander

1 tsp ground cumin
1 tsp garam masala
1½ cups fresh tomatoes, cubed
Juice of 1 lemon
3 tbsp fresh cilantro leaves, chopped
  (for garnish)

Soak and cook red beans until they are ²/₃ done (see page 137).

In a frying pan on medium-high, heat oil. Add onions, ginger, and garlic, reduce heat to medium and sauté until onions are caramelized, about 5–6 minutes. Add coriander, cumin, and garam masala and sauté for another 30 seconds. Stir in tomatoes and cook for about 5 minutes until tomatoes turn soft. Add mixture to cooked beans and cook for 15–20 minutes until beans are cooked through. Add lemon juice and adjust for salt. Garnish with cilantro and serve.

Makes 6 servings.

+ - +

 - - -

Variation 1: Substitute red kidney beans for small red beans.

Variation 2: Substitute Azuki beans for small red beans

+

-

slightly +

Doug's Favorite Beans

When my friend Doug invited me to Costa Rica, we ate fresh fish and beans almost everyday. I love the flavor and texture of the black-eyed peas combined with the coconut, veggies, and spices. Serve this dish with rice.

If you soak the black-eyed peas overnight they will only take 25 minutes to cook.

A vagar is a mixture of spices that is sautéed separately and added to the dish at the end.

Beans:
3 cups dried black-eyed peas (see note)
9 cups water
1 fresh green chili, slit at end
3 slices fresh ginger
½ tsp turmeric
2 tsp salt
1 stick kombu (optional)
2 large red bell peppers, cubed
2 large green bell peppers, cubed
2 cups coconut milk
 • *To reduce Kapha: use 1 cup coconut milk and 1 cup water*

6 tbsp lemon juice (or to taste)
1 tbsp gur (or brown sugar) (optional)

Vagar (see note):
1 tbsp ghee
 • *To reduce Kapha: use ½ this amount*
1 tbsp olive oil
2 cups onions, sliced
1 tbsp fresh green chilies, minced
 • *To reduce Pitta: use 1 tsp or omit*
1 tbsp fresh ginger, minced
½ cup fresh cilantro leaves, chopped (for garnish)

For the beans:
In a large pot on high heat, add beans, water, chili, ginger, turmeric, salt, and kombu (if using) and bring to a boil. Reduce heat to simmer and cook until beans are almost done, about 40 minutes. Add peppers, coconut milk, lemon juice, and gur (if using) and cook until done, about 10 minutes.

For the vagar:
While beans are cooking, in a large frying pan on medium-low, heat ghee and oil. Add onions, chilies, and ginger and sauté until caramelized, up to 30 minutes depending on how low your heat is; the slower the process, the sweeter the onions will be. When ready, pour over beans. Garnish with cilantro and serve.

Makes 8–10 servings.

Balancing Mung Dal

Split yellow mung is a lentil that cooks quickly and balances all three doshas. It is nourishing and easy on the digestive system.

Dal:
2 cups dried split yellow mung dal
5–6 cups water
1 fresh green chili, slit at end
  • *To reduce Pitta: use 1/4 or omit*
1 1-in (2½-cm) piece fresh ginger, sliced
2 tsp salt
¼ tsp turmeric
1 tsp olive oil

Vagar:
1 tbsp olive oil (I use half ghee and half olive oil)
1 tsp whole cumin seeds
¾ cup onions, sliced
1 tbsp fresh ginger, minced
1 tsp salt, or to taste
1 fresh green chili, minced
  • *To reduce Pitta: use 1/4 or omit*

¼ cup fresh cilantro leaves, chopped (for garnish)
1 tomato, sliced (for garnish)
  • *To reduce Pitta: omit*

For the dal:
In a large pot, combine all dal ingredients and bring to a boil. Reduce heat to medium and simmer until done, about 20–25 minutes.

For the vagar:
In a frying pan on medium-high, heat oil. Add cumin seeds and let sizzle for about 30 seconds. Add remaining vagar ingredients. Reduce heat to medium and sauté until onions are caramelized, about 7–8 minutes.

To serve, place cooked dal in a serving dish. Spread vagar on top and garnish with cilantro and tomato slices.

Makes 4–6 servings.

The King Dal

Whole mung (or "moong") beans are considered the "king" of beans and lentils because of their amino-acid content that balances and nourishes all the doshas.

½ cup dried whole green mung beans
3 cups water (for soaking)

1 tbsp good oil (see page 22)
¼ tsp mustard seeds
⅛ tsp hing
2 cups water
¼ tsp turmeric

¼ tsp cayenne pepper (optional)
  • *To reduce Pitta: omit*
Salt to taste
Juice of ½ a lemon
1 tbsp fresh cilantro leaves
  (or parsley), chopped (for garnish)

Soak beans in 3 cups water for at least 4 hours or overnight.

Drain beans and set aside. In a medium pot on medium-high, heat oil. Add mustard seeds, cover with lid, and let pop about 30 seconds. Immediately add soaked beans, hing, water, turmeric, cayenne, and salt. Bring to a boil, then reduce heat to simmer until done, about 40–60 minutes. (The longer the beans have soaked, the less water they need and time to cook.) Check from time to time in case you need to add more water. Add lemon juice, garnish with cilantro, and serve.

Makes 3–4 servings.

Sprouted Mung Dal

Sprouting mung beans before cooking increases their digestibility and nutritional value. This dal is a nourishing, gentle dish that can be served both hot and cold for a light lunch with rice and pickles.

4 cups sprouted whole green mung
  beans (see Sprouting page 25)
1½ cups water
¼ tsp turmeric
3 slices fresh ginger
1 fresh green chili, slit at end
  (optional)
  • *To reduce Pitta: omit*

Juice of 1 lemon (optional)
½ tsp cayenne pepper (optional)
  • *To reduce Pitta: omit*
Salt to taste

In a large pot, combine sprouted mung beans, water, turmeric, ginger, and green chili and bring to a boil. Reduce heat and simmer until done, 15–20 minutes. Add a little water as needed if liquid starts to dry out, but be sure that beans do not overcook. When cooked, the green husks will start to come off and mung will look yellow. Drain, then remove ginger slices and chili. Add lemon juice, cayenne, and salt (if using), then serve.

Makes 4 servings.

-

slightly +

slightly +

Granny's Dal

On Sundays, my grandmother would serve this with basmati rice or Whole Wheat Chapatis (page 218) for our large family gatherings. Urad dal has a calm, grounding effect on Vata, which is perfect for my highly active family!

Dal:

2 cups dried whole urad dal

6 cups water (for soaking)

6 cups water (for cooking)

1 tsp salt

1 1-in (2½-cm) piece fresh ginger, sliced

1 tsp good oil (see page 22)

5 cups water

1 fresh green chili, slit at end (optional)

• *To reduce Pitta: use ¼ or omit*

Vagar:

2 tsp good oil (see page 22)

¾ cup onions, sliced

1 tsp fresh ginger, minced

½–2 fresh green chilies, minced

• *To reduce Pitta: omit*

1 tsp salt

• *To reduce Pitta: use less or omit*

¼ cup fresh cilantro leaves, chopped (for garnish) (optional)

For the dal:

In a large bowl, soak urad dal in water for at least 4 hours or overnight. Drain before cooking. In a large pot, combine soaked dal and remaining dal ingredients and bring to a boil. Reduce heat to medium-low and simmer until done, about 1 hour. Add a little water as needed if liquid starts to dry out.

For the vagar:

In a medium frying pan on medium-low, heat oil. Add onions, ginger, green chilies, and salt, and sauté until onions are caramelized, about 8–10 minutes.

When dal is ready, remove ginger slices and whole chilies and place in a serving dish. Sprinkle vagar on top, garnish with cilantro, and serve.

Makes 6–8 servings.

+
-

Strengthening Tur Dal

This tur dal dish is always a hit at lunch or dinner parties. My maternal grandmother used to say that if the spices made you cough while making the vagar, the dish would taste good! Tur dal is a blood builder and strengthens muscles; it is also good for bones, joints, skin, and eyes. It goes well with basmati rice or Simple Pea Pilau (page 173).

Tur dal (also toor, tuvar, or arhar) are tan-colored when whole, but are usually sold skinned and split, exposing their yellow interior. Available at Indian or specialty grocery stores.

Dal:

2 cups dried tur dal (see note)
6 cups water (for soaking)
7 cups water (for cooking)
1 tsp salt
⅛ tsp hing
¼ tsp turmeric
1 tsp good oil (see page 22)
4–6 curry leaves (optional)

Vagar:

2 tsp good oil (see page 22)
2–3 dried red chilies
1 tsp black mustard seeds
1 tsp fresh ginger, minced

1 tsp garlic, minced
1 tsp salt
½ tsp turmeric
1 tsp ground cumin
1 tsp ground coriander
¼ tsp cayenne pepper, or to taste
  • To reduce Pitta: omit
1 cup tomatoes, chopped
2 tbsp tomato purée
2 tbsp lemon juice (see note)
1 tsp sweetener (optional) (see note)

¼ cup fresh cilantro leaves
  (or parsley), chopped (for garnish)

You could use
Tamarind Chutney
(page 261) in
place of the lemon
juice and sweetener.

Make this Tur Dal
a one-pot meal:
Add chopped car-
rots and quartered
potatoes to cook
with the dal.

For the dal:

Soak dal in 6 cups water for 1–2 hours. Drain before using. In a large pot on high heat, combine 7 cups water and tur dal and bring to a boil. Skim off froth with a slotted spoon. Add turmeric, salt, hing, oil, and curry leaves (if using). Reduce heat and simmer for 45 minutes.

For the vagar:

While the dal cooks, in a frying pan on medium-high, heat oil. Add chilies and sauté until they turn black. Immediately add mustard seeds, cover with a lid, and let pop for 30 seconds. Immediately add remaining vagar ingredients, except lemon juice and sweetener, and sauté until oil appears on the surface, about 5–7 minutes. You may want to reduce heat to medium if too hot.

Add vagar to cooked tur dal and stir. Add lemon juice and sweetener (if using) and simmer on medium or medium-low heat for another 10 minutes. Garnish with cilantro and serve.

Makes 2–4 servings.

–

+

slightly +

Urad Dal

Urad dal are black-skinned, cream-colored seeds with an earthy flavor. They are slightly heavy and therefore grounding and restorative for Vata. The cumin and hing aid digestion. Serve with rice or chapatis and a raita or plain yogurt.

1 cup dried urad dal

Vagar:
1 tsp ghee (or butter)
  • *To reduce Vata: increase to 2 tsp*
1 tsp olive or grapeseed oil
  • *To reduce Vata: increase to 2 tsp*
1 ½ tsp whole cumin seeds
1 cup onions, minced
2 tbsp fresh ginger, minced
4 tsp garlic, minced
  • *To reduce Pitta: omit*

¾ cup tomatoes, diced
1 tsp salt
2 tsp ground coriander
1 tsp fresh green chilies, minced
  • *To reduce Pitta: omit*
Salt to taste

1 tsp garam masala (for garnish)
¼ cup fresh cilantro leaves, chopped
  (for garnish)

Soak and cook urad dal (see page 137). Urad dal doesn't have to be soaked before cooking, but this will add an additional hour to the cooking time.

In a pot or frying pan on medium-high, heat ghee and oil. Add cumin seeds, cover with lid, and let sizzle for 30 seconds. Add remaining vagar ingredients, reduce heat to medium and sauté for 5–7 minutes until tomatoes are soft. Add vagar to cooked urad dal and mix well. Sprinkle with garam masala and cilantro, then serve.

Makes 4–6 servings.

– – + Variation: Before serving, add ¼ cup cream and heat through.

Ø

slightly +

 # Simple Brown Masoor Dal

 Brown or green lentils cook fast and are very satisfying. The cumin, coriander, and cilantro calm all the doshas. I often prepare this dish when I return from a run, and by the time I am out of the shower it is ready. Caution: do not overcook these lentils as they will become too mushy. Serve with chapatis or rice, and yogurt.

1 cup dried brown or green lentils	¾ tsp ground coriander
3 cups water or vegetable stock	¼ tsp garam masala
⅓ cup onions, chopped	¼ tsp fresh green chilies, chopped,
¾ cup tomatoes, chopped	or cayenne pepper
1 tsp tomate purée (optional)	• *To reduce Pitta: omit*
1 tsp fresh ginger, minced	½ tsp salt, or to taste
1 tsp good oil (see page 22)	1 tsp gur (or sweetener)
A pinch of hing (optional)	2 tbsp lemon juice
¼ tsp turmeric	¼ cup fresh cilantro leaves, chopped
¾ tsp ground cumin	(for garnish)

In a medium pot on high heat, bring lentils and water to a boil. Add all remaining ingredients except for gur, lemon juice, and cilantro. Reduce heat and simmer for approximately 20 minutes, or until lentils are done, adding more water if necessary. Add gur and lemon juice, mixing well to dissolve gur. Adjust for seasoning. Sprinkle with cilantro and serve.

Makes 2–3 servings.

Variation: Add 1 cup chopped vegetables to cook with other ingredients.

ø

slightly –

– # Quick & Easy Red Masoor Dal

These lentils are orange in their dried form and turn yellow once cooked. This is a great recipe if you're in a hurry or have unexpected guests. It has a light sweet and sour flavor and makes a balanced meal when served with rice or chapatis, the Dainty Cachumber (page 89), plain yogurt, and a green salad.

1 cup dried red lentils
  (no need to be soaked)
3 cups water
1 tsp salt
A pinch of hing (optional)
3 slices fresh ginger
1 fresh green chili, slit at end
  • *To reduce Pitta: use ¼ or omit*

½ cup tomatoes, diced
1 tsp tomato purée (optional)
½ cup onions, minced
¼ tsp turmeric
Juice of ½ a lemon
½ tsp gur (or maple syrup) (optional)
¼ cup fresh cilantro leaves
  (for garnish)

In a large pot, combine all ingredients except turmeric, lemon juice, gur, and cilantro. Bring to a boil, then reduce heat and simmer. Skim off froth with a slotted spoon. Add turmeric, stir, and cook until done, about 20 minutes. You may add more water if dal seems too dry. Add lemon juice and gur (if using), and stir to dissolve. Garnish with cilantro.

Makes 3–4 servings.

+

slightly +

- # Channa Dal

Channa dal is a split-lentil relative of whole chickpeas. It is a robust and tasty lentil that is yellow in color like tur dal, but can be heavier to digest, so only eat when your body has a strong digestive fire. Serve with chapatis or rice, a zucchini dish, and condiments for a complete meal.

2 cups dried split chickpeas

Vagar:
2 tbsp good oil (see page 22)
1 ½ tsp whole cumin seeds
1 ½ cup fresh tomatoes, chopped
1 ½ tsp ground coriander
¼ tsp turmeric
1 tsp garlic, minced
 • *To reduce Pitta: omit*

1–2 tsp fresh ginger, minced
Salt to taste
1–2 tsp fresh green chilies minced, or cayenne pepper
 • *To reduce Pitta: omit*
2 tbsp tomato paste
1 tsp maple syrup (or sweetener)
2 tbsp lemon juice, or to taste
½ cup fresh cilantro leaves, chopped (for garnish)

Soak and cook chickpeas (see page 137).

In a medium frying pan on medium-high, heat oil. Add cumin seeds and let sizzle for 30 seconds. Add remaining ingredients except maple syrup, lemon juice, and cilantro. Reduce heat to medium and sauté until tomatoes soften and spices are well cooked, about 8–10 minutes.

Add vagar to cooked chickpeas and mix over medium heat. Cook for 5 minutes, then add lemon juice and maple syrup. Garnish with cilantro.

Makes 6–8 servings.

Ameeta's Sliced Tofu with Green Onions & Cilantro

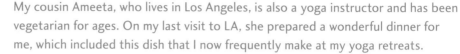

My cousin Ameeta, who lives in Los Angeles, is also a yoga instructor and has been vegetarian for ages. On my last visit to LA, she prepared a wonderful dinner for me, which included this dish that I now frequently make at my yoga retreats.

Ingredients such as ginger, soy, chili, and mustard warm the cool tofu and aid its digestion. Lemon juice stimulates the digestive fire (agni) and cilantro balances all the doshas. Eating tofu in excess will imbalance Kapha.

1 pkg firm tofu (about 1½ cups)
1 cup fresh cilantro leaves, chopped
½ cup green onions, sliced
2 tbsp sesame seeds
¼ tsp dried red chili flakes (optional)
  • To reduce Pitta: omit

Dressing:
¼ cup soy sauce or Bragg all-purpose seasoning
2 tbsp fresh ginger, grated
1 tbsp sesame seed oil
1 tsp Dijon mustard
¼ cup lemon juice

Drain tofu, wrap in a dish towel, and set aside to dry. Meanwhile, in a jar, combine all dressing ingredients, shake well to mix, and set aside. Slice tofu into ½-in (1½-cm) thick slices and place in a medium bowl. Pour dressing over tofu to marinate for at least 30 minutes. Add cilantro, green onions, sesame seeds, and chili flakes (if using). Toss and serve.

Makes 4–6 servings.

-
-

slightly + # Coconut Vegetable Tofu Medley

This is a complete meal when served with rice and includes all of the essential Ayurvedic tastes. I created this dish one day using whatever ingredients I had in the kitchen and it has since become a favorite. In Ayurveda, coconut is considered a sweet taste that calms Vata and cools down Pitta. It also is known to give strength, building Kapha properties.

1 tsp good oil (see page 22)
  • *To reduce Vata: add an extra tsp*
⅓ cup onions, chopped
1 clove garlic, minced
1 tsp fresh ginger, minced
¼ tsp turmeric
1 tsp salt, or to taste
1 fresh green chili, minced
  • *To reduce Pitta: use ¼ tsp or omit*
1 cup red bell peppers, diced

1 cup yellow bell peppers, diced
3 cups zucchini, quartered and sliced
  • *To reduce Kapha: use broccoli instead*
2 cups medium tofu, cubed
½ cup coconut milk
Juice of 1 lemon
1 tsp Agave nectar (or maple syrup)
  (optional)
¼ cup fresh cilantro leaves, chopped
  (for garnish)

In a medium pot on medium-high, heat oil. Add onions and sauté for 1–2 minutes. Reduce heat to medium, then add garlic, ginger, turmeric, salt, and chili, and sauté for another 1–2 minutes. Add peppers and zucchini, cover with lid, and cook until almost done, 4–6 minutes. Add tofu, coconut milk, lemon juice, and Agave nectar. Reduce heat to medium-low and simmer for another 5 minutes. Garnish with cilantro and serve.

Makes 3–4 servings.

-
-
+

Let's Tofu with Bok Choy & Yam Home Fries

Let, who cooks for my friends the Websters, often fuses her traditional Philippino cuisine with our "modern" ingredients. She once cooked this simple, tasty dish for lunch which left me feeling satisfied and energized without feeling heavy.

Arrowroot is a starch made from the swollen roots of a plant native to the West Indies and South America. It is a wonderful, clear thickener used in gravies and sauces that is more easily digested than other thickening agents.

1 tsp toasted sesame oil
1 cup medium-firm tofu, cubed
½ tsp ground arrowroot (see note)
¼ cup water
1 tsp soy sauce
½ tsp oyster sauce

1 cup bok choy, chopped
1 tsp ghee, (or good oil, see page 22)
1 cup yams, peeled and sliced
¼-in (¾-cm) thick
Water, enough to cover the yams in
   the skillet

In a frying pan on medium-high, heat oil. Add tofu and brown for about 2 minutes. In a cup or small bowl, dissolve arrowroot in water and stir. Add to tofu along with soy sauce and oyster sauce, mixing well. Bring to a boil, stirring constantly as it thickens, about 1 minute. Immediately add bok choy, cover with lid, reduce heat to medium, and cook for 3–5 minutes, or until done.

In another frying pan on high, heat ghee (or oil). Add yams and brown on each side. Add enough water to cover yams and cook, covered, for 4 minutes (you may want to reduce heat to medium-high). Remove lid and continue to cook until most of the water evaporates. Serve immediately with the tofu and bok choy.

Makes 2 servings.

-
slightly +
- Tandoori Tofu

After marinating in this delectable mixture overnight, the tofu becomes rich with flavor. Tandoori Tofu is great barbecued as well as baked, and can also be made into a tasty appetizer by cutting them into bite-sized squares and serving with toothpicks, Taramind Chutney (page 261), and yogurt.

1 ½ cups firm tofu, cubed
1 cup plain yogurt
  • *To reduce Kapha: use a lighter version*
2 cloves garlic, minced
  • *To reduce Pitta: use ½ clove or omit*
1 tsp fresh ginger, minced
¼ cup fresh cilantro leaves, choppe
Juice of 1 lemon
½ tsp ground cumin

½ tsp ground coriander
¼ tsp turmeric
1 fresh green chili, minced
  • *To reduce Pitta: omit or use ¼ tsp*
¼–½ tsp garam masala
¾ tsp salt, or to taste
¼ cup fresh cilantro leaves, chopped
  (for garnish)

In a large bowl, combine tofu with remaining ingredients except cilantro and toss until well mixed. Cover and refrigerate overnight.

Set oven to broil. Place tofu pieces in a single layer on a baking sheet. Pour any remaining marinade over top. Place on upper rack in oven and broil, stirring until lightly browned on each side, 3–4 minutes. Garnish with cilantro and serve.

Makes 4–6 servings (5 cubes per person).

For non-vegetarians: In place of tofu, use chicken (about 6 pieces on the bone, or for appetizers, 2 cups of chicken breast cut into bite-sized pieces) with this marinade and broil or barbecue at 350°F (180°C) until chicken juices runs clear, about 45 minutes.

-
+
- # The Modern "Pau" Baji

This baji is great as a meal any time and is easy to pack for lunch. It has a good mixture of protein and vegetables as well as all six Ayurvedic tastes. It is also complementary for Vata and Kapha.

2 cups texturized vegetable protein (TVP) (available in health food stores)
2 cups hot vegetable stock
½ cup onions, minced
¼ cup fresh cilantro leaves, chopped
1 fresh green chili, minced
½ tsp fresh ginger, minced
½ tsp garlic, minced
1 tsp dhanna jeera (see note on page 142)

4 tbsp lemon juice
1 tsp salt
¼ cup plain yogurt
2 eggs
2 tsp good oil (see page 22)
2 dried red chilies
1 tsp black mustard seeds
¼ cup celery, chopped
½ cup carrots, chopped
½ cup red bell peppers, diced
½ cup zucchini, sliced and quartered

In a large bowl, combine TVP and vegetable stock and let sit for about 10 minutes to reconstitute (it should double in size). Add onions, cilantro, green chilies, ginger, garlic, dhanna jeera, lemon juice, salt, yogurt, and eggs and mix well. Set aside.

In a frying pan on medium-high, heat oil. Add red chilies and sauté until blackened, 1–2 minutes. Immediately add mustard seeds, cover with lid, and let pop for 30 seconds. Add the celery and carrots and sauté for 3–4 minutes, then add peppers and zucchini. When liquid starts to dry out, add TVP mixture. Cook for another 5 minutes or until all moisture is absorbed.

Makes 4 servings.

+

-

- # Vegetarian Mixed Bean Chili

Chili lovers should try this great one-pot meal. After sharing this recipe among friends, they all told me it has become their family favorite. I love the TVP (texturized vegetable protein) in this chili as it absorbs all the flavors and has the texture of ground meat without the fat. Serve topped with yogurt or sour cream and grated cheese. (To reduce Kapha: omit or use light yogurt or sour cream.)

½ cup texterized vegetable protein (TVP) (available in health food stores)
2 tsp vegetable bouillon powder
1 cup hot water
1 tbsp good oil (see page 22)
1 cup onions, chopped in big chunks
1 cup celery, chopped
1 cup carrots, chopped
2 cloves garlic, minced
 • *To reduce Pitta: omit*
1 cup mushrooms, chopped

1 ½ cups mixed green, yellow, and red bell peppers, cubed
1 ½ cups tomatoes, chopped
1 ½ cups mixed beans (e.g., pinto, chickpeas, navy), cooked
1 tbsp chili con carne seasoning
1 tbsp wine (optional)
1 tbsp oyster sauce (or maple syrup or honey) (optional)
Dash of hot chili sauce
 • *To reduce Pitta: omit*
Salt to taste

In a medium bowl, combine TVP, vegetable stock powder, and hot water and let sit for 10 minutes to reconstitute TVP (it will double in size). In a large pot on medium, heat oil. Add onions, celery, and carrots and sauté for 3–4 minutes. Add garlic, mushrooms, and peppers and sauté for 2 minutes. Add remaining ingredients and TVP and simmer for 20 minutes. Check seasoning and add salt if necessary.

Makes 4–6 servings.

For non-vegetarians: Instead of the TVP and hot water: add 1 cup ground turkey or chicken; or add 1 cup ground beef.

-
-
+

Happy Cow Shepherd's Pie

This is another great one-dish meal that has become a regular comfort food for many of my family and friends. It uses texturized vegetable protein in place of beef. Using mashed sweet potatoes keeps this low on the Glycemic Index.

2 tsp vegetable bouillon powder
1 cup hot water
1 cup texturized vegetable protein (TVP) (available in health food stores)
1 tbsp good oil (see page 22)
⅓ cup onions, chopped
½ tsp fresh ginger, minced
1 clove garlic, minced
  • *To reduce Pitta: omit*
1 fresh green chili, slit at end
  • *To reduce Pitta: omit*
1 stalk celery, thinly sliced
½ bell pepper of your choice, diced

½ cup fresh green peas, cooked
¼ cup mushrooms, sliced
¼ cup fresh cilantro leaves (or parsley)
¼ cup water
1 tsp salt
1 tbsp oil
Freshly ground black pepper to taste
½ cup tomato sauce, (or ½ cup chopped fresh tomatoes)
3 sweet potatoes, cooked and mashed (about 5 cups)
  • *To reduce Kapha: use white potatoes*
1 tbsp grated Parmesan cheese

In a bowl, combine bouillon and hot water, then add TVP and soak for 5 minutes to reconstitute TVP (it will double in size). In a medium pot on medium-high, heat oil. Add onions, ginger, garlic, and chili and sauté for 2 minutes. Add TVP and remaining ingredients except sweet potatoes and Parmesan cheese. Reduce heat to medium and simmer until done, about 20 minutes. (If it starts to dry out, cover with lid.) Remove chili.

Preheat oven to 350°F (180°C). Spread TVP mixture evenly in a casserole or ovenproof dish. Cover with mashed sweet potatoes and flatten with fork.
Rake fork through for a nice design. Sprinkle Parmesan cheese on top. Bake for 20 minutes. Cut in squares and serve.

Makes 4–6 servings.

–

slightly +

ø # Vegetarian Kheema Matur

Kheema is ground meat, but I substitute it with TVP (texturized vegetable protein) and it turns out great. Serve with rice or chapatis.

2 tsp vegetable bouillon powder
1 cup boiling water
1 cup texturized vegetable protein (TVP)
3 tsp grapeseed oil (or good oil, see page 22)
½ cup onions, chopped
1 tsp garlic, minced
 • *To reduce Pitta: omit*
1 tsp fresh ginger, minced
1 tsp fresh green chilies, minced
 • *To reduce Pitta: omit*
¾ cup tomatoes, diced

2 tsp tomato paste
½ tsp ground cumin
½ tsp ground coriander
¼ tsp turmeric
½ tsp garam masala
1 cinnamon stick, 2-in (5-cm) long
2 cardamom pods, slit at end
½ tsp salt, or to taste
1 cup fresh green peas
1 cup water
Juice of a ½ lemon
¼ cup fresh cilantro leaves (or parsley), chopped

In a medium bowl, dissolve vegetable bouillon in hot water. Add TVP and set aside for 10 minutes to reconstitute TVP (it will double in size). In a large frying pan on medium-high, heat the oil. Add onions, garlic, ginger, and chilies and sauté until onions are soft, about 3 minutes. Add tomatoes, tomato paste, cumin, coriander, turmeric, garam masala, cinnamon stick, cardamom pods, and salt. Sauté until tomatoes become soft and oil rises to the surface, about 5 minutes. Add the reconstituted TVP, peas, and water and cook for 10 more minutes. Add lemon juice and stir. Remove cinnamon stick and cardamom pods, garnish with cilantro, and serve.

Makes 2–4 servings.

Rice

Almost every Indian meal includes rice. White basmati rice, known for its fragrance and delicious flavor, is the most common variety in Ayurvedic diets as it is easy and calming on the digestive system and benefits all doshas. (If reducing Kapha, eat in moderation.) When cooked al dente, basmati rice is also low on the Glycemic Index. Brown rice is high in fiber, B and E vitamins, and iron, and has some protein; however, it can aggravate Pitta and Kapha due to its heavier, moist qualities. If you feel you need to increase your fiber intake, use brown rice, but take note of how it affects your body and digestion.

Rice doesn't contain gluten, a protein in many grains that can be difficult for some to digest. This makes rice dishes suitable for those with gluten intolerance.

Tips for Cooking Rice:

- Wash rice by rinsing in water and draining 3 times; any more than this and you'll lose nutrients.

- An easy way to measure water for your rice is to make sure it covers the rice by 1 in (2½ cm).

- Use a pot with a tightly fitting lid as this allows the rice to cook in its own steam; and try not to peek, as this will slow the cooking process!

Cumin Rice

Cumin is a digestive aid and adds a wonderful flavor to this rice.

1 tsp good oil (see page 22)
¼ tsp whole cumin seeds
1 cup basmati rice

2 cups water
½ tsp salt, or to taste

In a medium pot on medium-high, heat oil. Add cumin seeds and let sizzle for 30 seconds. Add rice, water, and salt. Bring to a boil, then reduce heat to simmer, and cover tightly with lid. Cook for 20 minutes.

Makes 3–4 servings.

Aromatic Basmati Rice

This is the rice most often eaten at Indian meals.

1 cup white basmati rice
2 cups water
2 cloves
  • *To reduce Pitta: omit*
3 cardamom pods, slit at end

4 whole peppercorns
2 pieces cinnamon bark
  (1–2-in/2½–5 cm long) (see note)
Salt to taste

In a medium pot over high heat, combine all ingredients and bring to a boil. Reduce heat to simmer, cover with lid, and cook for 20 minutes.

Makes 3–4 servings.

Cinnamon bark is simply cinnamon sticks broken into smaller pieces. You can buy it at Indian grocery stores or specialty shops, or just break up regular cinnamon sticks yourself (although that is quite a lot of work!).

Make sure that you inform your guests that the whole spices are not to be eaten, as they are only there for flavoring. You may remove them before serving, but, if you leave them in they will continue to add flavor to the dish (and they look good too).

Saffron Rice

Saffron gives this rice dish a festive yellow color. It adds a subtle flavor and is known to revitalize the blood and circulation, as well as alleviate migraine headaches.

Saffron strands (or threads) are the dried stigmas from the saffron crocus. They can be found at general or specialty grocery stores; look for the brightest color. They're the world's most expensive spice, but a little goes a long way!

4 saffron strands (see note)
2 tbsp water
1 cup basmati rice

2 cups water
Salt to taste

In a bowl of water, soak saffron for 15 minutes. In a medium pot on high heat, combine saffron, including water it was soaking in, and the remaining ingredients. Bring to a boil, then reduce heat to simmer, cover with lid, and cook for 20 minutes.

Makes 3–4 servings.

Variation 1: Add 2 tbsp raisins (this will increase Kapha).

Variation 2: Add 2 tbsp dried cranberries (this will increase Vata and Pitta).

Variation 3: Add 2 tbsp slivered toasted almonds (this will increase Pitta and Kapha).

-
-
-  # Kitchari

 When I was growing up, kitchari – a popular Indian dish of rice, lentils, and spices – served with a dollop of ghee or butter, was a comfort food. Sometimes we would eat it with yogurt and pickles for a light lunch or supper. Kitchari is used in Ayurveda for healing and cleansing the system. It is calming for all the doshas, especially Vata. The split mung dal and rice create a complete protein that strengthens and nourishes the body. Kitchari is meant to be a bit softer and mushier than ordinary rice, I add about ½ cup water and cook it for about 5 minutes longer if I want it even softer and mushier. If using brown rice, cook for 45 minutes and let sit for another 10 minutes.

¼ cup split mung dal
   (see note on page 171)
½ cup basmati rice
2 cups water

Salt to taste
2 tsp flax or hemp oil
   (or ghee or butter)

In a medium pot on high heat, combine all ingredients, except oil, and bring to a boil. Reduce heat to simmer, cover with lid, and cook for 25–30 minutes. Drizzle with oil before serving.

Makes 2–3 servings.

 - - - Variation 1: Add ¼ tsp turmeric to cook with the other ingredients. Turmeric is a blood purifier and aids digestion of complete proteins. It reduces flatulence and inflammation, and is great for a sore throat. It also adds a lovely yellow color.

- + -
slightly
Variation 2: Add 1 piece cinnamon bark, 2 cloves, and 2 cardamom pods, slit at end, and cook with the other ingredients. Remove spices before serving.

slightly +
slightly +

Organic Brown Rice Kitchari

This healing dish is full of fiber and has a nice, nutty flavor.

If you have time, soak the split mung dal in ½ cup water for a few hours before cooking and drain before using. This activates the seed, increasing the nutrients and digestibility.

½ cup organic short-grain brown rice
¼ cup split mung dal (see note)
Salt to taste
¼ tsp turmeric (optional)

2 cups water
2 tsp flax or hemp oil (or ghee or butter)

In a medium pot on high heat, combine all ingredients, except oil, and bring to a boil. Reduce heat to simmer, cover with lid, and cook for 45 minutes. Let sit covered for 5 minutes. Drizzle with oil before serving.

Makes 2–3 servings.

Ø

-

- # Vegetable Rice Pilau

Pilau, or pilaf, has a rainbow of colors and is a wonderful way to get your vitamins and nutrients in one dish. The veggies in this pilau add a distinct flavor to the rice, because when they are cooked together their juices get absorbed in the grains.

2 tsp vegetable bouillon powder
1 cup hot water
1 tbsp oil
1 tsp whole cumin seeds
½ cup onions, chopped
1 tsp garlic, minced
   • *To reduce Pitta: omit*
1 tsp fresh ginger, minced
2 cups white basmati rice
1 fresh green chili, slit at end
   • *To reduce Pitta: omit*

1 cup potatoes, cubed
1 tomato, chopped
½ cup red bell peppers, cubed
1 cup fresh green peas
   • *To reduce Vata: use green beans*
¾ cup carrots, chopped
½ tsp turmeric
1 tsp salt, or to taste
¼ cup fresh parsley or fresh cilantro
   leaves, chopped (for garnish)

In a small bowl, dissolve bouillon in hot water and set aside. In a medium pot on medium-high, heat oil. Add cumin seeds and let sizzle for 30 seconds. Add onions, garlic, and ginger, and sauté for 30 seconds. Add rice and stir until it is coated with oil. Add green chili, potatoes, tomato, peppers, peas, carrots, turmeric, and salt. Add bouillon plus more water, enough to cover rice by 1 in (2½ cm). Bring to a boil, then reduce heat to simmer, cover with lid, and cook until done, about 20–25 minutes. Remove chili, mix well, and garnish with parsley or cilantro.

Makes 6–8 servings.

- - -   Mixed Vegetable Pilau with Tofu: Add ¾ cup medium tofu, cubed, at the same
    time as you add the vegetables.

slightly +

-

- # Simple Pea Pilau

 The peas and spices are delicious in this tasty side dish.

1 tsp good oil (see page 22)
½ tsp whole cumin seeds
½ cup white basmati rice
½ cup fresh green peas
  • *To reduce Vata: use green beans, chopped*
2 peppercorns (optional)

1 piece cinnamon bark (1-in/2½ cm long) (optional)
1 cardamom pods, slit at end (optional)
Salt to taste
¼ tsp turmeric (optional)
1¼ cups water

In a pot on medium-high, heat oil. Add cumin seeds and let sizzle for 30 seconds. Add remaining ingredients and bring to a boil. Reduce heat to a simmer, cover with lid, and cook for 20 minutes. Remove spices before serving.

Makes 2–3 servings.

-
slightly +
-

Bean Pilau

This dish is full of flavor from the mixture of spices and yogurt that are fully absorbed by the rice during the cooking process.

For non-vegetarians, omit azuki beans and add 2 cups lamb (will increase all doshas), beef (will increase Pitta and Kapha), or chicken (will reduce Pitta).

1 tbsp grapeseed oil (or other good oil, see page 22)
1 cup onions, thinly sliced
1½ cup tomatoes, chopped
1 cup plain yogurt
1 tsp garlic, minced
 • *To reduce Pitta: omit*
1 tsp fresh ginger, minced
2 tsp fresh green chilies
 • *To reduce Pitta: use only ½ tsp or omit*
½ cup fresh cilantro leaves, chopped
1 tsp ground coriander

1 tsp ground cumin
3 cloves
 • *To reduce Pitta: omit*
4 peppercorns
3 cardamom pods, slit at end (optional)
2 cinnamon sticks (1–2 in/ 2½–5 cm long)
Salt to taste
2 cups azuki beans, cooked
2 cups basmati rice

In a medium pot on medium, heat oil. Add onions and cook until golden, 4–5 minutes. Add all other ingredients except beans and rice and sauté for 7–8 minutes, until tomatoes soften. Add beans and rice and mix well. Add enough water to cover rice by 1 in (2½ cm). Bring to a boil, then reduce heat to simmer, cover with lid, and cook for 20–25 minutes. Remove from heat and let sit for 5 minutes. Remove whole spices before serving.

Makes 6–8 servings.

slightly +

+ # Organic Brown Rice Pea Pilau

This is packed with fiber, flavor, and nutrients.

If you have an aversion to onions, you can omit them. In Ayurveda, raw onions are pungent and therefore increase Vata. Cooked onions are sweeter and lighter and are usually balancing for Pitta and Vata in small quantities. Onions, raw or cooked, are most balancing for Kapha.

2 tsp good oil (see page 22)
1 tsp whole cumin seeds
1 onion, sliced length-wise (about 1 ½ cups) (see note)
1 cup tomatoes, chopped
2 cloves
  • *To reduce Pitta: omit*

2 cloves garlic, minced
  • *To reduce Pitta: use only one or omit*
¼ tsp turmeric
1 cup organic short-grain brown rice
½ tsp salt
2 ¼ cups water
¾ cup peas

In a medium pot on medium-high, heat oil. Add cumin seeds and let sizzle for 30 seconds. Reduce heat to medium; add onions and sauté until golden, about 3–4 minutes. Add tomatoes, cloves, garlic, and turmeric, and sauté until tomatoes soften, then stir in rice and salt. Add water and bring to boil. Reduce heat to simmer, cover with lid, and cook for 35 minutes. Stir in peas, cover again, and cook until rice is done, another 10–15 minutes. Remove cloves before serving.

Makes 3–4 servings.

Vegetables

In Indian cooking, vegetable dishes, traditionally served in combinations of two or more, form an essential part of a meal. They can be prepared many ways, providing a wide assortment of textures and spices that both stimulate the digestive juices and satisfy the doshas. This section includes mild vegetable dishes as well as some that are spicier to give your palate a tasty mix.

I hope you have as much fun as I do combing ethnic stores for spices as well as organic and local markets for the freshest vegetables possible for your meals.

slightly +

-

slightly + # Persian Greens

 I frequent Persian markets because I find they have the freshest selection. One day I found this tasty greens dish in the deli section and wanted to learn how to make it. My wish came true when I met Ensiah, who had recently moved to Canada from Iran, who not only knew how to make it, but even translated the ingredients for me!

1 ¼ cups kidney beans, dried
2 tbsp good oil (see page 22)
1 ½ cups onions, minced
½ tsp turmeric
Freshly ground pepper to taste
1 ½ cups hot water
2 tbsp good oil (see page 22)
½ cup fresh parsley, minced
1 cup spinach, minced

¼ cup garlic chives, minced (see note)
¼ cup fenugreek leaves, minced
  (see note)
1 tbsp fresh mint leaves, minced
5 dried limes (available in Persian
  grocery stores)
3–4 tbsp lime juice, or to taste
Salt to taste

Soak kidney beans in water overnight or for at least 1 hour before cooking.

In a pot on medium, heat 2 tbsp oil. Sauté onions until golden, about 6 minutes. Add turmeric and sauté for 1 minute. Add kidney beans, pepper, and hot water. Cover with lid and simmer gently until beans are half cooked.

In a separate pot on medium, heat 2 tbsp oil. Add parsley, spinach, garlic chives, and fenugreek leaves and cook until spinach is wilted, about 3–4 minutes. Add to beans and then add dried limes. Cover with lid, reduce heat to medium-low, and simmer for 30 minutes. Add lime juice and salt. Simmer for another 5–10 minutes. Serve with rice.

Makes 4 servings.

Continued on next page

+  + + For non-vegetarians: Use only ¾ cup kidney beans. After adding turmeric, add 26 oz (750 g) boneless stewing lamb, browning on all sides. Continue with rest of recipe. Lamb is considered sweet and cooling in Ayurveda. Although it increases all the doshas, it is considered a strengthening food.

Garlic chives (tareh) are flat leaves used in Asian and European cuisine since ancient times. This vegetable has a strong aromatic flavor that is fresh and zesty, resembling the subtle onion flavor of both chives and garlic. Pungent, warming, and stimulating, it is sometimes recommended to alleviate depression, and like garlic, it has antibiotic properties and promotes blood flow. Garlic chives are also a good source of calcium phosphates as well as other vitamins.

Fenugreek leaves (methi) are the green leaves of the herb grown from fenugreek seeds and are considered a delicacy in Indian cuisine. They have a strong distinct flavor, imparting the important bitter taste in Ayurveda. They are a good source of protein and are rich in essential amino acids. They are used medicinally to reduce flatulence, chronic coughs, dysentery, and loss of appetite.

Spinach & Broccoli Baji

The secret to this recipe is caramelizing the onions; the longer you take to cook them, the sweeter they get. Traditionally, Indian women slow-cooked this for up to two days. I prepared this dish at an Ayurvedic cooking course and Sherry Doman, one of the participants, later told me that she gave my recipe to her Indian mother; I was mortified as I had not kept in line with tradition. But Sherry reported that her mother loved it, saying she wished that she had always made it this way! Serve with chapatis or rice with onions, sliced daikon, fresh green chilies, and a yogurt raita (pages 267–269).

Spinach cleanses the blood, clears the lungs, and is good for the eyes. It is packed with vitamins A and C, iron, and dietary fiber.

See the Palak Paneer recipe that follows for a cheesy variation on the baji.

1 tsp butter (or ghee)
2 tsp olive oil
1 large or 2 small onions, sliced (about 1 ½ cups)
1 tbsp fresh ginger, minced

1 fresh green chili, slit at end (optional)
  • *To reduce Pitta: omit*
5–6 cups spinach, chopped (see note)
1 head broccoli, roughly chopped
1 tsp salt, or to taste

In a large pot on medium-low, heat butter and oil. Add onions, ginger, and chili and sauté until onions caramelize, about 8 minutes. Add spinach, broccoli, and salt and cover with lid. Reduce heat to low and cook for 20–30 minutes. Remove from heat, then in a blender or food processor, purée (be careful when blending hot ingredients).

Makes 4 servings.

-
-
+ # Palak Paneer

"Palak" means spinach and "paneer" is an Indian cottage cheese. Here are two variations on the preceding Spinach & Broccoli Baji recipe.

1 cup paneer, 1-in (2½-cm) cubes (page 24),
  or buy ready-made in Indian grocery stores

Follow recipe for Spinach & Broccoli Baji (page 179). After puréeing, add paneer. Toss and serve.

Makes 4–5 servings.

Michelle's Palak Paneer

Michelle, a fellow yoga instructor, came up with this variation at a cooking class I taught at her house, and it tasted delicious!

Substitute paneer with 1 cup crumbled goat's feta or goat's cheese to add to Spinach & Broccoli Baji, or serve separately in a bowl so guests can help themselves. Treat it like the Indian version of Parmesan cheese in pasta dishes!

African Spinach

My Pamoja Foundation colleague, Elizabeth Madoka, who is the wife of a Member of Parliament in Kenya, gave me this typical Swahili recipe (called *sukuma weeki*). After working tirelessly one day arranging meetings for us with citizens in the area, she cooked this dish for our supper from vegetables she'd grown in her garden. She prepares meals with the utmost care and appreciation, aware that there are people who regularly go hungry. Serve with Ugali (page 223) and a bean dish.

When eaten occasionally, spinach calms all the doshas. To reduce Kapha, eat spinach often.

1 tsp ghee
1 tsp olive oil
1–2 tsp garlic, crushed
  • *To reduce Pitta: omit*

6 cups spinach, packed (see note)
2 tsp vegetable bouillon powder
Salt to taste

In a pot on medium heat, melt ghee and oil. Add garlic and sauté for 30 seconds, then add spinach and vegetable bouillon. Cover and cook for 8–10 minutes. Add salt and serve.

Makes 2 servings.

You can vary this recipe by substituting spinach with kale, chopped.

Steamed Swiss Chard with Balsamic Vinegar

Swiss chard offers the prized bitter and pungent tastes in Ayurveda. I love the contrasting colors of the chard's vibrant pink stems and deep green leaves that are filled with vitamins A, C, and K and iron, among other essential nutrients.

2 tsp olive oil
5 cups (packed) Swiss chard, chopped
  (leaves only)
Salt to taste

Freshly ground pepper to taste
1–2 tbsp olive oil (for tossing)
1–2 tbsp balsamic vinegar

In a large pot or frying pan on medium-high, heat oil. Add Swiss chard, salt, and pepper. Toss then cover with lid, and steam for 1–2 minutes. Toss again. Cover and steam for another 3–4 minutes. Remove from heat, then toss with olive oil and balsamic vinegar to your taste. Serve while still warm.

Peg's Chard

Peg is a dear friend, an award-winning Canadian filmmaker, a practicing yogini, and a great cook who prefers warming foods and avoids dairy products to alleviate her chronic cough (from a bout with pneumonia) while balancing out her Vata-Kapha body type.

Follow the above recipe, except add 1–2 tsp fresh ginger, minced, sauté for 30 seconds before adding Swiss chard, and use lemon juice instead of balsamic vinegar.

+

-

slightly +

Mama's Mushroom & Spinach Pie

My longtime friend Monica learned this recipe from my mother and then passed it back to me! It is delicious for lunch or dinner and her kids love it. Serve with a salad.

If you prefer to use fresh spinach, use 5–6 cups, chopped. In a large pot, combine 1 cup boiling water and spinach. Cook until wilted, 1–2 minutes. Drain and squeeze dry.

Monica uses filo pastry that she buys; simply follow directions on the package, or use your favorite pastry shell.

2 tsp good oil (see page 22) (I use half ghee and half olive oil)
1 cup mushrooms, sliced and quartered
½ cup green onions, sliced
½ tsp fresh ginger, minced
½ tsp garlic, minced
  • To reduce Pitta: omit
½ tsp fresh green chilies, minced
  • To reduce Pitta: omit
Salt to taste

Freshly ground pepper to taste
10-oz (300-g) pkg frozen chopped spinach, thawed and excess liquid removed (see note)
1 egg
1 cup Mozzarella cheese, grated

Pastry shell (see note)
1 egg white

Preheat oven to 350°F (180°C).

In a pot on medium, heat oil. Add mushrooms, green onions, ginger, garlic, and green chilies and sauté until mushrooms soften. Add salt and pepper to taste and stir. Add spinach and mix well. Cook for about 3 minutes. Remove from heat and let cool. In a large bowl, beat egg. Add cheese and mix well. When spinach mixture is cool, add to egg mixture, mix, and set aside.

Roll out pastry into a rectangular shape, about 12×18-in (30×45-cm). Place filling in the center and fold pastry into a log, ensuring all ends are well sealed, pinching together with your fingers. On an oiled baking sheet, place pastry seam-side down. Brush egg white over pastry for glaze. Bake for 45 minutes. Slice in 2-in (5-cm) pieces to serve.

Makes 3–4 servings.

slightly +

slightly +

Eat Your Curried Green Peas

Find out why no one has to say, "Eat your peas!" at Indian dinner tables. Apart from enriching the flavor, spices warm the cool peas and make them calming for Vata. Serve with rice.

To serve this with chapatis, this recipe should be less liquid, so add ¼ cup plus one tbsp water instead of 1 cup. If this is too dry, add a little more water, 1 tbsp at a time.

1 tbsp good oil (see page 22)
½ cup onions, minced
1 tsp garlic, minced
  • *To reduce Pitta: omit*
1 tsp fresh ginger, minced
1 tsp ground cumin
1 tsp ground coriander
½ tsp turmeric
¼–1 tsp cayenne pepper
  • *To reduce Pitta: omit*
2 cups tomatoes, diced
  (with their juices)
  • *To reduce Pitta: omit*

1 tbsp tomato purée
  • *To reduce Pitta: omit*
1 ¼ tsp salt, or to taste
1 ½ tbsp fresh cilantro leaves, chopped
4 cups fresh green peas
1 cup water
Juice of ½ a lemon
½ tsp garam masala
1 ½ tbsp fresh cilantro leaves, chopped
  (for garnish)

In a pot on high, heat oil. Add onions, garlic, and ginger. Reduce heat to medium and sauté until onions are golden, about 3–5 minutes. Add cumin, coriander, turmeric, and cayenne and sauté for another 30 seconds. Add tomatoes, tomato purée, salt, and 1½ tbsp cilantro. Sauté for 5 minutes until tomatoes soften. Add peas and mix well. Add water, increase heat to high, and bring to a boil. Cover with lid, reduce heat, and simmer until done, about 10 minutes. Adjust for salt and add lemon juice. Sprinkle with garam masala and cilantro.

Makes 4 servings.

Mutter Paneer: Follow the recipe above, then add ¾ cup paneer, cubed (page 24), just before adding garam masala and cilantro.

+

−

−  # Fresh Green Pea & Potato Curry

When my sister and I returned from boarding school (in the highlands of Kenya, 500 miles away from home!) for holidays, my mother would cook for us this curry, one of our favorite dishes. Serve with chapatis or rice, a raita (pages 267–269), and the Dainty Cachumber (page 89).

Green peas balance out Pitta and Kapha; to reduce Vata eat them in moderation. Peas are energizing as they are full of fiber, vitamins, nutrients, and some protein.

2 tsp good oil (see page 22)
1 tsp whole cumin seeds
½ cup onions, chopped
1 tsp fresh ginger, minced
1 clove garlic, minced
1 cup tomatoes, diced
2 tsp tomato purée
¼ tsp turmeric
½ tsp salt, or to taste
1 tsp cumin
1 tsp ground coriander

½ tsp garam masala
½ tsp cayenne pepper, or 1 tsp fresh green chilies, chopped
  • To reduce Pitta: reduce or omit
2 cups potatoes, cubed
2 cups fresh green peas
1 cup water
½ tsp salt, or to taste
Juice of ½ a lemon
¼ cup fresh cilantro leaves, chopped (for garnish)

In a pot on medium-high, heat oil. Add cumin seeds and let sizzle for 30 seconds. Add onions, ginger, and garlic, reduce heat to medium, and sauté until onions are golden, about 4–6 minutes. Add tomatoes, tomato purée, turmeric, salt, cumin, coriander, garam masala, and cayenne and sauté for 3–4 minutes. Add potatoes and cook until they start to soften. Add peas and water, increase heat to high, and bring to a boil. Reduce heat and simmer until peas until done, about 10 minutes. Add lemon juice and adjust for salt. Garnish with cilantro and serve.

Makes 2–4 servings.

slightly +

-

- # Pea & Mushroom Curry

The spices add flavor and aid digestion in this pea and mushroom medley.

1 tbsp good oil (see page 22)
½ tsp black mustard seeds
¾ cup onions, minced
½ tsp turmeric
1 tsp garam masala

⅓ cup plain yogurt
1 tsp salt, or to taste
3 cups fresh green peas
3 cups mushrooms, sliced

In a pot on medium-high, heat oil. Add mustard seeds, cover with lid, and let pop for 30 seconds. Add onions, reduce heat to medium-low, and sauté until golden, about 6–8 minutes. Add turmeric and garam masala, and stir for about 30 seconds. Add yogurt and salt, increase heat to medium-high, and bring to a boil. Reduce heat to medium and add peas. Cook for 3 minutes, then add mushrooms. Cover with lid and continue cooking for 10–15 minutes, until peas and mushrooms are done. Adjust for salt and serve.

Makes 4 servings.

ø

ø

– # Alu Methi

My family always quickly polishes off this dish. The fenugreek provides the bitter (and acquired) taste that is prized for cleansing the liver and creating clarity of mind and sight.

1 tbsp good oil (see page 22)
½ tsp whole cumin seeds
1 cup onions, minced
1–2 fresh green chilies, minced
  • To reduce Pitta: reduce or omit
1 tsp fresh ginger, minced
½ tsp turmeric

Salt to taste
1 cup tomatoes, diced
  • To reduce Pitta: omit
4 cups potatoes, boiled, peeled, and diced
1 cup fenugreek leaves, chopped (available at Indian grocers)

In a pot on medium-high, heat oil. Add cumin seeds and let sizzle for 30 seconds. Add onions and sauté until just golden, about 3–4 minutes. Add chilies, ginger, turmeric, salt, and tomatoes and stir. Reduce heat to medium and cook until tomatoes soften, about 5–7 minutes. Add potatoes and fenugreek leaves and cook until fenugreek wilts, about 5 minutes. Stir to mix well, then serve.

Makes 4 servings.

– + – Potato & Spinach Curry: Add 4 cups spinach, chopped and ½ cup water in place of fenugreek leaves and cook for 2–3 minutes longer.

−

 +

 +

Lata's Green Masala with Paneer

Whenever our family was invited to my close friend Lata and her late husband Vinod's home for dinner, we looked forward to it for days. They always served spectacular meals with the freshest ingredients and spices they would grind just before cooking. Lata likes her Green Masala hot, so to reduce Pitta, cut down on the chilies! Serve with rice.

2 tbsp ghee (or 1 tbsp ghee or butter + 1 tbsp light oil)

1 ½ cups onions, minced

2 tbsp fresh green chilies, chopped
- *To reduce Pitta: use 2 tsp*

5 tbsp fresh ginger, minced

3 tsp garlic, minced

12 whole peppercorns

4 bay leaves

5 cloves

2 tsp olive oil (or ghee)

1 ½ tsp black mustard seeds

½ tsp turmeric

3 cups paneer, cut into ¾-in (2-cm) cubes (page 24)

2 cups fresh cilantro leaves (packed), roughly chopped

1 cup sour cream
- *To reduce Kapha: use a light version*

In a large frying pan on medium-low heat, melt ghee. Add onions and sauté until caramelized, about 8–10 minutes. Add chilies, ginger, garlic, peppercorns, bay leaves, and cloves. In another small frying pan on medium-high, heat oil. Add mustard seeds, cover with lid, and let pop for 30 seconds. Immediately reduce heat to medium, add turmeric and sauté for 30 seconds. Add paneer and sauté for another minute. Add to onion mixture. Remove from heat, add cilantro, and mix. Remove peppercorns, bay leaves, and cloves. In a small bowl, combine 2 tbsp of mixture with sour cream and stir well (this prevents curdling). Return to rest of mixture and stir.

 − − −

For non-vegetarians: You can substitute fish (Vata should use fresh halibut) for the paneer, searing the fish 3–4 minutes per side, depending on its thickness, before coating in the masala mixture.

+

 +

 - # Fit for a King Eggplant Bharta

 In my opinion, Eggplant Bharta is the pièce de resistance in an Indian vegetarian menu. The secret is broiling the eggplant until it is very soft, sizzling the cumin seeds, and slow-cooking the onions and vegetables. I think the reason some people do not like eggplant is because it is often undercooked. Serve with chapatis and plain yogurt.

2 large eggplants
A little olive oil to rub on eggplants
2 tbsp olive oil
  • *To reduce Kapha: use light*
1 ½ tsp whole cumin seeds
2 medium onions, chopped
1 ½ tsp fresh ginger, minced

3 medium tomatoes, diced
1 tsp salt, or to taste
1–2 tsp fresh green chilies, minced
  • *To reduce Pitta: use ½ tsp or omit*
¼ cup fresh cilantro leaves, chopped
  (for garnish)

Set oven to broil.

Wash and dry each eggplant. Pierce both ends with a fork, coat eggplant all over with oil, and broil for about 20 minutes on each side, until very soft on all sides. (It will look completely collapsed, and mushy.) Remove from oven and let cool completely. Scoop out eggplant pulp and chop or mash it. Set aside in a bowl and discard peel.

In a large frying pan on medium-high, heat oil. Add cumin seeds and let sizzle for 30 seconds. Add onions, reduce heat to medium, and sauté until onions are golden, about 5–7 minutes. Add ginger, tomatoes, salt, and chilies and cook until tomatoes soften, about 4–5 minutes. Add mashed eggplant, reduce heat to medium-low, and cook for another 10 minutes, stirring occasionally. Eggplant tastes especially good if you cook it until it begins sticking to the bottom of the pan. Garnish with cilantro.

Makes 2–4 servings.

slightly +

 # Indian Fusion Ratatouille

One day my friend, journalist Lyn Cockburn, walked into my clothing store and said she was procrastinating on a newspaper assignment about "exotic" fruits and vegetables available in Vancouver, but she was less than enthusiastic. I, on the other hand, thought it was a great idea, and accompanied her on her search. After exploring our local ethnic stores, I created this recipe with our day's bounty. Lyn liked it so much that she published it with her article on our adventures!

Shing qua, also known as Chinese okra, tastes and looks like a cross between a zucchini and a cucumber, but with deep, long ridges in its dark green skin. The best ones to use are 12–18 in (30–45 cm) long. If bought fresh, they do no not have to be peeled, as this vegetable absorbs flavors easily. When mature, it tastes very bitter. Shing qua is available at Chinese grocers.

2 tbsp olive oil
¾ cup onions, minced
1 tsp fresh ginger, minced
2 cloves garlic, minced
 • *To reduce Pitta: omit*
1 fresh green chili, minced
½ cup fresh cilantro leaves
  (or parsley), chopped
½ tsp turmeric
½ tsp cayenne pepper
 • *To reduce Pitta: omit*

1 tsp ground cumin
1 tsp ground coriander
Salt to taste
3 tomatoes, cubed
1 long Japanese eggplant, sliced
  (about 1½ cups)
1 small round eggplant, cubed
1 shing qua, cubed (see note)
1 chayote, thinly sliced (see note)

In a large pot on medium-high, heat oil. Add onions, ginger, garlic, and chilies and sauté until onions are golden, about 3–4 minutes. Add cilantro, turmeric, cayenne, cumin, coriander, and salt and stir. Add remaining ingredients, cover with lid, reduce heat to medium, and cook for 6–8 minutes. Stir, cover again, reduce to medium-low, and simmer for 30–40 minutes. Adjust seasoning. Serve over rice.

Makes 2–4 servings.

Chayote is the Spanish name for this vegetable commonly used by Aztecs and Mayans. It looks like a large "vegetable pear," its English name. Part of the gourd family, chayote has a mild flavor, somewhat of a cross between a potato and a cucumber.

Soft & Spicy Eggplant Curry

 The soft texture of the eggplant is delicious when combined with peas and spices. Serve this on rice.

1 tbsp good oil (see page 22)	1 cup tomatoes, chopped
1½ tsp black mustard seeds	6 cups eggplant, cubed
1½ cups onions, chopped	1½ cups fresh green peas
1 tsp salt, or to taste	¾ cup water
½ tsp turmeric	1 tbsp fresh cilantro leaves, chopped
¼ tsp cayenne pepper, or to taste	(for garnish)
⅛ tsp hing (optional)	

In a large pot on medium-high, heat oil. Add mustard seeds, cover with lid, and let pop for 30 seconds. Add onions, salt, turmeric, cayenne, and hing and sauté until onions are golden, about 4–5 minutes. Add tomatoes and eggplant, mix well, cover with lid, and cook for 10 minutes. Add peas and water and cook for another 5 minutes, or until peas are done. Check for seasoning. Garnish with cilantro.

Makes 4–6 servings.

+ – – Variation: Add 1 cup potatoes, cubed and ½ cup water along with tomatoes and eggplant.

Meena's Zucchini & Squash Medley

My cousin Meena Nanji's primary dosha is Pitta, which brings her passions into reality. An award-winning filmmaker, she recently finished a documentary exploring the history of women's rights in Afghanistan entitled *View from a Grain of Sand*. When she needs to calm Pitta, she cooks this colorful and nourishing dish.

Meena serves this dish with French green lentils cooked very plainly, with a little salt and, when almost done, a squeeze of lime. Serve lentils on the side or stir into the dish.

1–2 tbsp olive oil
2 cups zucchini, diced
2 cups squash, diced
1 tsp ground coriander

Salt to taste
Juice of ½ a lime
¼ cup fresh cilantro leaves, chopped (for garnish)

In a frying pan on medium-high, heat oil. Add zucchini and squash and sauté for 4–5 minutes, tossing regularly. Reduce heat to medium, add coriander, stir, cover with lid, and cook for about 5–7 minutes, until vegetables are soft. Add salt and lime juice, toss, and garnish with cilantro.

Makes 2–4 servings.

+

-

-

Broccoli, Cauliflower & Potato Baji

This is an adaptation of the cauliflower baji my grandmother used to make. Broccoli was not as easy to find in Africa or I'm sure she would have used it! This is one of the tastiest ways to eat it.

Slitting chilies releases their flavor and heat. Use a sharp knife, keeping the end intact. Chilies are always optional. If you have excess Pitta, use very little or omit.

2 tsp good oil (see page 22)
¾–1 cup onions, quartered
1 tsp fresh ginger, minced
¼ tsp turmeric
1 fresh green chili, slit at end
  or minced (see note)
  • *To reduce Pitta: use ¼ tsp or omit, or*
    cayenne pepper to taste

1 cup potatoes, thinly sliced
2 cups broccoli, chopped into florets
2 cups cauliflower, chopped into florets
Salt to taste
½ tsp garam masala
Freshly ground pepper to taste
¼ cup fresh cilantro leaves, chopped
  (for garnish)

In a large frying pan on medium, heat oil. Add onions, ginger, turmeric, and chili and sauté for 2–3 minutes, until onions start to soften. Add potatoes, broccoli, and cauliflower. Mix well, stir in salt, cover with lid, and cook until vegetables are softened, about 15 minutes. (If it needs more liquid, add up to ¼ cup water, but avoid if possible.) Stir in salt. Cook until done, about 15 minutes. Sprinkle with garam masala and pepper. Garnish with cilantro and remove chili before serving.

Makes 4–5 servings.

slightly +
-

Delectable Curried Cauliflower with Ginger & Tomatoes

This is a tasty cauliflower dish. To reduce Pitta, eat in moderation or omit the tomatoes.

1 tbsp good oil (see page 22)
1 tsp whole cumin seeds
1 tbsp fresh ginger, minced
¾ tsp turmeric
½–1 tsp cayenne pepper
  • *To reduce Pitta: omit*
3 cups tomatoes, chopped
  • *To reduce Pitta: omit*

1 large head cauliflower, chopped
  into florets
Salt to taste
¾ tsp garam masala
¼ tsp garam masala (for garnish)
¼ cup fresh cilantro leaves, chopped
  (for garnish)

In a pot on medium-high, heat oil. Add cumin seeds and let sizzle for 30 seconds. Add ginger, turmeric, cayenne, and tomatoes and sauté for 3–4 minutes. Add cauliflower, salt, and ¾ tsp garam masala. Stir, cover with lid, and cook for 10–15 minutes, until cauliflower is softened. Garnish with garam masala and cilantro.

Makes 4–6 servings.

French Bean

& Tomato Cumin Sauté

My friend Peg says these are the best beans that she has ever had, and eats them straight from the pan. She once added 1 tsp cayenne pepper by accident, which turned out to be a delicious mistake!

2 tsp coconut oil (or good oil, see
  page 22)
1½ tsp whole cumin seeds
⅓ cup onions, chopped
½ cup tomatoes, chopped

1½ cups long French green beans
½ tsp turmeric
¼–1 tsp cayenne pepper
Salt to taste

In a large frying pan on medium-high, heat oil. Add cumin seeds and let sizzle for 30 seconds. Add onions and sauté for 1–2 minutes. Reduce heat to medium, then add tomatoes, beans, turmeric, cayenne, and salt. Stir, cover with lid, and cook for 5–10 minutes, until vegetables are done. If it needs more liquid, add up to ¼ cup water.

Makes 2 servings.

ø
slightly + # Basia's No Fuss
- French Green Beans

French green beans, a thin variety, are tender, sweet, and crisp when fresh (the only way to have them). This recipe from my friend Basia preserves the natural flavor and freshness of the beans while adding color and zest. The lemon and vinegar not only add extra zing, but provide the sour taste, which aids digestion.

5 cups French green beans
6 cups iced water
1 cup red bell peppers, finely diced
½ cup red onions, finely diced
  • *To reduce Vata and Pitta: omit*
½ cup goat's cheese, crumbled
4–5 tbsp olive oil

3 tbsp balsamic vinegar
Juice of ½ a lemon
¼ tsp dry mustard (or 1 tsp Dijon)
Salt to taste
Freshly ground pepper to taste

In a large pot of boiling water, add beans. Reduce heat to medium-high and blanch for 3–5 minutes until tender and bright green. Remove beans and immediately plunge in a bowl of iced water to stop the cooking process. Drain beans and add to serving bowl. Add all remaining ingredients and toss well. Check for seasoning and serve.

Makes 6–8 servings.

 – – – Variation: Sauté chopped onions in 1 tsp olive oil on medium heat for 4–5 minutes, then add to beans.

-

+

-

Traditional Vegetable Curry

This curry is even more traditional when you serve it with rice or chapatis, a raita (pages 267–269), the Dainty Cachumber (page 89), and a pickle.

2 tsp good oil (see page 22)
1 cup onions, minced
1 tsp garlic, minced
1 tsp fresh ginger, minced
½–1½ tsp fresh green chilies, minced
 • *To reduce Pitta: use less or omit*
1½ cups tomatoes, chopped
 (with their juices)
2 tbsp tomato paste
1 cinnamon stick, broken
 (about 2-in/5-cm long)
2 cardamom pods, slit at end
4 whole black peppercorns

¼ tsp turmeric
½ tsp cayenne pepper
 • *To reduce Pitta: omit*
1 tsp ground coriander
1 tsp ground cumin
1 tsp salt, or to taste
6 cups mixed vegetables
1 cup water
Juice of ½ a lemon
½–1 tsp garam masala
¼ cup fresh cilantro leaves, chopped
 (for garnish)

Continued on next page

In a large pot on medium-low, heat oil. Add onions and sauté until soft, about 3–4 minutes. Add garlic, ginger, and chilies and sauté for 4–5 minutes, until the onions are caramelized. Add tomatoes, tomato paste, cinnamon sticks, cardamom pods, peppercorns, turmeric, cayenne, coriander, cumin, and salt. Increase heat to medium and sauté for 5–10 minutes until tomatoes are softened. Add mixed vegetables and water, cover with lid, and cook for 25 minutes. If curry needs more liquid, add water, 1 tbsp at a time. Add lemon juice and stir. Sprinkle with garam masala and cilantro. Remind guests not to eat cinnamon sticks, cardamom pods, or whole peppercorns; you can discard these before serving, but they continue to add flavor if you leave them in the dish.

Makes 4–6 servings.

Chicken Curry: Instead of vegetables, add 1 whole chicken, skinned and cut into pieces, or 6 chicken pieces (legs and thighs add the most flavor). Sauté chicken in tomato sauce to brown for 3–4 minutes before adding water. Cook for 25–35 minutes until chicken is tender.

Chicken & Potato Curry: To the above Chicken Curry, add 2 medium potatoes, quartered, after chicken has cooked for 5–10 minutes. Add 1 extra cup water and continue to cook.

slightly +

ø

- # Karela

Karela, also known as bitter gourd, is one of my favorite dishes. It takes time to prepare, but it's worth it if you enjoy bitter gourd (an acquired taste). Although the tomatoes increase Pitta, the bitter gourd calms it.

Bitter gourd is a diuretic, a great liver cleanser, and regulates blood sugar, alleviating diabetes; it's available in ethnic markets.

Bitter tastes are prized in Ayurveda for balancing salty, sour, and sweet flavors and helping people to see clearly. They calm Pitta and Kapha and stimulate Vata.

4 cups bitter gourd, peeled and sliced into ¼-in (¾-cm) rounds (see note)

2 tsp salt

½ cup good oil (see page 22)
  • To reduce Kapha: use a light oil

4 cups potatoes, peeled and sliced

1 cup onions, thinly sliced

2 cups tomatoes, diced

2 tsp tomato paste

1 tsp garlic, minced
  • To reduce Pitta: omit

1 tsp fresh ginger, minced

2 tsp fresh green chilies, minced
  • To reduce Pitta: omit

1 tsp ground cumin

1 tsp ground coriander

1 tsp garam masala

¼ tsp turmeric

A pinch of hing

½ tsp cayenne pepper
  • To reduce Pitta: omit

Salt to taste

2 tsp gur (or brown sugar)

Juice of ½ a lemon

½ tsp garam masala (for garnish)

¼ cup fresh cilantro leaves, chopped (for garnish)

In a large bowl, add gourd and sprinkle with salt. Place a plate with a heavy can on top and leave to sweat for 4 hours. Rinse well, then squeeze out excess liquid.

In a frying pan on medium-high, heat oil. Add gourd and fry on both sides for 3–4 minutes, until crispy. Remove from pan and set aside. Add potatoes to pan and fry on both sides until crispy. Remove from pan and set aside. Reduce heat to medium, add onions, and sauté until golden, about 5–7 minutes. Remove half the onions and set aside. Add remaining ingredients to pan except gur and lemon juice, and sauté for about 7 minutes. Return gourd, potatoes, and onions to pan and sauté for another 5 minutes. Add gur, ensuring it dissolves. Add lemon juice and stir. Just before serving, sprinkle with garam masala and cilantro.

Makes 6–8 servings.

Matteo's Simply
Delicious Asparagus

Matteo grew up in Lugano, Switzerland, so close to Italy that I think he inherited their love of cooking. Here I include one of his simplest, tastiest dishes. His secret: always buy the thinnest, freshest stalks of asparagus.

Asparagus is a diuretic and is sweet, cooling, and astringent. It is full of vitamins A, B, and C, folate, and fiber.

1 bunch thin asparagus
   (about 4-in/10-cm thick in diameter)
   (see note)
1 tbsp ghee (or butter)

¼ cup Parmesan cheese, grated
Salt to taste
Freshly ground pepper to taste

Set oven to broil.

In a large pot of boiling water, add asparagus. Reduce heat to medium-high and cook for 4–5 minutes, until asparagus start to soften yet are still crisp. In a baking dish, place asparagus. Dot with ghee all over. Sprinkle with Parmesan, salt, and pepper. Broil for 2–3 minutes or until Parmesan starts to brown. Serve immediately.

Makes 4 servings.

Malu's Bhindi

Malu is a family friend who has lived in both India and Canada. On Diwali (the Hindu New Year), a group of us would meet for a potluck amid a festival of lights. One year we decided we would give a Cook of the Year award, and Malu got our vote!

Okra's superior fiber alleviates constipation and acid reflux, and regulates blood sugar and cholesterol

1 tbsp good oil (see page 22) (I use half ghee and half grapeseed oil)
½ tsp mustard seeds
1 tsp whole cumin seeds
⅛ tsp hing (optional)
4 cups okra, sliced into 1-in (2½ -cm) pieces

½ tsp turmeric
½ tsp cayenne pepper
  • *To reduce Pitta: omit*
Salt to taste

In a heavy-bottomed or non-stick frying pan on medium-high, heat oil. Add mustard seeds, cover with lid, and let pop for 30 seconds. Add cumin seeds and hing and let sizzle for 20 seconds. Add okra and mix well. Reduce heat to medium and add remaining ingredients. Mix well and cook for about 10 minutes, until okra is softened. If it needs more liquid, add up to ¼ cup water.

Makes 4 servings.

–

–

+ # Squash Heaven

Pauline Le Bel (also a Bowen Island resident) writes songs, plays, and musicals. She shared with me one of her scrumptious, nourishing meals that she puts together in a jiffy. The sweetness and softness of the squash compliments the saltiness of the feta and the texture of the rice and nuts.

1 ½ cups brown rice, cooked with 1 tsp vegetable bouillon powder

1 large butternut squash (or acorn or other winter squash)
1 tsp maple syrup
½ cup feta cheese, crumbled

¼ cup walnuts or sunflower seeds, toasted
1 tsp gomasio (see note)
½ cup fresh parsley, chopped
¼ cup fresh herbs, chopped (e.g., oregano, chives, basil)
Freshly ground pepper to taste

Preheat oven to 350°F (180°C).

Cut squash in half, scoop out seeds and discard. Place cut side down on a baking sheet. Bake for about 45–60 minutes until soft, depending on the size of squash. (Test with a fork.) Remove from oven, coat with maple syrup, and set aside.

In a medium bowl, toss together cooked rice and remaining ingredients. Stuff squash with rice mixture and serve.

Makes 2 servings.

Gomasio is sesame salt often found ready-made in Japanese grocers or health food stores. It adds tons of flavor and nutrients to your brown rice, salads, stews, and soups; it is also rich in calcium, protein, fiber, and vitamin E. Here is how to make it yourself: ¼ cup unhulled toasted sesame seeds (to toast seeds, place in frying pan on medium heat, toss continuously for 3–5 minutes) and 1 tsp salt, or to taste. Grind seeds and salt lightly in a coffee grinder (not one you regularly use for coffee) to retain some texture.

+

+

- # Grandma's Turnip Curry

Turnips are packed with vitamin C. When buying, choose smaller ones if possible, as they are often sweeter and softer. After cooking this, my neighbor Janis, who is a passionate vegetarian cook, said, "It was just perfect." Serve with rice or chapatis.

2 tsp good oil (see page 22)
½ tsp whole cumin seeds
1 small onion, chopped
1 tsp garlic, minced
1 tbsp fresh ginger, minced
8 cups large turnips, peeled and cubed

¼ cup water
½ tsp turmeric
1 tsp sea salt
Cayenne pepper to taste
1 tsp maple syrup

In a large pot on medium-high, heat oil. Add cumin seeds and let sizzle for 30 seconds. Add onions and sauté for 4–5 minutes until golden. Add garlic and ginger and sauté for 1 minute. Add turnips, water, turmeric, salt, and cayenne. Toss to mix. Reduce heat to medium, cover with lid, and cook for 30–40 minutes, until turnips are softened. If it needs more liquid, add a bit more water. Add maple syrup and mash. Adjust seasoning and serve.

Makes 2–4 servings.

+

ø

- # Sweet & Sour Sambaro

 This is a deliciously sweet, sour, and spicy vegetable dish and condiment that adds rich flavor and texture to a meal.

If green chilies are too hot, remove white pulp and seeds before using.

3 cups cabbage, chopped
1 tbsp salt
1 tbsp good oil (see page 22)
2 dried red chilies
½ tsp black mustard seeds
½ cup carrots, julienned

2 fresh green chilies, slit at end
 (see note)
½ tsp turmeric
1 tbsp gur
Juice of 1 lemon
Salt to taste

In a colander over a bowl or in the sink, add cabbage and sprinkle with salt. Place a plate and a heavy can on top and leave to sweat for 1–2 hours. Rinse cabbage and squeeze out excess moisture. Set aside.

In a large pan on medium-high, heat oil. Add dried red chilies and sauté until blackened. Add mustard seeds, cover with lid, and let pop for 30 seconds. Immediately add cabbage, carrots, green chilies, and turmeric and sauté for 3–4 minutes. Add gur (if hard, mince first) and lemon juice. Sauté for another 1–2 minutes while gur dissolves. Remove from heat and place in a serving bowl to stop the cooking process. Taste for salt, adding if needed. Remove chilies before serving.

Makes 4–6 servings.

Pasta

Pastas balance both Vata and Pitta, and generally increase Kapha. To reduce Kapha, use buckwheat flour soba noodles, which are available in health food stores or Japanese grocers. There are so many kinds of pasta available on the market, it is fun to experiment and find out what types are best for your body and constitution. I love both brown rice pasta and soba noodles, which are also useful if you are avoiding gluten products. And remember, as long as pasta is cooked al dente, it remains low on the Glycemic Index.

–

 +

 + # Spicy Tomato Pasta

This is one of my favorite dishes that's easy to make anytime, especially when tomatoes are in season. If you grow your own tomatoes as well as cilantro or basil, you can throw this together in mere minutes.

Tomatoes are rich with vitamins A and C, and potassium. They are high in antioxidants, and are known to help prevent cancer and combat high blood pressure.

2–4 cups pasta of your choice, uncooked (1 cup per serving)
2 tsp olive oil
¼ cup onions, chopped
1½ tsp garlic, minced
2–3 tsp fresh green chilies, minced
• *To reduce Pitta: omit*

4 cups Roma tomatoes, chopped, with their juices (about 8 tomatoes)
½–1 cup fresh cilantro leaves, chopped
Salt to taste
Freshly ground pepper to taste
Parmesan cheese, grated, to taste

In a large pot of boiling salted water, add pasta. Reduce heat and cook until al dente. While pasta is cooking, in a frying pan on medium-high, heat oil. Add onions and sauté for 2–3 minutes. Add garlic and chilies and sauté for 1–2 minutes. Add tomatoes and cook until softened, about 4–5 minutes, stirring often. Reduce heat to medium, then add cilantro, salt, and pepper. Toss and cook for 1 minute. Remove pasta from heat and drain. Garnish sauce with Parmesan and serve over pasta.

Makes 2–4 servings.

Variation 1: Substitute ½–1 cup chopped fresh basil for cilantro leaves.

Variation 2: Substitute crumbled goat's feta cheese for Parmesan cheese.

Variation 3: Add ¼ cup chopped black olives and 1 tbsp capers with the tomatoes.

slightly +

+ # Amrita's Pasta

I put this together one day when I was staying at my friend Kathy's place; she liked it so much she wrote down the ingredients. A few years later, she made it for me at her house and I asked for the recipe. She laughed and said, "This is yours. We've been eating it at our house ever since you cooked it and we even call it Amrita's Pasta!" Serve with a fresh salad.

8 cups penne or farfelle (bow tie) pasta, cooked al dente

16-oz (171-ml) jar artichoke hearts with liquid

2–3 tbsp sun-dried tomatoes in oil
  • *To reduce Kapha: use ½ this amount, or use dry and reconstitute in water*

½–¾ cup feta cheese, crumbled

⅓ cup pine nuts, lightly toasted

⅓ cup black olives, chopped (optional)

½–1 cup fresh basil, chopped (see note)
  • *To reduce Pitta: use mint*

Salt to taste

Freshly ground pepper to taste

In a large bowl, combine all ingredients. Toss together to mix well.

Makes 6 servings.

Basil is considered a holy plant in India and is revered in Ayurvedic herbalism. It is antibacterial, an antiseptic, and a diuretic; it also calms the nerves and clears the aura. It's also good for alleviating colds, flus, and lung problems, increasing prana (breath, or "life-force energy"), and strengthening the immune system. Basil is considered pungent and heating and therefore good for calming Vata and Kapha, but not to be used if there is excessive Pitta.

slightly +
+

Kamut Spaghetti with Cilantro Pesto

One day I made this recipe with cilantro in the pesto instead of the traditional basil and loved it. It's so easy to make and very tasty. Cilantro is balancing for all the doshas.

Kamut spaghetti is made with whole grain kamut which is full of protein and fiber. It is available in most groceries and health food stores.

Kamut spaghetti, uncooked (enough for 4–6 people) (see note)
3–4 tsp garlic
½ tsp fresh green chilies (optional)
  • *To reduce Pitta: omit*
3 cups fresh cilantro leaves (packed)
¾ cup fresh parsley (packed)
½ cup pine nuts

½ cup olive oil
  • *To reduce Kapha: use a light version*
¾ cup Parmesan cheese, grated
¼ cup sun-dried tomatoes in oil
  • *To reduce Kapha: use dry and reconstitute in water*
Salt to taste

In a large pot of boiling water, add spaghetti. Reduce heat and cook until al dente. While pasta is cooking, in a blender or food processor, combine garlic and chilies, and pulse until minced. Add cilantro and parsley and pulse again. Add remaining ingredients and blend until it becomes a smooth paste. Remove spaghetti from heat and drain. Toss sauce with pasta and serve.

Makes 4–6 servings.

 – – – 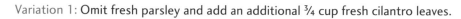 Variation 1: Omit fresh parsley and add an additional ¾ cup fresh cilantro leaves.

– – + Variation 2: Omit sun-dried tomatoes and add an additional ¼ cup Parmesan cheese.

Spaghetti with Garlic & Red Chili Peppers

This recipe always reminds me of my Uncle Arjun, who would take us to the best Italian restaurants and ask the chef especially for this dish even though it was never on the menu! I love the flavors of the oil and sautéed garlic, which is more like a vegetable in this dish. I have added the Indian flavoring of the blackened red chili instead of the Italian crushed red peppers.

I like to leave these chillies in my pasta while I'm eating it as they continue to add flavor, however they are not to be eaten.

Spaghetti, cooked al dente
  (enough for 4–6 people)
  • *To reduce Kapha: use soba noodles*
1–2 tsp olive oil
1–2 tsp ghee (or butter)

3 whole dried red chilies (see note)
6–8 cloves garlic, thinly sliced
Salt and freshly ground pepper to taste
½ cup Parmesan cheese, grated

In a frying pan on medium-high, heat olive oil and ghee. Add chilies and garlic slices and sauté until garlic starts to brown and chilies start to blacken, tossing regularly. Add spaghetti and toss to coat with butter and oil. Add salt and pepper to taste. Sprinkle Parmesan over dish and serve.

Makes 4–6 servings.

Eggs, Etc.

Eggs are a good source of balanced protein as they contain all the amino acids needed for the human body to function. Eggs are rich in minerals, iodine, phosphorus, and zinc as well as vitamins A, D, and E, B vitamins, selenium, calcium, and iron; they're considered one of nature's perfect foods.

Eggs calm Vata, increase Pitta, and are balancing for Kapha when eaten once or twice a week. They are hot, oily, and heavy in quality and can be difficult to digest according to Ayurveda, so make sure you eat these when your agni is good.

slightly +

+ # Mushroom, Leek & Red Bell Pepper Quiche

I've been making this quiche for years and still love it every time. It's simple to make; I usually buy or prepare the crusts ahead of time. I like it best paired with a colorful salad.

2 pre-made pie crusts
1 tsp ghee (or butter)
1 tsp olive oil
½ cup onions, chopped
1 leek, sliced, white parts only
3 cups mushrooms, sliced
¼ cup red bell peppers, finely diced
Salt to taste
¼ tsp thyme

4 eggs
1½ cups milk
3 tbsp unbleached white flour
¼ tsp salt
¼ tsp dry mustard
1½ cups Gruyere cheese, grated
¼ tsp cayenne pepper

Preheat oven to 375°F (190°C).

In a frying pan on medium-high, heat ghee and oil. Add onions and leeks and sauté until onions are translucent, about 2–3 minutes. Add mushrooms, peppers, salt, and thyme and sauté for 3–5 minutes. Set aside to cool.

In a mixing bowl, combine eggs, milk, flour, salt, and mustard. Beat until ingredients are well blended and mixture starts to foam. Divide cheese into two portions and spread evenly over bottom of both pie crusts. Divide vegetable mixture evenly and spread over cheese in each crust. Pour half the egg mixture into each crust. Sprinkle with cayenne. Bake for 40–45 minutes or until solid in center, but not hard. Slice into quarters.

Makes 2 medium-sized quiches (4–6 servings).

Crustless Quiche with Mushrooms, Leeks & Red Bell Peppers

This is a variation on the previous recipe; if you're watching your weight, this is a great way to still enjoy quiche without the calorie-laden crust. If you want to make this even lighter, use skim milk and low-fat cheese. Enjoy with a salad full of sprouts and greens to add the important bitter taste and to help cleanse the liver.

Use the same ingredients on the previous page, except for the pie crusts, then follow directions for sautéing the vegetables and beating the egg mixture. Add the cooled vegetables to egg mixture and mix. Pour vegetable-egg mixture into a lightly oiled pie pan. Spread cheese evenly on top and sprinkle with cayenne. Bake for 35–40 until solid in center, but not hard, and cheese begins to bubble and turn golden brown.

Makes 4–6 servings.

–

+

– # Curried Eggs

Ismail Merchant, the late filmmaker, was known to produce feasts on the spur of the moment no matter how remote his film location was. Curried eggs were one of his favorites. Here is my version; the spices, parsley, and cilantro make the eggs easier to digest for Vata and Kapha. To reduce Pitta, make this with egg whites. Serve with rice.

If entertaining guests, you can arrange the eggs in a serving dish first and then pour sauce over them.

4 eggs, hard-boiled and halved

1 tbsp good oil (see page 22)
½ cup onions, chopped
¼ tsp turmeric
2 cups tomatoes, chopped

½ tsp cayenne pepper, or to taste
Salt to taste
Juice of ½ a lemon
¼ tsp garam masala
¼ cup fresh parsley or fresh cilantro
   leaves, chopped (for garnish)

In a pot on medium-low, heat oil. Add onions and turmeric and sauté until onions turn golden, about 8–10 minutes, stirring often. Increase heat to medium and add tomatoes, cayenne, and salt. Cover with lid and cook until tomatoes soften, about 8–10 minutes. Add lemon juice and stir. Gently add cooked, halved eggs, keeping yolks intact. Carefully spoon tomato curry sauce over eggs. Sprinkle with garam masala and garnish with parsley or cilantro.

Makes 2–4 servings.

–

slightly +

slightly +

Spiced "Buttermilk" Curry

Here is a low-fat version of a traditional family favorite that is quick to make. Timing is everything, so have your ingredients ready for each stage, and don't leave the stove as this dish needs your constant attention. You'll love the flavor of the "buttermilk" and spices with the sweet and sour tastes coming from the sweetener and lemon juice. Serve with rice and kitchari.

For a full-fat version, use 2 cups buttermilk and ¾ cup water instead of the yogurt-water mixture.

Available at Indian grocery stores, fenugreek seeds are used to treat diabetes and hypoglycemia and also are known to alleviate diarrhea, dysentery, and rheumatism.

1¼ cups plain yogurt
1½ cups water
2 tbsp gram flour
1 tsp good oil (see page 22)
½ tsp mustard seeds
½ tsp whole cumin seeds
¼ tsp fenugreek seeds (see note)
1 fresh green chili, slit at end
  • *To reduce Pitta: omit or use ¼ chili*
3–5 curry leaves
2 cloves
  • *To reduce Pitta: omit*

½ tsp garlic, minced or pressed
1 tsp fresh ginger, minced
¼ tsp turmeric
½ tsp gur (or other sweetener)
1 tsp salt, or to taste
¼ tsp cayenne pepper, or to taste
Juice of ½ a lemon
¼ cup fresh cilantro leaves, chopped, (for garnish)

In a medium mixing bowl with a whisk, blend yogurt, water, and flour until mixture is smooth. In a pot on medium-high, heat oil. Add mustard seeds, cover with lid, and let pop for 30 seconds. Add cumin seeds, fenugreek seeds, green chili, curry leaves, cloves, garlic, and turmeric, and sauté for 30 seconds. Add yogurt mixture and bring to a boil while stirring or whisking continuously. Reduce heat and simmer until mixture thickens (to the consistency of whipping cream) for about 10 minutes, continuing to stir. Add gur and stir until it dissolves. Then add salt, cayenne (if using), and lemon juice. The curry leaves, chili, and cloves can be discarded or left in for flavor (but warn your guests not to eat them). Garnish with cilantro.

Makes 2–3 servings.

Breads and Grains

Whole grains, an important staple in the diets of people worldwide, are a rich source of minerals, fiber, and B vitamins. They are also grounding, as they produce serotonin in the brain (which help to regulate our moods, sleep, and appetite, among other things) and stabilize our bodies' metabolism. All doshas benefit from eating some grains each day, but to reduce Kapha, eat smaller portions.

In Indian cooking, many of the common breads are circular, unleavened, and flat. The ingredients are very simple, so once the art of making these breads is mastered, they are quick and easy to prepare. Hot buttered chapatis are a warm, soothing component to any Indian meal; adding spices, stuffing them, and using a variety of fibrous flours offer a rich assortment of flavors and textures. To appeal to contemporary tastes, I also have included Carrie's Spelt Oatmeal Bread (page 230), Banana Walnut Loaf (page 232), Flax Seed Raintree Crackers (page 235), and some muffin recipes. People who omit white or wheat flour from their diets will especially benefit from this chapter, as most of the recipes use alternative flours. In addition, almost all of these recipes are yeast-free.

-
-
+

Whole Wheat Chapatis

Making chapatis can be a therapeutic activity, with all the kneading and rolling. Even if they don't look perfect the first time, keep trying. Before long, you will be a chapati master! Serve with a variety of Indian entrées or for breakfast with a little ghee and honey or jam.

Ayurveda believes fresh food has the most prana – the Sanskrit word for breath or "life force" – however, these chapatis do freeze well for up to a few weeks.

In traditional Indian dinners, chapatis and a vegetable or lentil dish are often served first, followed by a curry and rice as the second course.

2 cups whole wheat flour (see note)
½ tsp salt (optional)
1½ tbsp ghee (or good oil, see page 22)
 • *To reduce Kapha: use light oil*

1 cup boiling water (may need another tbsp)

In a large bowl, combine flour and salt. Add ghee and mix together with hands. Pour in boiling water and mix with a wooden spoon; let sit until mixture cools. Once cooled, knead with your hands to form a firm, smooth dough. Cover and let sit for 5 minutes. Knead again lightly for another 4–5 minutes. Divide into 10 evenly-sized balls and place on a plate. Cover with a slightly damp cloth or another plate.

On a lightly floured surface with a rolling pin, roll out each ball evenly into a 7-in (17½-cm) circle. (This gets better with practice; sometimes edges become too thick while the center gets too thin. If this happens, simply reform the dough into a ball and roll out again.)

In a dry heavy-bottomed or non-stick frying pan on medium-high heat, cook each chapati by placing it top-side down in the pan. When it begins to bubble, after about 1 minute, gently press edges with a non-metal spatula to allow it to gather air and rise. Flip and cook the other side for 1 minute. Set aside in an ovenproof dish. Repeat with remaining dough. If pan gets too hot, reduce heat. Experiment to determine the optimal heat to cook the chapatis; the more they bubble and rise, the lighter they are.

Stack chapatis on top of each other in a dish, separated with wax paper or coated with a little ghee, to prevent sticking. Cover dish with lid to prevent drying and place in a warm oven until ready to serve.

Makes 10 chapatis.

Whole wheat is a grounding, moist grain that can balance ingredients such as beans and lentils. If you have a wheat intolerance – headachy, sluggish, or find it hard to digest – avoid this recipe and try the Spelt, Corn Chapatis, or Spelt & Gram (pages 220–222) for a period as you acclimate yourself to the healthier Ayurvedic lifestyle. Gradually, you can try re-introducing wheat into your diet.

Chapatis are usually torn off a little piece at a time, wrapped around a bit of food, and eaten with the fingers. It takes time to learn to do this gracefully!

-
-
+ # Spelt Chapatis

When I had dinner at my friend Jeto's house, she made this age-old chapati recipe with spelt flour. The chapatis were delicious, and we enjoyed them right off the stove with a tasty vegetable subji. Serve with any Indian entrée or for breakfast with honey.

Spelt is an ancient grain and although it is a close relative of wheat, most people with wheat intolerances can digest it due to its low-gluten content. Spelt has 15–20 percent protein content and more complex carbohydrates than wheat. Spelt flour does not rise quite as high as wheat flour and needs slightly less liquid to bind it.

2 cups spelt flour (see note)
½ tsp salt
½ cup warm water

1½ tbsp ghee, melted
   (or good oil, see page 22)
   • Vata can add 1 tbsp more

In a large bowl, combine flour and salt. Add water and mix together with hands. Knead with your hands to form a firm, smooth dough. If too sticky, add more flour, 1 tbsp at a time; if too dry, add more water, 1 tbsp at a time. Cover and let sit for 5 minutes. Pour melted ghee over dough and knead again. Divide dough into 10 evenly-sized balls. On a lightly floured surface with a rolling pin, roll out each ball evenly into a 7-in (17½-cm) circle.

In a dry heavy-bottomed or non-stick frying pan on medium-high heat, cook each chapati by placing it top-side down into the pan. When it begins to bubble, after about 1 minute, gently press edges with a non-metal spatula to allow it to gather air or rise. Flip and cook the other side for 1 minute. Set aside in an ovenproof dish. Repeat with remaining dough. If pan gets too hot, reduce heat. Experiment to determine the optimal heat to cook them. Stack chapatis on top of each other in dish, separated with wax paper or coated with a little ghee, to prevent sticking. Cover dish with lid to prevent drying and place in a warm oven until ready to serve.

Makes 10 chapatis.

+

+

- # Corn Chapatis

This is a rustic Indian farmer's flat bread. I love these chapatis served hot with spinach baji. They are also wonderful eaten with other vegetable bajis and curries.

To get rid of ama, (toxins) from your body, add these ingredients to your dough when you add the salt: $^1/_8$ tsp hing (a spice available in Indian markets); $^3/_4$ tsp whole cumin seeds; a pinch of black pepper; $^1/_2$ tsp fresh ginger, minced; $1^1/_2$ tsp turmeric; $1^1/_2$ tsp ground coriander; and 3 tsp non-pasteurized honey.

1 cup ground corn flour
½ tsp salt
1 tbsp ghee (or olive oil)
  • To reduce Kapha: use 1 tbsp

1 tbsp plain yogurt (optional)
½ cup cornmeal, cooked
½ cup cold water (may need more)

In a large bowl, combine corn flour, salt, ghee, and yogurt then mix. Add cooked cornmeal and mix again. Add water, 1 tbsp at a time, and knead with your hands to form a dough. If too moist, add more corn flour, 1 tbsp at a time; if too dry, add more water, 1 tbsp at a time. Divide dough into 6 evenly-sized balls. Rub hands with a little oil and on a lightly floured surface, shape balls into 5-in (12-cm) flat circles.

In a dry heavy-bottomed or non-stick frying pan on medium-high heat, cook each chapati for 2–3 minutes on each side. Set aside in ovenproof dish. Repeat with remaining dough. If pan gets too hot, reduce heat. Experiment to determine the optimal heat to cook them. Stack chapatis on top of each other in dish, separate with wax paper or coat with a little ghee, to prevent sticking. Cover dish with lid to prevent drying and place in a warm oven until ready to serve.

Makes 6 chapatis.

slightly +

-

- # Spelt & Gram Flour Chapatis

The combination of fresh cilantro with the gram flour make it hard to stop eating these chapatis. Luckily they are quite filling, so a little goes a long way. These are delicious dipped into plain yogurt or eaten with curries. (I often carry these with me to enjoy as a mid-morning snack.)

Gram flour is available in Indian or specialty markets.

To vary this recipe, add ¹/₂ tsp fresh green chilies, minced. (To reduce Pitta: omit.)

½ cup gram flour (see note)
½ cup spelt flour
½ tsp salt
1 tbsp fresh cilantro leaves, chopped

¼ cup water
1 tbsp buttermilk
1 tsp good oil (see page 22)

In a large bowl, combine flours, salt, and cilantro, then mix well. Add water, buttermilk, and oil. Knead mixture with your hands until it forms a smooth dough. If too sticky, add more spelt flour, 1 tbsp at a time. Divide mixture into 6 evenly-sized balls. On a lightly floured surface with a rolling pin, roll out balls into 6–7-in (14–16-cm) circles.

In a dry heavy-bottomed or non-stick frying pan on medium-high heat, cook each chapati by placing it top-side down into the pan. When it begins to bubble, after about 1 minute, gently press edges of chapati with a non-metal spatula as this allows it to gather air or rise. Flip and cook the other side for 1 minute. Set aside in an ovenproof dish. Repeat with remaining dough. If pan gets too hot, reduce heat. Stack chapatis on top of each other in dish, separated with wax paper or coated with a little ghee, to prevent sticking. Cover dish with lid to prevent from drying and keep in a warm oven until ready to serve.

Makes 6 chapatis.

+

+

-  # Ugali

vegan

Ugali is a staple food in Kenya that warms and soothes the senses. It is often eaten with African Spinach (page 181) or vegetable, bean, or lentil curries. Elizabeth Madoka, my hostess in Mwatate, Kenya where I worked with the Pamoja Foundation, gave this recipe to me.

Use your fingers to eat ugali. Form a bite-sized ball, make a dent in it with your thumb, then scoop up some curry with it and pop it into your mouth. Now you are eating the African way!

4 cups water
1 tsp salt, or to taste (optional)

2 cups white maize flour
   (may substitute grits, sorghum,
   or yellow cornmeal) (see note)

In a pot on high heat, bring water and salt to a boil. Add flour, 1 tbsp at a time, while stirring constantly with a whisk to avoid lumps, until all the flour is used. Reduce heat to medium-low and cook until mixture reduces and thickens and does not stick to the sides of the pot, about 5–6 minutes. Let sit for about 5 minutes, then remove from heat. Let sit for another minute, then serve.

Makes 4 servings.

White maize flour is difficult to find in North America, unlike the more common yellow cornmeal or corn flour. If you do find white maize flour, it will make this dish more authentic.

slightly +

+ # Alu Roti

These are a real treat in Indian homes. My family enjoys them on holiday weekends when we can all gather for a long lunch or late breakfast. This recipe takes a bit longer to make, but it is well worth it. Eat these hot off the griddle dipped into some yogurt and green chutney (see pages 259 or 260) or Coconut Mint Chutney (page 262) and/or Tamarind Chutney (page 261). Add some Milky Masala Chai (page 282) and enjoy!

These roti may be cooked ahead of time and reheated in a dry frying pan for a minute or two on each side just before serving.

Roti:
4 cups whole wheat flour
9 tbsp ghee
1 cup cold water

Filling:
3 medium potatoes, peeled and
    quartered (about 1 lb, or ½ kg)
3 tbsp good oil (see page 22)
½ cup onions, minced
½ tsp salt

½ tsp ground cumin
½ tsp garam masala
¼–½ tsp fresh green chilies, minced
  • To reduce Pitta: omit
½ cup fresh cilantro leaves, minced
Juice of ½ a lemon

¼ cup ghee, melted (for brushing)

For roti:
In a large bowl, combine the flour and ghee with your hands until mixture resembles breadcrumbs. Add water and knead with your hands until it forms a firm, smooth dough. If too dry, add more water, 1 tbsp at a time, and knead again. Set aside in a bowl, covered, for 30 minutes.

For filling:
While dough rests, in a large pot of salted, boiling water, cook potatoes in water until they are softened, about 20 minutes. Drain and mash, then set aside. In a medium frying pan on medium, heat oil. Add onions and sauté for 4–5 minutes, until soft. Add salt, cumin, garam masala, green chilies, and mashed potatoes. Stir until ingredients are well mixed. Remove from heat and stir in cilantro and lemon juice.

To stuff roti:

Divide dough into 12 evenly-sized balls. On a lightly floured surface with a rolling pin, roll out dough into 5-in (12-cm) circles. Place $\frac{1}{12}$th of the filling into the center of each circle. Fold the edges over and pinch them together to enclose the filling (it will look like a stuffed wonton), then pat into a flat circle. Gently roll them out again into 6-in (14-cm) circles. Keep them covered with a damp cloth until done.

In a dry heavy-bottomed or non-stick frying pan on medium-high heat, cook roti for about 1 minute. Flip over and cook other side. Brush with a little melted ghee, cook for 2 minutes, then flip over again. Brush other side with melted ghee and cook for 1 minute, until lightly brown on both sides.

Makes 12 roti.

– + + Mooli Roti

This recipe uses daikon (mooli) and chilies in the stuffing instead of potatoes (alu). Serve each roti with 2–3 tbsp plain yogurt and 1 tsp of green chutney (see page 259 or 260). You can also add Coconut Mint Chutney (page 262) and/or Tamarind Chutney (page 261).

Roti:
4 cups whole wheat flour
9 tbsp ghee
1 cup cold water

Filling:
3 cups daikon, grated
1½ tsp salt

1½ tsp fresh green chilies, minced, or
  to taste (see note)
  • *To reduce Pitta: omit*
¼ cup fresh cilantro leaves, chopped
1½ tsp fresh ginger, minced
1 tbsp lemon juice

¼ cup ghee, melted (for brushing)

For roti:
In a large bowl, combine flour and ghee with your hands until mixture resembles breadcrumbs. Add water and knead with your hands until it forms a firm, smooth dough. If too dry, add more water, 1 tbsp at a time, and knead again. Set aside in a bowl, covered, for 30 minutes.

For filling:
In a large bowl, combine all ingredients and mix well.

To stuff roti:

Divide dough into 12 evenly-sized balls. On a lightly floured surface with a rolling pin, roll out dough into 5-in (12½-cm) circles. Place ¹⁄₁₂th of the filling into the center of each circle. Fold the edges over and pinch them together to enclose the filling (it will look like a stuffed wonton), then pat into a flat circle. Gently roll them out again into 6-in (15¼ cm) circles. Keep them covered with a damp cloth until done.

In a dry heavy-bottomed or non-stick frying pan on medium-high heat, cook roti for about 1 minute. Flip over and cook other side. Brush with a little melted ghee, cook for 2 minutes, then flip over again. Brush other side with melted ghee and cook for 1 minute, until lightly brown on both sides.

Makes 12 rotis.

Chilies do not always pack the same heat, so the amount of green chili to use really depends on how hot it is. To test, brave souls can slice a tiny bit off the end (i.e. the size of 4 grains of salt) and try it. Another way to tell is by scent – the stronger it is, the stronger the heat. Serrano chilies (the thin green ones) are generally hotter than the common jalapeño. Always remember to wash your hands after handling chilies, and avoid rubbing your eyes.

+

ø

- # Traditional Rotlo

Serve this wholesome bread with any curry. I love eating the leftovers for breakfast; I crumble about a quarter of a slice into a cup of plain yogurt and season it with salt and pepper. This bread is dry, which reduces Kapha, and is known to help offset cold symptoms.

Millet flour is dark gray in color, high in iron and B vitamins, and available in Indian groceries or health food stores.

1¼ cups millet flour (see note)
½ tsp salt

2 tsp grapeseed or olive oil (or ghee)
 • *To reduce Kapha: use 1 tsp*
¼ cup cold water

In a large bowl, combine all ingredients and knead with your hands until you form dough with the consistency of wet clay. If too dry, add more water, 1 tbsp at a time; if too mushy, add more flour, 1 tbsp at a time.

On a lightly floured surface, with a rolling pin or the palms of hands, flatten dough into an 8-in (20-cm) circle. If it gets crumbly or starts to fall apart, wet your fingers and press it back together.

Lift it off the surface with a large, flat spatula so that it does not break apart. In a dry heavy-bottomed or non-stick frying pan on medium-high heat, cook rotlo for 2–3 minutes, then flip over and cook other side for 2–3 minutes until slightly brown. Note that the rotlo is quite solid and will not bubble up or rise when cooking. Flip again if necessary; if pan is too hot, reduce heat. The bread is ready when both sides are crisp and brown. Cut into quarters and serve immediately, or store for up to 2 days.

Makes 2–4 servings.

+

slightly +

- # Upma

Millet has been a part of Indian diets for thousands of years, and is a staple in the diet of the Hunza people, who live in the foothills of the Himalayas and known for their long life spans. This upma is nicely spiced, and tasty with or without onions. Serve it warm; any leftovers can be enjoyed eaten cool the next day for lunch.

Toasting millet before using removes allergens, glutamine, and other Kapha qualities of this grain.

1 cup yellow millet (see note)
1 tbsp ghee (or olive oil)
1 tbsp black mustard seeds
5 curry leaves
¼ tsp turmeric
1 tsp fresh green chilies, minced
 • *To reduce Pitta: omit*

½ cup shallots (or onions), chopped
½ tsp salt
3 cups water
 • *To reduce Vata: add an extra ½ cup*
Sprig of fresh cilantro or parsley (for garnish)

Preheat oven to 350°F (180°C).

In a non-stick baking pan, place millet and toast for 7–8 minutes, until slightly brown. Remove from oven and set aside. In a pot on medium-high heat, melt ghee. Add mustard seeds, cover with lid, and let pop for 30 seconds, then immediately add curry leaves, turmeric, chilies, and shallots. Reduce heat to medium-low and sauté until shallots are golden brown. Add salt and water, increase heat, and bring to a boil. Gently add toasted millet, stirring constantly to avoid lumps. Allow mixture to come to a rolling boil for 1–2 minutes. Reduce heat to low, cover with lid, and cook for 25–30 minutes, or until millet is light and fluffy. Towards the end, if the millet is not yet done you can add an extra ¼ cup of water. Remove from heat and serve immediately.

Makes 4–6 servings.

-
-
slightly +

Carrie's Spelt Oatmeal Bread

I noticed how vibrant Carrie, a fellow Bowen Islander, looked after she removed wheat and refined sugar from her diet. She said the results are worth it – she's healthier, has more energy, and can easily maintain her weight. I asked Carrie to share one of her great wheat-free recipes for the book.

2 cups boiling water
1 cup rolled oats
⅓ cup honey
  • *To reduce Pitta: use maple syrup*
2 tbsp butter (or ghee)
2 tsp salt
1 pkg (¼ oz/8g) active dry yeast

½ cup warm water (110°F/43°C)
1 large egg
4½ cups spelt flour
2 tbsp honey, slightly warmed
  (for brushing)
2 tbsp rolled oats (for sprinkling)

In a large bowl, combine boiling water, oats, honey, butter, and salt and set aside. In a small bowl, dissolve yeast in warm water and let stand about 10 minutes. (Some yeasts, such as RiZE Organic Yeast, do not require this step.) Pour the yeast mixture into the oat mixture and mix well. Add the egg and mix, then add flour and mix again until dough is smooth and elastic; if too sticky, add more flour, 1 tbsp at a time. (Be careful not to over-knead as spelt flour is more delicate than wheat flour.) Lightly oil a large bowl and add dough, turning to coat with oil. Cover with a damp cloth and set aside to rise in a warm place until dough doubles in volume, about 1 hour.

Preheat oven to 375°F (190°C). Punch down dough, then on a lightly floured surface, divide dough into 2 equal pieces and form into loaves. Place loaves into 2 lightly oiled 9×5-in (22×12-cm) loaf pans. Cover with a damp cloth and let rise again until doubled in volume, about 40 minutes. Bake for about 30 minutes, or until the top of each loaf is golden brown and the bottom sounds hollow when tapped. Remove loaves from pans, brush tops with honey, and sprinkle with oats.

Makes 2 loaves (10–12 slices per loaf).

-
-
slightly +

Spelt Oatmeal Bread: Bread Machine Version

Carrie says her bread recipe (opposite page) is really easy to make if you have a bread machine.

½ cup old fashioned oats
1 cup boiling water
2 tbsp butter
1½ tsp salt
3 tbsp honey

1 tbsp dark molasses (optional)
1 large egg, lightly beaten
3 cups light spelt flour
2 tsp active dry yeast

In the bread machine's mixing bowl, add oats and cover with boiling water. Once oats have cooled but are still warm, add remaining ingredients according to bread machine manual. Bake on the light setting.

Makes 1 loaf.

−

 ∅

 +

Banana Walnut Loaf

This is another delicious, never-fail recipe. I am addicted to banana bread, so I save a lot of money and calories while increasing my nutritional intake by making my own. Serve it on its own, or with fruit and frozen yogurt for dessert.

Gur (jaggery) is similar to molasses but without the heavy taste, and is high in B vitamins and minerals.

Although Ayurveda recommends fresh food, this loaf freezes well for up to 2 weeks.

½ cup olive oil
¾ cup brown sugar (or ¼ cup gur [see note] and ½ cup brown sugar)
2 large eggs
1¾ cups ripe bananas, mashed
1 tsp vanilla extract

1¼ cups whole wheat flour
¼ cup wheat germ
1 tbsp flax seeds, ground
1 tsp baking soda
1 tsp baking powder
¼ cup walnuts, chopped

Preheat oven to 350°F (180°C).

In a large bowl, combine oil, sugar, eggs, bananas, and vanilla and stir until just mixed. Add flour, wheat germ, flax seeds, baking soda, and baking powder. Fold and combine until just moistened. Stir in chopped walnuts and pour into a lightly oiled 9×5-in (22×12-cm) loaf pan. Bake for 45 minutes–1 hour, or until a toothpick or fork comes out clean.

Makes 6–8 servings.

-
-
slightly +

Banana, Oat & Berry Muffins

Use ripe bananas for these low fat and healthy carb muffins.

1 1/3 cups whole wheat flour
  • *To reduce Kapha: use spelt flour*
1 tbsp flax seeds, ground
2 tbsp wheat germ
1 cup 12-grain cereal
  (or porridge oats)
2 tsp baking powder
1 tsp baking soda
1/2 tsp salt
1 large egg

1/4 cup vegetable oil
3/4 cup ripe bananas, mashed
  • *To reduce Kapha: substitute additional*
    1 cup berries
1/2 cup sweetener (e.g., brown sugar,
  maple syrup, honey)
  • *To reduce Kapha: use honey*
3/4 cup milk
1/2 cup mixed berries

Preheat oven to 400°F (205°C).

In a large bowl, combine the first 7 ingredients, then mix and set aside. In a separate bowl, beat egg, then add oil, bananas, sweetener, and milk, and mix well. Add liquid ingredients to dry ingredients and mix to incorporate, then stir in berries. Lightly oil a muffin tin or cover with olive oil spray and spoon mixture evenly into muffin cups. Bake for 18–20 minutes, or until a toothpick or fork comes out clean. Let cool on a cake rack.

Makes 12 muffins.

+
-

Sascha's Blueberry Almond Eggless Muffins

I met my friend Keri when she was leading camping safaris around North America (including driving the bus!). She put me in touch with her brother Matthew, who recently opened the Lettus Café Organic restaurant in San Francisco. Lettus chef Sascha Weiss shared this delicately flavored muffin recipe. The toasted almonds and the lemon zest combined with the blueberries and very little flour create a medley of flavors and textures. No eggs in this recipe make these easy on the digestive system.

Barley is a cool, light, and dry grain that alleviates Pitta and Kapha. Barley tea (¼ cup barley to 8 cups hot water) relieves fever and calms the urinary tract.

Soak almonds overnight to blanch them, then peel and toast them in the oven just before using. Soaking almonds increases their nutritional value as it returns the nut back to its live form.

1 ¾ cups barley flour (see note)
  • *To reduce Vata: use spelt flour*
¾ tsp baking powder
¼ tsp baking soda
¼ tsp salt
1 tbsp lemon zest, packed
7 tbsp grapeseed oil (or canola oil)
½ cup maple syrup

½ cup plain soy milk
½ tsp lemon juice
1 tsp vanilla extract
¾ cup blueberries
¼ cup almonds, peeled, toasted, and roughly chopped (see note)

Preheat oven to 350°F (180°C).

In a bowl, sift together flour, baking powder, baking soda, and salt and set aside. In a separate bowl, whisk together all remaining ingredients except berries and almonds. Add berries and mix. Pour liquid mixture into dry and mix well, then stir in almonds. Lightly oil a muffin pan and spoon mixture evenly into muffin cups. Bake for 15–18 minutes, or until a toothpick or fork comes out clean. Let cool on a cake rack.

Makes 12 muffins.

–

slightly +

slightly + # Flax Seed Raintree Crackers

I belong to a group of Bowen Island painters. One day, fellow member Penny brought these wonderful crackers to our plein-air painting class. They're a wonderful, nutritious snack that are easy to carry with you (try them instead of trail mix), and are delicious alone or with your favorite cheese.

To turn these crackers into tea cakes: after baking them the first time, thinly slice them and serve.

The mixed seeds can be a combination of some or all of the following: pumpkin seeds, sesame seeds, sunflower seeds, poppy seeds.

2 cups raisins (or currants)
  • *To reduce Kapha: use cranberries*
¾ cup mixed chopped nuts
  (e.g., almonds, pecans)
  • *To reduce Pitta and Kapha: substitute with more seeds, see note*
¼ cup flax seeds
1 cup mixed seeds (see note)
  • *To reduce Kapha: omit sesame seeds*

1 large egg
2 tbsp milk
1 cup buttermilk
¾ cup strong black tea
  (or decaf black tea or Rooibos tea)
1 tsp salt
½ cup brown sugar
3¼ cups plus 2 tbsp spelt flour
2 tsp baking soda

Preheat oven at 325°F (160°C).

In a large bowl, combine raisins, nuts, and seeds. In another bowl, beat egg and milk together. Add buttermilk, tea, salt, and sugar and beat again. Sift flour and baking soda over nut mixture. Pour in liquid ingredients and mix well. Pour into a lightly oiled 9×9-in(22×12-cm) pan and bake for 60–75 minutes, until a toothpick or fork comes out clean. Cover and refrigerate overnight.

The next day, preheat oven to 290°F (145°C). Cut loaf lengthwise into 4 logs. Cut each log into very thin slices about ¼-in (6-mm) thick. Spread on a baking sheet and bake for about 45 minutes until dry, but not browned. Turn oven off and leave crackers to dry out and crisp further for another 45 minutes. Store in an airtight container for up to 3 months.

Makes 60–70 crackers.

Desserts

It's possible to enjoy a wide range of tempting desserts on an Ayurvedic diet, so long as you use healthy ingredients. This chapter also includes contemporary takes on traditional Indian desserts like Rasgouli Homemade Cheese Patties in Sweet Syrup (page 240), Sweet Shikand (pages 242), and Traditional Indian Rice Pudding with Nuts (page 239).

Sugar was once considered a rare and costly commodity. Today, it is easily refined and stored, so we consume more than we should; much of the excess sugar eaten today is hidden in processed and packaged foods. Be aware that sugar creates a nutritional debt in the body that must be compensated by increasing your intake of vitamins, minerals, protein, and healthy fats that are all necessary to burn off sugar. Many recipes in this chapter can use Sucanat, Rapadura, or gur, all of which are made from sugar cane juice and, unlike white sugar, retain some of their natural nutrients.

-
- # Sonita's Norwegian Rice Pudding
+ with an Indian Twist

My half-Norwegian cousin Sonita lives in London, England with her husband, Paul, who does most of the cooking. However, this is one dish she says she does make because it practically cooks itself. I've modified this family favorite to include short-grain brown rice, which adds a nutty flavor to the caramelized, spice-infused milk.

Butter (to grease baking dish)
2½ cups short-grain brown rice, cooked
½–¾ cup brown sugar
2–3 cinnamon sticks, 2-in (5-cm) long

1 cup heavy cream
4–5 cardamom pods, slit at end
½ cup raisins
2½ cups whole milk

Preheat oven at 350°F (180°C).

Grease an ovenproof baking dish with butter. Cover bottom of dish with rice. Add remaining ingredients and stir. Bake for 30–40 minutes.

Makes 4–6 servings.

-
-
+

Traditional Indian Rice Pudding with Nuts

A perfect dessert when you have leftover rice. The spices warm the cooling milk.

1 cup rice, cooked and mashed
4 cups whole milk
  • *To reduce Kapha: use low-fat or goat's milk*
¼ tsp nutmeg
¼ tsp ground cinnamon (or 2-in piece of cinnamon bark or stick)

4 tbsp sweetener
3 tbsp raisins
1 tsp pistachios, coarsely chopped (for garnish)
1 tsp almonds, coarsely chopped (for garnish)

In a large pot on high heat, combine all ingredients except nuts, and bring to a boil. Reduce heat and simmer, stirring occasionally, for 20 minutes. Garnish with nuts and serve.

Makes 4 servings.

 - - Variation: Apart from adding a lovely subtle flavor and rich color, saffron is a digestive aid and reduces food allergies. Add ¼ tsp broken saffron strands to 2 tbsp milk and set aside for 10 minutes. Then add with other ingredients to the pot.

 Rasgouli Homemade Cheese Patties in Sweet Syrup

Ragouli is often made with sugar, but my version uses maple syrup. I love the subtle flavor of the fresh cheese combined with the syrup.

To make a traditional sugar syurp, substitute 3 cups white sugar for the maple syrup and add another 1 1/2 cups water.

Cheese:
6½ cups whole milk
1 cup plain yogurt
3 tbsp lemon juice
1½ tbsp semolina flour

Syrup:
1½ cups maple syrup (see note)
¼ tsp cream of tartar
1½ cups water
½ tsp rose water

For the cheese:

In a large pot on high heat, add milk and bring to a boil. Remove pot from heat and add yogurt and lemon juice. Stir gently to blend (the curds will separate from the whey). Strain through cheesecloth. Allow cheese to cool in cheesecloth for about 10 minutes. Pull in edges of cheesecloth to tighten around cheese, and squeeze out excess liquid whey. Discard whey. Place cheese on a baking sheet and knead for 2 to 3 minutes. Add semolina gradually, ½ tsp at a time, and knead for 8–10 minutes until cheese becomes firm and smooth and does not crumble.

For the syrup:

In a medium pot on high heat, combine maple syrup, cream of tartar, and 1½ cups water and bring to a boil, stirring to dissolve. Continue to cook for about 5 minutes. Remove from heat and add rose water. Pour off 1 cup of syrup and set aside. Return to stove on lowest heat setting.

Roll 1 tbsp of cheese mixture into small balls, then add to pot of hot syrup on stove. Stir occasionally, adding reserved syrup 1 tbsp at a time; ensure cheese balls are always covered by syrup as they simmer, about 30 minutes. Remove from heat and refrigerate for at least 30 minutes to overnight to allow cheese to absorb flavors. Serve in bowls with the syrup, warm or cool.

Makes 6 servings.

slightly +

slightly +

Light Carrot Halva

This is a lighter version of my mother's recipe. Gently cooking the carrots reveals the depth of their sweetness. In this recipe, the spices warm the carrots while the reduced milk, cream, and nuts enrich the flavor.

This recipe is still delicious if you do not have saffron.

¼ tsp saffron strands, broken (see note)
2 tbsp whole milk
  • *To reduce Kapha: use low-fat or goat's milk*
1 tbsp good oil (see page 22)
1 tbsp ghee (or butter)
3 cloves
4 cardamom pods, slit at end
2–3 pieces cinnamon bark
  (2-in/5-cm long)

6–8 cups carrots, grated
  (about 2½ lbs/1 kg)
1 cup whole milk
  • *To reduce Kapha: use low-fat or goat's milk*
½ cup cream
½ cup sweetener
10 almonds or pistachios
  (or combination), coarsely ground
  (for garnish)

In a small bowl, soak saffron strands in 2 tbsp milk. In a medium pot on medium, heat oil and ghee. Add cloves, cardamom pods, and cinnamon bark and stir for 1 minute. Add carrots and cook for 25–30 minutes, stirring frequently so carrots are not charred; add a little more ghee or oil if this occurs. Add milk, cream, and saffron-milk and cook for 10 minutes, stirring occasionally until liquid is absorbed. Add sweetener, reduce heat to low, and continue to cook until the mixture no longer clings to the side of the pot. Pour onto a flat serving plate and garnish with nuts. You may discard cloves, cardamom pods, and cinnamon bark or leave in as they continue to add flavor (warn your guests not to eat them).

Makes 6–8 servings.

Variation: Add ¼ cup raisins or currants when you add the sugar.

Sweet Shikand

Saffron adds a subtle flavor and a warm pale yellow hue to this sweetened sour cream dessert. When combined with a hint of cardamom and garnished with almonds, this shikand is a finger-licking delight.

2 cups light sour cream
4 tbsp sugar
¼ tsp ground cardamom
¼ tsp saffron strands, broken

2 tbsp almonds, coarsely ground
1 tsp almonds, coarsely ground
 (for garnish)
3 fresh mint leaves (for garnish)

In a bowl, combine all ingredients except for garnishes, and mix well. Refrigerate for at least 3 hours so saffron has time to color and flavor the dish. Before serving, stir to mix again. Garnish with almonds and mint leaves and serve.

Makes 4 servings.

Michele's Shikand

Michele is an Ayurvedic masseuse from Switzerland who has worked with physically challenged people for over twenty years. She said her favorite dessert is shikand because "it makes people very sweet in their hearts."

Use all ingredients from the Sweet Shikand recipe opposite except substitute 1 cup ricotta cheese and 1 cup whipping cream for the sour cream and add an extra tbsp of ground almonds. Then add from variations below:

 – + In a pot on medium-high, heat ½ tsp ghee, then add ¼ tsp minced ginger and a 2-in (5-cm) piece cinnamon bark. Sauté for 30 seconds to 1 minute. Add 1 cup sliced bananas and or ¼ cup raisins, stir through, and add to shikand before refrigerating. Remove cinnamon bark before serving.

 – + Mix 2 tbsp grated coconut and/or ½ tsp fennel seeds into shikand before refrigerating.

  – – In a pot on medium-high, heat ½ tsp ghee. Add ¼ tsp freshly ground red peppercorns and ¼ tsp cinnamon, then add 1 cup chopped pear and cook until pear softens into a compote (may need 2 tbsp water). Mix into shikand before refrigerating. (A little ghee helps Kapha to digest fruit when mixed with dairy.)

slightly +

Saffron, Cranberry & Almond Vermicelli

The warm, fragrant flavors of cardamom and cinnamon combined with the red cranberries and the yellow saffron make this dessert both a visual and tasty treat. I created this recipe when I did not have raisins on hand, which are commonly used in this traditional Indian dessert.

¼ tsp saffron strands, crushed
½ cup water (for soaking)
2 tbsp good oil (see page 22)
6 cardamom pods, slit at end
2 cinnamon sticks
2 cups roasted vermicelli, broken into pieces (available in Indian grocery stores)

1 cup water
½ cup skim milk
 • *To reduce Vata: use whole milk*
⅓ cup Agave nectar (or other sweetener)
1 ½ tbsp dried cranberries
1 ½ tbsp almonds, coarsely ground (for garnish)

Preheat oven to 350°F (180°C).

In a small bowl, combine saffron and ½ cup water and set aside. In a pot on medium, heat oil, add cardamom pods and cinnamon sticks and sauté for 30 seconds. Add vermicelli and sauté until it is evenly browned. Add 1 cup water, milk, Agave nectar, cranberries, and saffron-water, increase heat, and bring to a boil. Remove from heat, pour into an ovenproof dish, cover with lid, and bake for 10 minutes. Remove lid and bake for another 10 minutes until liquid has evaporated. Remove cardamom pods and cinnamon sticks. Garnish with almonds and serve.

Makes 4 servings.

+  Lapsi

This is a rich, grainy dessert that goes well with any Indian meal. Although Ayurveda emphasizes freshness, this freezes well for a few weeks.

2 tbsp ghee (or good oil, see page 22)
1 cinnamon stick
1 cup cracked wheat
1 cup whole milk
   • *To reduce Kapha: use low-fat, goat's, or soy milk*
2 cups water
¼ tsp saffron strands, broken (optional)

2 tbsp coconut, shredded
3 cardamom pods, slit at end
½–¾ cup sweetener
2 tbsp raisins
1 tsp almonds, coarsely ground (for garnish)
1 tsp pistachios, coarsely ground (for garnish)

Preheat oven to 300°F (150°C).

In a pot on medium heat, melt ghee. Add cinnamon stick and cook for 30 seconds. Add cracked wheat and cook for about 6 minutes, stirring constantly. Add milk, water, saffron, coconut, and cardamom pods, and cook for 10 minutes, stirring occasionally. Add sweetener and raisins. Mix well and simmer until the liquid has been absorbed, continuing to stir, about 15 minutes. Remove from heat, pour into an ovenproof dish, cover with lid, and bake for 20 minutes. Garnish with almonds and pistachios and serve. You can remove cinnamon stick and cardamom pods before serving, or leave in as they continue to add flavor (warn guests not to eat them).

Makes 4–6 servings.

-
-
+  Kara

Kara, also known as Shiro, is traditionally served in Hindu temples as an offering, or "prasad," to the Gods. Eating as little as 1–2 tbsp of Kara can be very satisfying. When I was a child, my siblings and cousins would eagerly await the moment when the Kara would be dropped into the palms of our hands after a religious ceremony at the temple. I am sure this is what helped keep us quiet for hours on end, listening to the prayers and the chanting that as adults we now embrace.

1 cup water
½ cup brown sugar
¼ cup ghee (or butter)
1 cup whole wheat flour

1 cup whole milk
• *To reduce Kapha: use low-fat, goat's, or soy milk*

In a pot on high heat, combine water and sugar and bring to a boil, then reduce heat to medium. In another pot on medium heat, melt ghee. Add flour and stir constantly until mixture is golden brown. In a third pot on medium-high, heat milk until it just starts to boil, then remove from heat. Add water and sugar mixture to flour and ghee mixture. Whisk until smooth and thick. Add hot milk, reduce heat to low, and cook for about 20 minutes, stirring often.

Makes 4–6 servings.

- +
slightly

Variation 1: Substitute ¾ cup gur for the brown sugar.

Variation 2: Add ¼ tsp broken saffron strands, ¼ tsp nutmeg, and ½ tsp ground cardamom to milk as it's heating.

Variation 3: Garnish with 1 tbsp slivered almonds, 1 tbsp crushed pistachios, and 1 tsp white poppy seeds.

China Grass Pudding with Nuts

This is a refreshing dessert made with agar agar, a gelatin base sometimes called China grass. Serve with fruit, or on its own.

Made from seaweed, agar agar is a powerful, natural, flavorless gelatin that looks like transparent straw. Medicinally, it alleviates constipation.

Rose water is calming for Pitta.

2 ½ tbsp agar agar flakes (see note)
1 cup water
1 cup sweetener
4 cups whole milk
 • To reduce Kapha: use low-fat or goat's milk

1 cup whipping cream
1 tsp vanilla extract (or a few drops of rose water, see note)
1 tbsp almonds, slivered
1 tbsp pistachios, coarsely ground (for garnish)

In a large pot on high heat, combine agar agar and water and bring to a boil for 2 minutes while stirring until agar agar dissolves. Add sweetener and stir to dissolve. Add milk and whipping cream and cook for 2 minutes, stirring constantly. Remove from heat. Add vanilla extract and let cool slightly. Pour into a serving bowl. When completely cooled, garnish with nuts and refrigerate until firm, about 4 hours.

Makes 6–8 servings.

Variation: Add ¼ tsp broken saffron strands to milk and let sit for 10 minutes before adding to pot.

Fruity "Jello"

This is a light, simple dessert that is good for you!

2 cups fruit of your choice, sliced or
chopped
1 cup water

1 tbsp agar agar flakes
1 ½ cups apple juice

Place fruit in a serving bowl. In a medium pot on high heat, combine water and agar agar and bring to a boil for 2–3 minutes while stirring until agar agar dissolves. Remove from heat, add apple juice, and stir. Pour over fruit. Refrigerate until it sets, about 45–60 minutes.

Makes 4 servings.

The Long-Awaited Chai Crème Brûlée

Chef Nathan Wright of the Galley Bistro on Bowen Island created this fusion recipe after working in a restaurant called Mango Shiva in Calgary, where he learned the original from an Indian colleague.

Masala mix:
½ cup fennel seeds
1 tbsp cloves
1½ tbsp cardamom seeds
2 cinnamon sticks
1 large slice fresh ginger

4 cups whipping cream
2–3 Earl Grey tea bags
  (may use decaf)
2 tbsp black tea leaves (or 2–3 black
  tea bags) (may use decaf)
12 egg yolks
1 cup sugar
½ cup sugar (for sprinkling)

Preheat oven to 300°F (150°C).

In a small bowl, combine all masala mix ingredients.

In a pot on medium-high heat, combine masala mix, whipping cream, tea bags, and tea leaves and heat until mixture just starts to foam and bubble. Immediately remove from heat. Cover and leave to steep for 10 minutes. Strain into a pot to discard spices, tea bags, and tea leaves. Return to heat and bring to a boil, uncovered. Remove from heat. In a separate bowl, combine egg yolks and 1 cup sugar and mix well. Add this mixture, 1 tbsp at a time, into hot liquid, stirring constantly to temper the eggs. Strain and pour into 12 individual crème brûlée ramekins. Place ramekins in a deep baking dish filled ½-inch (1¼ cm) high with water. Bake in this water bath for 1 hour (the water bath prevents curdling). Remove from oven, cool, and refrigerate to set. Sprinkle ½ cup sugar on top of custards. Heat a spoon over a stove element, then rub heated spoon over sprinkled sugar so it melts and forms a hard crust on top of the custard (or use a small blow torch).

Makes 12 servings.

-
-
+

Caroline's White Chocolate Cardamom Mousse

Caroline Rechia, owner of Chocolibrium.com, is a registered nutritionist and has some great desserts in her repertoire. This cardamom-infused coconut milk combined with the chocolate makes this dessert irresistible.

Chocolate contains anandamine, a protein used by our brain to produce pleasurable sensations. Ananda is the Sanskrit word for bliss.

6 cardamom pods, crushed
1¾ cup coconut milk
7 oz (200 g) white chocolate at room temperature, chopped into small pieces (see note)

1 pkg gelatin (for 4 servings)
1 tbsp confectioner's sugar (icing sugar) (optional)
2 tsp vanilla extract
2 egg whites

In a large pot on high, combine cardamom and coconut milk and bring to boil. Remove from heat, and remove pods with a slotted spoon (some cardamom bits may remain in pot). In a double boiler or in a separate pot on very low heat, melt chocolate while stirring constantly. Return coconut milk to heat and sprinkle with gelatin while stirring to completely dissolve. Sift in confectioner's sugar (if using), and stir to dissolve.

Remove coconut milk from heat, then add vanilla and melted chocolate. Whisk vigorously until well combined. Pour into a bowl, cover, and refrigerate for 30 minutes. In a medium bowl, beat egg whites until stiff. Remove mousse from refrigerator and fold in egg whites. Refrigerate for another 90 minutes to set.

Makes 4 servings.

-

slightly +

+

Creamy Extra Dark Chocolate Fondue

Cocoa West Chocolatier on Bowen Island creates inspired organic chocolate in the French and Belgian artisan traditions. Founder and maître chocolatier Joanne Mogridge shared this dessert with me, which is delicious, easy to prepare, and fun for guests. Dark chocolate is a rich source of magnesium and has the bitter taste valued in Ayurveda. Chocolate is also acidic, but this is counterbalanced by the alkaline nature of the fruit.

1 cup 70% cocoa mass dark chocolate, chopped or broken (see note)
1 cup soy milk (or whipping cream)

5–6 cups mixed fruit (e.g., orange segments, strawberries, sliced bananas, cherries, sliced pineapple)

Place chocolate in an ovenproof bowl. In a medium pot on high heat, bring soy milk to a boil. Immediately remove from heat and pour over chocolate. Stir until smooth.

Arrange fruit on a platter. Serve with forks or fondue sticks to dip fruit into the chocolate.

Makes 6 servings.

Recent studies indicate that dark chocolate with a high cocoa mass content (70% and above) is a good source of flavanoids, which are beneficial as antioxidants. This type of chocolate is also low on the Glycemic Index and does not produce the highs and lows of other sweets. Known to be a mood enhancer because it stimulates the release of serotonin in the brain, chocolate is often used in courtship rituals and called the food of love.

slightly +

+

Caroline's Carob Almond Cookies

Carob is a delicious, potassium-rich placebo for chocoholics.

Almond meal is finely ground almonds and is also known as almond flour.

½ cup coconut oil (or butter) (at room temperature)
½ cup maple syrup (at room temperature)
½ cup carob powder
1 cup almond meal (see note)
• *To reduce Pitta: use blanched almonds, ground*

⅔ cup oat flour (or kamut or unbleached white flour)
Pinch of salt
⅓ cup carob chips (or nuts of your choice)

Preheat oven to 325°F (160°C).

In a bowl, combine coconut oil and maple syrup until well mixed. In a separate bowl, combine carob powder, almond meal, oat flour, and salt, until evenly blended. Stir in carob chips. Add oil and maple syrup mixture and stir until it forms a dark-colored dough.

On a lightly greased baking sheet, place tbsp-sized balls of dough. Press down dough into circles and bake for 12 minutes and bake for 12 minutes or until edges are crisp. Allow to cool on baking sheet before transferring to a cooling rack. These will be a bit soft on the inside, like brownies. Serve warm or cool.

Makes 14–18 cookies.

Caroline's Vanilla Cardamom Shortbread Cookies

Cardamom gives these cookies an Indian twist that reminds me of the "katchori" cookies my grandmother used to make. I make these with Rapadura sugar and spelt flour, which is more filling than traditional shortbread cookies, so a little goes a long way.

1 cup butter
½ cup sugar (e.g., Sucanut, Rapadura, or gur)
2 tsp vanilla extract

4 cups spelt or unbleached white flour
1 tbsp ground cardamom
½ cup almonds, sliced

Preheat oven to 350°F (180°C).

In the bowl of an electric mixer or in a food processor, cream butter and sugar. Add vanilla and blend. In a separate bowl, combine flour and cardamom and mix. Fold flour into creamed butter and sugar to make a stiff, crumbly dough.

On a greased baking sheet, press dough to form an even 1-in (2½-cm) thick rectangle. Bake for 30 minutes. Remove from oven, then sprinkle with almonds and press them into the dough. Bake for another 10 minutes until dough begins to turn golden brown. Remove from oven and let cool while still on baking sheet for 10 minutes. Slice into squares and continue to let cool on baking sheet. When completely cool and crisp, remove from sheet and serve or store.

Makes 25–30 cookies.

-
-
+

Blackberry-Apple Oat Bars

These wonderful dessert bars are from Moreka Jolar, the chef at the rejuvenating Hollyhock retreat center on Cortes Island, BC, where many come to share wisdom, be inspired, and honor their minds, bodies, and spirits.

¾ cups unbleached white flour
¾ cups whole wheat flour
2 cups rolled oats
1½ cups almonds, slivered, or mix of
  sunflower and pumpkin seeds
2 tsp baking powder
1 tsp cinnamon

1 cup ghee (or unsalted butter,
  softened)
1 cup Sucanat (or raw cane sugar or
  brown sugar)
4 apples, cored and cut into slivers
3 cups blackberries

Preheat oven to 350°F (180°C).

In a blender or food processor, combine all ingredients except apples and blackberries and mix well. Set aside half of mixture. Press remaining half into the bottom of a lightly oiled 10×15-in (25×38-cm) baking sheet. Bake for 10–12 minutes until it turns lightly brown. Lay apple slivers over the crust, then top with blackberries and reserved crumble mixture. Bake for another 15–20 minutes. Allow to cool before cutting into bars.

Makes 12–15 bars.

-
-
+ # Creamy Banana-Berry Ice

(vegan)

This is another refreshing contribution from the kitchen at the Hollyhock retreat center, which exists to nourish and support people making the world better. This recipe is delicious garnished with fresh berries, toasted coconut, or chocolate shavings.

4 frozen bananas
Zest and juice of 1 lime
2 cups frozen raspberries, blueberries,
  or strawberries
1 cup coconut cream

In a blender or food processor, combine bananas with the lime zest and juice and blend until soft and creamy, about 2 minutes. Add frozen berries and coconut cream and continue to blend until desired consistency is reached. Serve immediately. This will keep frozen for up to 1 month.

Makes 8–10 servings.

Condiments

Condiments are an integral part of any Indian meal; they add color and flavor to dishes and take them from merely good to sensational. Condiments are also a good way to incorporate raw ingredients in your diet, as well as some of the six essential tastes (see page 20) important to a balanced Ayurvedic meal. All the recipes here are relatively simple to prepare; in some, the vegetables, fruits, and spices are cooked lightly or marinated.

These condiments are best served separately (ideally in small bowls decoratively placed on the table) and eaten in small quantities: one or two tablespoons of the raitas, and one or two teaspoons of the chutneys and pickles, are enough for one person. Condiments are useful for getting the digestive juices flowing, or as it is said in Ayurvedic terms, activating *agni*.

–

+

–

Tomato Chutney

vegan

This chutney is a great replacement for ketchup with most dishes. Tomatoes are a rich source of vitamins A and C. Although this will keep in the refrigerator, I prefer to make it fresh each time I need it, so this recipe only makes half a cup. If you want to make a full cup, double the quantity and use a larger frying pan, as the chutney should spread out in a thin layer on the pan as it cooks. This is a hot, pungent, and spicy chutney and only a little (about ½ tsp) adds great flavor to snacks and other dishes. It is often served with the Endvo Savory Squares (page 68) and Savory Dokra Squares (page 71).

The oil in this chutney works as a preservative. If for any reason you omit the oil, it will only last for up to 2 days.

¾ cup tomatoes, grated
3 tbsp tomato paste
½ tsp garlic, crushed
½ tsp fresh ginger, crushed
1 tsp ground cumin

¾ tsp salt, or to taste
2 tsp lemon juice
½ tsp sugar
½ tsp chili powder, or to taste
1 tbsp olive oil (see note)

In a small frying pan on medium heat, sauté tomatoes. When liquid from tomatoes has almost evaporated, add tomato paste, garlic, ginger, cumin, salt, lemon juice, sugar, and chili powder. Sauté for 1 minute, then add oil, and stir for 30 seconds. Remove from heat and serve. If desired, store in a sealed container in the refrigerator for up to 2 weeks.

Makes ½ cup.

Cilantro Mint Chutney

This chutney is balancing to all the doshas. In many Indian homes, the refrigerator is never without it, as it adds flavor to numerous dishes and snacks. This is one of two green chutneys in this chapter (see next page).

To preserve chutney, place in a sealed container and add 1–2 tsp of olive oil on top. It will last up to 2 weeks in the refrigerator.

Ayurveda always recommends using fresh food, but this chutney freezes well (for up to 1 month).

2 bunches fresh cilantro leaves
   (about 6 cups)
1 bunch fresh mint leaves
   (about 3 cups)
2 tsp salt, or to taste
3 tbsp olive or grapeseed oil
   • *To reduce Kapha: use a light version*

6 tbsp lime juice (1–2 limes)
   (may use lemons)
1 tbsp Agave nectar
   (optional)
1–2 tsp olive oil (for preserving)
   (optional) (see note)

In a blender or a food processor, combine all ingredients and blend to a pulp.

Makes 1½ cups.

If chutney is too chunky, while blending add an additional 1–2 tbsp olive oil (will reduce Vata) or lime juice.

-
+
-

Cilantro Garlic Chutney

 vegan

This second of two green chutneys (see previous page) is a delicious and pungent combination. Be careful, though, this chutney is addictive.

To preserve chutney, place in a sealed container and add 1–2 tsp of olive oil on top. It will last up to 2 weeks in the refrigerator.

4–5 cloves garlic
  • *To reduce Pitta: use 2 or omit*
1–3 fresh green chilies
  • *To reduce Pitta: omit*
2 bunches fresh cilantro leaves
  (about ¼ lb/115g)

2 tsp salt
3 tbsp olive oil
5 tbsp lime (or lemon) juice
1 tsbp Agave nectar (optional)

In a blender or a food processor, combine garlic and green chilies and chop. Add all remaining ingredients and blend to a pulp.

Makes 1–1½ cups.

  – – +
slightly

Variation: Cilantro Garlic Coconut Chutney

Add 2–3 tbsp grated coconut to the above mixture. The chutney should have a paste-like consistency; if it needs more liquid, add 1–3 tbsp lime juice. Serve with South Indian Dosas (page 35), Baked Pakoras (page 61), or Endvo Savory Squares (page 68).

Tamarind Chutney

Tamarind pods, which grow on the tamarind tree – a large evergreen native to tropical Africa – contain a pulp that has a distinctly rich, sour flavor; it is mouth-wateringly delicious and enhances digestion. Tamarind chutney is a great addition to any meal and is wonderful with Baked Pakoras (page 61), Vegetable Samosas (page 62), and Endvo Savory Squares (page 68). It also can be used in place of lemon and honey for a sweet and sour flavor in dals (lentil dishes) or curries.

Tamarind pulp is available in Indian grocery stores or specialty markets.

Make sure you rub as much tamarind juice as you can out of the pulp. Discard pits and threads.

The flavor of this chutney is slightly sweeter when made with brown sugar instead of gur.

½ cup tamarind pulp (see note)
2 cups water
½ cup gur (or brown sugar) (see notes)

2–2½ tsp chili powder, or to taste
¼ tsp ground cumin

Rinse tamarind pulp once under running water and then, in a bowl, soak pulp in water for 30 minutes. In a medium pot on high heat, bring tamarind pulp and water to a boil. Reduce heat to simmer and add all other ingredients. Simmer for 5 minutes and remove from heat. Once cooled, rub with the back of a spoon through a sieve into a bowl (see note). Store in a sealed container in the refrigerator for up to 2 weeks.

Makes 1 ½ cups.

Gur, also called jaggery, is the first derivative of sugar cane with just the fiber and water removed, thus preserving its rich mineral and nutrient content – iron, magnesium, and potassium. It has a rich flavor resembling molasses and looks like a semi-solid form of brown sugar.

slightly

Coconut Mint Chutney

A mere teaspoonful is delicious served with Baked Pakoras (page 61), snacks, and curries.

2 tbsp unsweetened dry coconut, grated
½ cup plain yogurt
• *To reduce Kapha: may omit*
1–3 fresh green chilies
• *To reduce Pitta: use ½ green chili or omit*

1 cup fresh mint leaves
½ tsp salt
Juice of 1 lemon
½ tsp sweetener
¼ cup tomatoes, chopped (optional)
• *To reduce Pitta: omit*

In a blender or food processor, combine all ingredients and purée until smooth. Let mixture sit for at least 30 minutes before using to allow the coconut to absorb the liquid and start to thicken.

Makes about 1 cup.

Ripe Mango Chutney

In many cultures, mangoes are considered the king of fruits; they are rich in vitamins A and C. Ripe mangoes are balancing to all three doshas when eaten in moderation. They are slightly warming, so Pittas should only eat in small amounts. I love the orange color and rich flavor this fresh chutney adds to a meal.

If you use nectarines, this recipe will yield 1 ¾ cups instead of 2.

3 ripe mangoes (or nectarines), diced (see note)
⅓ cup apple cider vinegar

¼ cup maple syrup
Salt to taste
¼ tsp fresh red chilies, minced

In a pot on high heat, combine all ingredients and bring to a boil, then reduce heat and simmer for 15 minutes. Remove from heat and let cool. Store in a sealed container in the refrigerator for up to 1 week.

Makes 2 cups.

–

+

slightly + # Lime Pickles

vegan

Here is a delicious sweet and sour condiment that can be served with any curry dish. In Indian households, lime pickles are also often eaten in very small amounts alongside eggs at breakfast or with cheese and toast.

Make sure the syrup covers the lime slices by 1/4–1/2-inch (1/2–1-cm). If this reduces during the 2 weeks of storage, top up with vinegar.

12 limes (or lemons), thinly sliced in circles
2–3 tsp pickling salt (or regular salt)
1 tsp turmeric
2 cups apple cider vinegar
3 cups sugar (I use gur or brown sugar)

4 bay leaves
4 cinnamon sticks
6 cloves
6 peppercorns
1 tsp whole cumin seeds
1 tsp cayenne pepper

Spread out lime slices on a baking sheet, and sprinkle evenly with 1/2 the pickling salt and 1/2 the turmeric. Turn each lime over and sprinkle evenly with rest of salt and turmeric. Let sit on the counter (or in the sun, if possible) for 2–3 days. In a pot on low heat, bring remaining ingredients to a simmer for 30 minutes until syrup thickens. Add lime slices, simmer for another 10 minutes, and remove from heat. Cool and store in a jar with a lid (see note). Let this sit on the counter for 2 weeks before using and shake from time to time. This will keep in the refrigerator for 2–3 months.

Makes 2 1/2–3 cups.

slightly

Carrot Pickles

This is a "must have" in your refrigerator and a great way to add the raw ingred-ients essential to a balanced Ayurvedic meal. Patrick, a friend of mine from Vancouver, opened a restaurant in Montreal called the Titanic. After eating these carrot pickles on several occasions at our family dinners, he added them to his restaurant menu where they have become a staple.

If you do not have both lemon juice or vinegar on hand, you can use 2½ tbsp of either ingredient.

3 carrots, sliced into 2½-in (6-cm) long thin sticks (1 carrot is about ¾ cup)
½ tsp lemon juice (see note)
2 tbsp apple cider vinegar (see note)
1 tsp salt
½ tsp chili powder, or to taste

1 tsp yellow mustard seeds, crushed (available in Indian grocery stores)
2 slices fresh ginger (optional)
2 fresh green chilies, slit at end (optional)
¼ tsp turmeric (optional)

Combine all ingredients in a jar with a lid and shake well. Refrigerate for at least 2 hours before serving. Shake the jar from time to time. This will keep in the refrigerator for at least 1 week.

Makes 2–2½ cups.

Green Mangoes with Salt & Cayenne

Green mangoes add the sour taste that in small amounts aids digestion.

Green mangoes are the unripe fruit, and are often featured in Indian dishes as well as Thai and Malaysian.

2 raw green mangoes, diced (see notes)

1 tsp salt, or to taste
½ tsp cayenne pepper, or to taste

In a bowl, combine all ingredients and serve.

Makes 1½–2 cups.

To cut a mango, slice on either side of the seed or "the bone" to create two slices. Then cut the remaining mango from around the seed. Discard the seed and dice each slice and the remaining flesh.

Raitas

Raitas are yogurt-based condiments that aid digestion. They are eaten in small quantities (about 1–2 tablespoons) as an accompaniment to a meal. The spices increase the digestibility of the yogurt and the vegetables add texture, flavor, color, and nutrients. Homemade yogurt does not increase Pitta as store-bought yogurt does. A little yogurt is beneficial for all constitutions.

Homemade Yogurt

In Swahili, yogurt is called *maziwa lala*, which literally means milk that sleeps. If you make this in the early evening, it will be ready for your breakfast when you wake up the next morning. Once you make this you will wonder why you ever used store-bought, as it is so delicious and easy to make. Freshly-made yogurt is full of beneficial bacteria that aids the digestion and kills some harmful bacteria. It also contains protein, B vitamin complex, calcium, potassium, phosphorus, and folic acid. People who have difficulty digesting milk often find fresh yogurt much easier to digest.

People who have to take antibiotics often eat yogurt to replace the healthy bacteria that the antibiotics destroy.

Here is an Indian remedy for an upset stomach: ¼ cup fresh yogurt and ¼ tsp whole cumin seeds, crushed.

4 cups organic whole milk

2 heaping tbsp organic yogurt (at room temperature)

In a pot on medium, heat milk until it foams up. Turn off heat and allow it to cool. Test with your finger; when it feels lukewarm (or about 100°F or 38°C), then pour milk into a very clean or sterilized bowl. Whisk in the yogurt. Cover bowl and let sit in a warm place where there is no draft (such as in the oven with the oven light on or on top of a toaster oven set at the lowest temperature) for 8–12 hours before using.

Makes 4 cups.

Save some of this yogurt to use for making the next batch.

- + + # Cumin Raita

Cumin adds flavor to this raita and aids digestion. The cayenne gives it wonderful color and a little punch. This is a simple, elegant way to complete your meal.

1 cup plain yogurt
¼ tsp whole cumin seeds, crushed
  (see note)
¼ tsp salt (optional)

Pinch of cayenne pepper (for garnish)
1 sprig fresh mint or cilantro leaves
  (for garnish)

In a bowl, combine yogurt, cumin, and salt. Sprinkle with cayenne and garnish with cilantro.

Makes 1 cup.

To crush cumin seeds, place in a brown paper bag and roll with a rolling pin; or use a coffee grinder, ensuring it remains coarse, not powdered. (Use a different coffee grinder from the one you use for coffee beans.)

- + + # Cucumber Raita
slightly

A wonderful, cooling accompaniment to any curries or dals. This raita offers both the sour and bitter tastes in Ayurveda.

¼ tsp salt (for cucumbers)
½ cucumber, grated
1½ cups plain yogurt
¼ tsp salt (for mixture) (optional)

Pinch of cayenne pepper (for garnish)
1 sprig fresh cilantro leaves
  (for garnish)

In a bowl, lightly salt grated cucumber and leave it to drain in a sieve for ½ hour. Squeeze out excess water. In a bowl, combine yogurt, cucumbers, and salt and mix well. Sprinkle with cayenne and garnish with cilantro.

Makes 1¾ cups.

- + + # Tomato Raisin Raita

I love the sweet and sour flavor of this raita.

To decrease Pitta: add an additional ¼ cup fresh cilantro leaves, chopped.

¼ cup raisins
2 cups plain yogurt
½ cup tomatoes, diced

½ tsp ground cumin (for garnish)
1 sprig fresh cilantro leaves
  (for garnish) (see note)

In a small bowl of water, soak raisins for 5 minutes. In a serving bowl, combine yogurt and tomatoes and mix well. Drain raisins and stir into yogurt mixture. Sprinkle with cumin, garnish with cilantro, and serve.

Makes 2¾ cups.

- + + # Spinach Raita

slightly

3 cups spinach, chopped
2 cups plain yogurt
½ tsp salt

½ tsp whole cumin seeds,
  toasted and ground
Cayenne pepper to taste

Bring a pot of water to a boil. Add spinach and blanch for 1 minute. Drain, squeeze out excess water, and set aside. In a bowl, combine all ingredients including spinach and mix well.

Makes 2¾ cups.

Coconut & Banana Raita

The mustard seeds mixed with the bananas and coconut add texture and flavor to this raita.

1 ¼ cups plain yogurt
1 cup bananas, sliced
1 tsp salt
1 tbsp olive oil
1 tsp black mustard seeds

2 ½ tbsp coconut, grated
1 ½ tbsp plain yogurt
1 tsp fresh cilantro leaves, chopped
   (for garnish)

In a bowl, combine 1 ¼ cups yogurt, bananas, and salt. Mix well and set aside. In a small frying pan on medium-high, heat oil. Add mustard seeds, cover with lid, and let pop for 30 seconds. Immediately add coconut. Stir for a few seconds, then add 1 ½ tbsp yogurt and continue stirring for a few more seconds until well mixed. Add mixture to bowl of yogurt and bananas. Mix well. Garnish with cilantro, cover, and refrigerate for 1 hour before serving.

Makes about 3 cups.

Beverages

According to Ayurveda, cold beverages suppress digestive juices and therefore are generally not recommended; instead, sip on room temperature water or warm tea with or without lemon. Also try to consume most of your liquids between meals for optimum hydration and cleansing. The milk beverages, lassis, and non-alcoholic cocktails in this chapter can be enjoyed at room temperature or slightly cooler.

Beverages and teas can be snacks in themselves, select ones to calm your dosha, which changes with the season or time of day (see page 292). Try some of these tasty, nourishing drinks instead of caffeinated tea or coffee and notice how your sense of well-being improves.

-
-
+ # Almond Milk

Soaking almonds activates their seed enzymes and thus increases their nutritional value dramatically. A small glass of almond milk is a wonderful way to get your protein and omega-3 oils, which enhance clear thinking and lubricate the skin from the inside out. If you need to reduce Kapha, drink a smaller amount and omit the maple syrup, or use a little honey instead.

1 cup almonds
2 cups purified water (for soaking)
3 cups purified water (for blending)

Maple syrup to taste (or honey)
    (optional)

In a bowl, soak almonds with 2 cups purified water overnight.

The next morning, drain almonds and remove skins by pouring boiling water over them. Allow them to cool slightly, then pop off skin by squeezing each almond gently between your fingers.

In a blender or food processor, blend almonds until very smooth. Add 3 cups purified water and continue blending for 3 minutes. Pour almond mixture through cheesecloth into a pitcher to drain off liquid; squeeze to extract any remaining liquid. Add maple syrup to liquid and mix. Save leftover almond mixture to add to other recipes calling for nuts and seeds, or sprinkle over your breakfast cereal.

Makes 3 cups.

-
-
+ # Spicy Almond Milk

I love the flavor and texture of the ground poppy seeds. It'll do wonders for your complexion!

Poppy seeds have been grown for thousands of years. In Ayurveda, they are prized for calming the mind.

Anise (aniseed) is known in Ayurveda for reducing acidity and aiding digestion.

2 tbsp fresh ginger, roughly chopped (see note)
4 tsp poppy seeds (see note)
1 tsp ground anise (see note)
1 tsp freshly ground black pepper

4 tbsp maple syrup (or honey), or to taste
½ cup water
2 cups Almond Milk (page 272)
2 cups water

In a blender or food processor, purée ginger into a paste. Add poppy seeds, anise, pepper, and maple syrup and blend. Add ½ cup water and blend. Add almond milk and 2 cups water and continue blending until well mixed. Pour into a pitcher and serve.

Makes 4 servings.

Ginger is known in Ayurveda for reducing acidity and aiding digestion. Chewing on a piece of fresh ginger also helps ease motion sickness.

Cinnamon & Sweet Warm Almond Milk

This is a lovely warm protein drink for winter. I ladle this into mugs straight out of the saucepan; however, you may want to pour it into a teapot to serve. The cinnamon stick will continue adding flavor.

3½ cups Almond Milk (page 272)   1 tbsp honey
1 cinnamon stick

In a large saucepan on medium heat, combine almond milk and cinnamon stick and gently heat. As soon as mixture is warmed through, remove from heat. Add honey and serve.

Makes 3 servings.

The Cold Feet Cure: Almond Milk with Crushed Pistachios & Rose Water

This is a traditional wedding drink. Full of flavor, it will calm the guests' excitement as well as the bride and groom's pre-wedding jitters!

4 cups Almond Milk (page 272)   Sweetener to taste
2 tbsp unsalted pistachios, crushed   A few drops of rose water
¼ tsp ground cardamom   A few strands of saffron (optional)
⅛ tsp nutmeg

In a pitcher, combine all ingredients, mix well, and serve.

Makes 4 servings.

slightly +

slightly + # Nice & Nutty Brown Rice Milk

 This non-dairy milk is full of fiber and nutrients. Once you discover how easy this is, you may never buy it ready-made again.

½ cup short-grain organic brown rice, uncooked

8 cups water
½ tsp salt

In a large pot on high heat, combine rice, water, and salt and bring to a boil. Reduce heat to a simmer, cover with lid, and cook for 1½ hours. Remove from heat, then in a blender or food processor, purée until smooth and serve. This will keep in the refrigerator for 7 days.

Makes about 6 cups.

Variation 1: Add melted, 70% cocoa mass dark chocolate.

Variation 2: Add ground cinnamon to taste and sweeten with maple syrup.

Variation 3: Add 1–2 tbsp of flax seeds to increase omega-3 oils and the nutritional value.

- - -

The Salty Lassi

Lassi is a natural yogurt drink that is sometimes served with ice and fresh mint leaves in summer. The cumin aids the digestion and adds a delicate note. The Salty Lassi is a staple in Indian cuisine.

1 cup plain yogurt
1 tsp whole cumin seeds, crushed

1 tsp salt
3 cups water

In a pitcher, combine all ingredients and whisk until smooth.

Makes 4 servings.

 - - -

The Bonny Sweet Lassi

A sweet lassi with a hint of ginger.

1 cup plain yogurt
2 tbsp sweetener
½ tsp ground cardamom

3 cups water
½ tsp fresh ginger, grated (optional)

In a pitcher, combine all ingredients and whisk until smooth.

Makes 4 servings.

ø +

Pineapple & Coconut Cocktail

Feast your eyes and taste buds on this tropical treat.

3 cups pineapple juice
1 cup coconut milk
2 tsp maple syrup (optional)

½ tsp lime juice
4 strawberries (for garnish)
4 fresh mint leaves (for garnish)

In a pitcher, combine all ingredients except garnishes and mix well. Pour evenly into 4 glasses. Slit ends of strawberries to place on the lip of each glass and add a mint leaf on top of each cocktail, then serve.

Makes 4 servings.

 - -

Ginger Mint Cocktail

This refreshing drink aids digestion.

4 tsp fresh ginger, roughly chopped
¼ cup fresh mint leaves, roughly
   chopped
¼ cup lime juice

4 tsp maple syrup (or honey)
1 cups water
4 fresh mint leaves (for garnish)

In a blender or food processor, purée ginger into a paste. Add mint leaves and purée into a paste. Add all remaining ingredients and blend. Strain through cheesecloth, pour into glasses, and garnish with mint leaves.

Makes 4 servings.

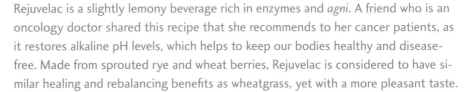

Rejuvelac

Rejuvelac is a slightly lemony beverage rich in enzymes and *agni*. A friend who is an oncology doctor shared this recipe that she recommends to her cancer patients, as it restores alkaline pH levels, which helps to keep our bodies healthy and disease-free. Made from sprouted rye and wheat berries, Rejuvelac is considered to have similar healing and rebalancing benefits as wheatgrass, yet with a more pleasant taste.

This recipe takes about 1 week to prepare, but will keep for up to 6 weeks when refrigerated in tightly sealed glass jars. In spite of the lengthy process, Rejuvelac is wonderful to make, especially with children, as each day you can watch the seeds grow, and "come to life".

Equipment:
6 1–2 qt (1–2 l) glass jars with wide mouths with tightly fitting lids.
Thick elastic bands (that will stretch around jar mouths)
18-in (½-m) mesh window screen (available in hardware stores), cut in squares wide enough to cover tops of jars and be secured with elastic bands
Dish rack

Ingredients (available at health food stores):
½ cup rye berries
½ cup hard wheat berries
1½ cup soft wheat berries
3 medium beets

Day 1 (morning):

In a large bowl, combine rye berries and hard and soft wheat berries and mix well. Add equal portions of berry mixture to each of the 6 jars (ensure the jars are only ⅓ full). Fill the rest of each jar with water and stir so berries are submerged. Attach mesh screens to the mouth of each jar with an elastic band. Let jars sit in indirect sunlight for 8–16 hours.

Day 1 (evening):

With screens still attached, drain off all the water from jars and rinse seeds with cold water by filling jars and pouring out through screens 3 times. Place jars on dish rack, leaning mouth-down at a 45-degree angle so mixture can aerate and water can drip out.

Day 2 (morning):

Repeat process from Day 1 (evening).

Day 2 (evening):

Repeat process.

Continued on next page

Days 3–5:

Repeat process in morning and evening until berries have sprouted, i.e. grow tails that are quite long (about ⅓–¾ in/1–2 cm) and tangled with each other.

Day 4 or 5 (morning):

Once tails are long and matted, remove sprouted berries from jars, place in a large bowl, and cover with water. With clean hands, gently disentangle sprouts and discard any seeds that have not sprouted. Rinse 3 times. Return equal portions of sprouts to each jar (ensure jars are only ⅓ full). Clean and peel beets. Cut beets into quarters and place 2 pieces in each jar (ensure pieces are large enough so they sink). Fill jars with lukewarm water, washing down the insides of each jar as you fill them. Secure mesh screens over jar mouths with elastic bands. Place jars in indirect sunlight. Let sprouts ferment for 48 hours.

Day 6 or 7

After 48 hours of fermenting, the sprouts should be ready as there will be a grayish foamy layer on the surface. (Scrape off the foam and rub into your skin. It will feel soft as a baby's!) The Rejuvelac is ready when it tastes somewhat lemony; if not, let it sit for another 12 hours. Drain through a cheesecloth into clean jars and serve. Cover remaining Rejuvelac with tightly fitting lids and refrigerate. Drink up to 1 glass of Rejuvelac a day.

Makes about 1 gallon (4 liters).

Rooibos Chai

Rooibos is a non-caffeinated tea from South Africa that can be served with or without milk and sweetener. It contains polyphenols, powerful antioxidants known to keep skin healthy. It also has a wonderful calming effect on the body and joints.

To dry the orange peel: chop the washed peel of an orange into small pieces. Dry by leaving out, covered, in the sun for a few days, or by baking at 200°F (95°C) for 15–20 minutes.

It is important to steep Rooibos tea for 3–8 minutes before drinking to get the full health benefits.

2–3 plain Rooibos tea bags
(or 2 heaping tsp loose tea leaves)
1 cinnamon stick (or 2–3 broken
pieces cinnamon bark)
2–3 cardamom pods, slit at end
2–4 whole peppercorns
1 tbsp dried orange peel, chopped into
small pieces (optional) (see note)

2–3 cloves
1–2 slices fresh ginger (optional)
1 cup milk (or water)
2 cups water

In a large pot on high heat, combine all ingredients. Bring to a boil, then reduce heat and simmer for 5 minutes. Pour into a teapot and set aside for 3–8 minutes (see note). Serve.

Makes 3 servings.

- -

Masala Chai Mix

Masala is a blend of flavorful spices added to chai, which is the Indian word for tea, and is derived from the Chinese character for tea, cha (tea originated in China). Masala chai is a staple in Indian households. Add this mix to a pot of tea ($\frac{1}{8}$–$\frac{1}{4}$ tsp per cup). Over time you may increase or decrease the various spices, depending on your taste.

1 tsp cloves
1 tsp freshly ground black pepper
1 tsp cardamom seeds
½ tsp nutmeg, grated

1 2-in (5-cm) piece cinnamon bark
  (or 1 tsp ground cinnamon)
1 tsp ground ginger

In a dry frying pan on medium heat, combine all ingredients and toast for 3–4 minutes, stirring constantly. Remove from heat. In a coffee grinder (one that you don't normally use for coffee), grind masala in batches, then mix together and store in an airtight container.

Makes about ¼ cup.

 - -

Milky Masala Chai

Here is a recipe for the milky version of masala chai, now popular worldwide.

Milk products in general increase Kapha and are good for balancing Vata. In India, they are consumed with ginger, pepper, and other pungent spices to make them easier to digest for the other doshas.

3 cups water
1 cup milk (or soy milk)
½–¾ tsp Masala Chai Mix
  (see above)

1–2 tsp loose leaf black tea
  (or 1–2 tea bags)
Sweetener to taste (optional)

In a large pot on high heat, combine all ingredients. Bring to a boil, stirring to ensure milk does not burn, then reduce heat immediately and simmer for 5 minutes. Strain, add sweetener if desired, and serve.

Makes 4 servings.

Tea Fit for a Yogi

My mother discovered the recipe for this calming yet energizing tea.

6 small pieces cinnamon bark
1 tsp whole fenugreek seeds
1 tsp cardamom pods
1 tsp cloves

1 tsp whole peppercorns
2 tsp fennel seeds
2 tsp fresh ginger, chopped

In a brown paper bag, crush all ingredients except for ginger by using a rolling pin or gently tapping with a hammer.

In a large bowl, combine all ingredients and mix together. Use 1–2 tsp per pot of hot water and steep to your taste. Store leftover tea mixture in an airtight container.

Makes 4–5 tablespoons.

Lemongrass, Mint & Ginger Tea

A refreshing tea that's great any time, but especially during summer. I make this tea for dinners and retreats, letting it simmer in a big pot on the stove before guests arrive. They are always thrilled to be greeted by its soothing scent.

1 bunch fresh mint leaves, chopped
2 sticks lemongrass (available in
  Thai or other ethnic grocers)
4 ginger tea bags (or 3 tbsp fresh
  ginger, chopped)

5 cloves
5 cardamom pods, slit at end
4–5 pieces broken cinnamon bark
8–10 cups water

In a large pot on high heat, combine all ingredients. Bring to a boil, then reduce heat and simmer for 5–10 minutes, depending on desired strength. Strain before serving.

Makes 8–10 servings.

- + -

Daikon Tea

 (vegan)

Flush fats out of your body with this tea.

¼ daikon, roughly chopped   4 cups hot water

In a large pot on high heat, combine all ingredients. Bring to a boil, then reduce heat and simmer for 15–20 minutes. Remove from heat, strain, and serve.

Makes 3–4 cups.

+ - -

Dandelion Tea

(vegan)

This tea is a liver cleanser and its main ingredient can be picked from your lawn. Next time you see dandelions, don't ignore them!

2 cups dandelions (flower, leaves,   4–6 cups water
    and stems)

In a large pot on high heat, combine all ingredients. Bring to a boil, then reduce heat and simmer for 30 minutes. Remove from heat, strain, and serve.

Makes 3–5 cups.

- -

slightly

Parsley Tea

This tea is high in iron, vitamins A and C, potassium, and calcium. It cleanses and strengthens the body at the same time.

1 bunch fresh parsley, include stems   Juice of 1 lemon
3 cups water

In a large pot on high heat, combine parsley and water. Bring to a boil, then reduce heat and simmer for 30 minutes. Strain, add lemon juice, and serve.

Makes 3 servings.

 - -

Turmeric Tea

Turmeric cleanses the blood, is wonderful for the complexion, and is a natural anti-inflammatory remedy.

1 tsp turmeric   2 tsp honey (optional)
4 cups boiling water

In a large pot, combine turmeric and water and stir. Add honey (if using) and serve.

Makes 4 servings.

- -

Calming Ginger Tea

My creative writing teacher Melba used to have this tea ready whenever we arrived. Warming, good for calming the nerves, and delicious – just what we needed before churning our creative wheels!

4 tsp fresh ginger, chopped
4–6 cups water

Maple syrup to taste (or honey)
 (optional)

In a large pot on high heat, combine ginger and water. Bring to a boil, then reduce heat and simmer for at least 5 minutes. Add maple syrup and serve.

Makes 4 servings.

 + -

Shelley's Garlic Ginger Tea

My friend Shelley swears by this tea whenever she catches a cold or cough that she can't seem to shake.

4 cloves garlic
Pinch of cayenne pepper
4 tsp fresh ginger, chopped
4–6 cups water

Maple syrup to taste (or honey)
 (optional)
Squeeze of lemon (to taste)

In a large pot on high heat, combine garlic, cayenne, ginger, and water. Bring to a boil, then reduce heat and simmer for 30 minutes. Strain, serve with maple syrup (if using) and a squeeze of lemon.

Makes 4 servings.

slightly

How to Start Your Day
Lemon Drink

I thank my lucky stars I met Joan, who became my private trainer when I got off the roller coaster of workaholism. In only three months, she trained me to run 10K (6.2 miles) in one hour. Joan drinks this fat-breaking and cleansing lemon tea first thing every morning.

Juice of ½ lemon
1 cup boiling water
Pinch of cayenne pepper (optional)

Maple syrup to taste (or honey)
  (optional)

In a mug, combine all ingredients and stir.

Makes 1 serving.

slightly

vegan

Autumn Tea

This is a warming tea that's good for the throat and for when you have a cold.

I recommend using the Japanese brown rice teas, Genmai Cha or Yama Moto Yama.

2 brown rice tea bags (see note)
2–3 cardamom pods, slit at end
2–3 cloves

2 cinnamon sticks
½ tsp turmeric
8–10 cups water

In a large pot on high heat, combine all ingredients. Bring to a boil, then reduce heat and simmer for 5–10 minutes, depending on desired strength. Strain before serving.

Makes 8–10 servings.

Winter Tea

This tea warms the body when the cold weather sets in.

More water can be added to use the same simmering ingredients for a second batch of tea.

2 tea bags ginger tea (or 1 tbsp fresh ginger, chopped)
2 sticks lemongrass (available in Thai or other ethnic grocers)
2–3 cardamom pods, slit at end

2–3 cloves
2 cinnamon sticks (or 4–5 pieces cinnamon bark)
½ tsp turmeric
8–10 cups water

In a large pot on high heat, combine all ingredients. Bring to a boil, then reduce heat and simmer for 5–10 minutes, depending on desired strength. Strain and serve

Makes 8–10 servings.

Cooling Summer Tea

I make this for my summer yoga retreats; everyone loves its soothing and refreshing flavor.

You may add more water to pot as ingredients get more potent and use same ingredients for a second round (which your dosha-calmed guests are sure to want!).

3 tbsp fresh ginger, chopped
2 cinnamon sticks
3 cardamom pods, slit at end

½ bunch fresh mint leaves
6 cups water
Honey to taste (optional)

In a large pot on high heat, combine all ingredients. Bring to a boil, then reduce heat and simmer for 5–10 minutes. Strain then serve in mugs.

Makes 6 servings.

- - -

Papa's Non-Alcoholic Mulled Wine

My father made this one day while entertaining at our family home in Kenya. The sun had just gone down and a nice cool breeze was blowing. This drink was a perfect way to greet our guests.

4 cups unsweetened grape juice
2 cups unsweetened apple juice
2 cups unsweetened pineapple juice
1 cup unsweetened cranberry juice

4 tbsp maple syrup (or honey) (optional)
1 4-in (10-cm) cinnamon stick
¼ tbsp cloves

In a large pot on medium-low heat, combine all ingredients and slowly bring to a boil. Once boiling, remove from heat immediately, strain, and serve in mugs.

Makes 8 servings.

ø   - -

Hot Apple Cider

5 cups apple juice
2 pieces broken cinnamon bark

2 cloves

In a large pot on high heat, combine all ingredients. Bring to a boil, then reduce heat and simmer for 10–15 minutes. Strain before serving.

Makes 4 servings.

-
+ # Spicy, Hot &
+ # Extra Dark Chocolate

Joanne from Cocoa West Chocolatier on Bowen Island shared one of my absolute favorite chocolate drinks with me. Savor each sip. Thanks, Joanne!

⅔ cup 2% milk (or soy milk or water)
Pinch of cayenne pepper
Pinch of ground nutmeg

2–3 tbsp bittersweet chocolate, 70% cocoa mass (use a little less if making with soy milk so it isn't too thick)

In a medium saucepan on medium-high heat, combine milk, cayenne, and nutmeg. Watching carefully, bring milk almost to boil, then remove from heat immediately. Add chocolate and stir briskly until chocolate melts. Whisk to create froth on top and serve in warmed cups. May be sweetened slightly to taste.

Makes 1 serving.

Appendix

Seasons of the Year

Just as food affects each dosha, so does each season. For example, winter and early spring have Kapha qualities that are cool, moist, and dormant, so every body type should compensate with more warming Pitta-increasing foods. The Pitta season, late spring and summer, gives Pittas a "double dose" of fire. All body types should follow more cooling recipes and practices during this time, especially Pittas. The Vata season, fall and early winter, tends to be full of movement — leaves are falling and people are going back to their routines. During this time, all doshas should be mindful of being grounded and follow a diet that will decrease Vata.

See guidelines below for more information on balancing your primary doshas. Also see information on yoga (pages 302), and other alternative Ayurvedic therapies (pages 313).

The Kapha season is winter and early spring. Balance by including extra outdoor activities in your regular exercise routine and increasing the amount of hot spices in your meals. Eat warm, light foods such as vegetable soups, as well as foods that are more pungent, bitter, and astringent. You should also decorate your surroundings with warm, vibrant colors.

The Pitta season is late spring and summer, when the heat is on. Balance by eating lighter, cooling, less spicy foods, as well as more fruits and salads. Decorate your surroundings with cool, soothing colors. Also try to rest and relax as much as possible near water or in the shade when it is hot.

The Vata season is fall and early winter. This is a time to eat warmer, grounding foods, like cooked root vegetables and comfort foods like Happy Cow Shepherd's Pie (page 164) and Beat the Cold Soup (page 117). Rest and restrict yourself to relaxing activities when possible; sit by a warm fire, or take a walk in the forest. Decorate your surroundings with earth tones to ground your energy.

Menu Plans

When planning your own Ayurvedic menus, it is important to include the Six Tastes of Ayurveda – sweet, salty, sour, pungent, bitter, and astringent – to calm the doshas and thus restore the body's natural balance (pages 20). You can adjust any recipe or meal plan to suit your individual constitution by choosing foods that will balance out your particular dosha and omitting those that will aggravate your it; simply follow the dosha symbols accompanying each recipe and read the tips that show you how to modify it. When cooking for guests, you can serve tridoshic dishes (appropriate for all three doshas), or a variety of dishes that will balance each dosha. You also can offer each of the six tastes as condiments or side dishes so guests can adjust meals themselves to suit their constitution. In addition, whether you are dining alone or with others, your surroundings greatly influence the Ayurvedic benefits of your food and your ability to properly digest your meal, so pay attention to ambiance: avoid eating while watching television, keep conversation light and amicable, and select background music that will enhance, not stifle, the sensual enjoyment of your meal.

The particular season and time of day are important factors when planning a menu. Once you are aware of the general principles of the seasonal and daily cycles, you can fine-tune your food preparation according to the time of year and day – e.g., serve Pitta-reducing dishes at midday and in the heat of summer, which are common Pitta-aggravating times. (See opposite page for more seasonal tips.)

Here is a summary of the seasons and times of day (year-round) that can aggravate (+) each dosha, and therefore require dishes that reduce or calm (−) that dosha:

Vata: Fall and early winter; 2 am–6 am and 2 pm–6 pm

Pitta: Summer and late spring; 10 am–2 pm and 10 pm–2 am

Kapha: Winter and early spring; 6 am–10 am and 6 pm–midnight

Sonf are fennel seeds, which act as a digestive aid and a mouth freshener. At the end of a meal, place about ¼ cup sonf in a small bowl on the table. Guests can take about ¼ tsp and gently chew them, swallowing once they liquefy.

Papadums are circular, thin, crispy wafers that come in a variety of flavors and are served with appetizers and/or entrées. Papadums can be purchased at any Indian grocery store. To toast, place one papdum on a cooling rack (with legs) directly over the stove element on medium-high, flipping it until each side is evenly toasted.

The menu plans that follow suit all doshas, and therefore all six tastes. They should be used as a general guideline so that once you become familiar with the principles of Ayurveda, you will be able to modify and create menu plans that work for you.

In general, an Indian-style party meal should include: an appetizer and some chutneys, restorative drinks appropriate to the season, a few vegetable dishes, a protein dish (e.g., lentil or bean dish), some pickles, a raita, salad, and dessert. For your own everyday meal, simply eliminate the appetizer and dessert. Of course, you can really simplify things by choosing a one-pot dish – for example, a Bean Pilau (page 174), Coconut Vegetable Tofu Medley (page 159), or Happy Cow Shepherd's Pie (page 164); add a salad or a grain dish for a complete and balanced meal.

Summer Dinner Party

As a fundraiser for the Pamoja Foundation, I prepared this menu for an Ayurvedic cooking class and dinner at Vancouver's well-known Barbara-Jo's Books to Cooks. This menu is also great to prepare with friends.

Appetizers:
Vegetable Samosas (page 62)
Lemon wedges (to squeeze into
  samosas)
Cilantro Mint Chutney (page 259)
Papadums (see note)

Drinks:
Cooling Summer Tea (page 288)
Water with lime slices
Ginger Mint Cocktail (page 277)

Entrée:
Palak Paneer (page 180)
Simple Brown Masoor Dal (page 155)
Fit for a King Eggplant Bharta
  (page 189)

Aromatic Basmati Rice (page 168)
Chapatis (choose from pages 218–
  222)
Fresh Daikon and Endive Salad
  (page 88), or the Bittersweet Salad
  (page 90), or your choice of bittersweet, raw vegetables

Condiments:
Ripe Mango Chutney (page 262)
Tomato Raisin Raita (page 268)

Dessert:
China Grass Pudding with Nuts
  (page 247)
Sonf (see note)

Lazy Winter Evening

I cooked this menu for *City Cooks*, a TV cooking show, to demonstrate how one can prepare a delicious Ayurvedic meal in under an hour. After filming, the staff came on set and devoured all the food; they were so impressed, they ordered Indian spice boxes from me so they could try making these dishes at home!

Appetizers:
Baked Pakoras (page 61)
Coconut Mint Chutney (page 262)

Drink:
Winter Tea (page 288)

Entrée:
Whole Wheat Chapatis (page 218) (or
  purchase freshly made)
Vegetable Rice Pilau (page 172)
French Bean & Tomato Cumin Sauté
  (page 195)

Quick & Easy Red Masoor Dal
  (page 156)
The Dainty Cachumber (page 89)

Condiments:
Daikon sticks or carrot sticks
Cumin Raita (page 267)

Dessert:
Sweet Shikand (page 242)

Warming Autumn

Try this menu to strengthen the body and satisfy the taste buds when the cool weather sets in. Make the tamarind chutney in advance to quicken the cooking time.

Appetizer:
Spiced Pumpkin Soup (page 115)

Drink:
Autumn Tea (page 287)

Entrée:
Strengthening Tur Dal (page 152)
Broccoli, Cauliflower & Potato Baji
  (page 193)
Grandma's Turnip Curry (page 203)

Chapatis (choose from page 218–222)
Tomato, Feta & Mint Salad (page 87)

Condiments:
Tamarind Chutney (page 261)
Coconut & Banana Raita (page 269)

Dessert:
Sonita's Norwegian Rice Rudding with
  an Indian Twist (page 238)

African-Indian Fusion

This menu, appropriate for lunch or dinner, includes some of my favorite African and Indian flavors, reminding me of the wonderful meals I enjoyed in Kenya.

Appetizer:
Khandvi Rolls (page 67)

Drinks:
Spicy Almond Milk (page 273)
Papa's Non-Alcoholic Mulled Wine
   (page 289)

Entrée:
Ugali (page 223)
African Spinach (page 181)
Small Red Bean Curry (page 146)

Delectable Curried Cauliflower with
   Ginger & Tomatoes (page 194)
The Great White Salad (page 89)

Condiments:
Green Mangoes with Salt & Cayenne
   (page 264)

Dessert:
Caroline's White Chocolate Cardamom
   Mousse (page 250)

Easy Lunch

I have this menu down to an art: chop the veggies for the dal, keeping some aside to artfully arrange for the raw salad platter. Cook the rice, lentils, and veggies at the same time, place the yogurt in a small bowl on the side, and in twenty minutes, your lunch is ready!

Drink:
Water with lime slices

Entrée:
Simple Brown Masoor Dal (veggie
   variation) (page 155)
Cumin Rice (page 167)
Raw salad with fresh veggies of your
   choice

Condiment:
Plain yogurt, garnished with a pinch
   of cayenne pepper and some fresh
   parsley or mint leaves

Dessert:
Blackberry-Apple Oat Bars (pre-made)
   (page 254), or Creamy Banana-Berry
   Ice (pre-made) (page 255), or fresh
   fruit according to your dosha.

Summer Picnic

I prepare this light menu at my summer yoga retreats and serve it buffet-style outdoors; it's always well-received.

Drinks:
Tea Fit for a Yogi (page 283)
Water with lemon slices

Appetizers:
Endvo Savory Squares with Tomato
   Chutney (page 68 and 258)
Soothing Guacamole (page 54) with
   sliced veggie sticks of your choice
Indian-Style Hummus (page 57)
   with chapatis (choose from pages
   218–222)

Salads:
Sprouted Mixed Bean Salad (page 101)
The Perfect Pomegranate & Spinach
   Salad (page 91)
Tabouleh Twist with Olives & Walnuts
   (page 95)
The Bittersweet Salad (page 90)
Rainbow Wild Rice Salad (page 98)

Desserts:
Light Carrot Halva (page 241)
Banana Walnut Loaf (page 232)

Mais Oui Brunch

Appropriately, I serve this brunch to my French conversation group that meets on the first Sunday each month.

Appetizer:
Fresh fruit salad of your choice

Carrie's Spelt Oatmeal Bread (page
   230 or 231)

Drinks:
Milky Masala Chai (page 282)
Almond Milk (page 272)

Condiments:
Carrot Pickles (page 264)
Lime Pickles (page 263)

Entrée:
Indian Omelet (page 50)
Tofu Scramble (page 40)

Dessert:
Banana, Oat & Berry Muffins
   (page 233)

Breakfasts

Here are three breakfasts to nourish and satisfy you whether you are running late or have all the time in the world.

Chai (choose from pages 281–282)
Almond milk (choose from pages 272–274)
Porridge with Stewed Berries (page 37)
or
Adrian or Nevenka's breakfast shake (page 31)
or
Nice & Nutty Brown Rice Milk (page 275)
or Lemongrass, Mint & Ginger Tea (page 283)
Tofu Veggie Breakfast Wrap (page 41)

Cleanses

Why should I do a cleanse?

There are many types of cleanses that restore the body by eliminating toxins, thereby improving our ability to absorb nutrients. After cleansing, people usually find that their digestion improves, resulting in clear skin, more energy, and a healthier weight. Additionally, cleanses can balance moods and improve mental clarity, making you feel clear-headed and present. It is advisable to do a cleanse one to four times a year. Always consult a health professional or doctor before commencing any cleanse.

General tips:

Be creative when preparing a cleansing menu. Experiment with various tea recipes. Discover the variety of fruits and vegetables available in your local markets. Make your salads colorful and adventurous; for example, add beets, carrots, avocados, nuts, watercress, dandelion greens, sprouts, radicchio, onions, and/or nuts. Prepare tasty, invigorating dressings using lemon juice and cold-pressed oils (e.g., olive, flax seed, hemp, or sesame oils). Add garlic, ginger, salt, and herbs, and raisins, dried cranberries, and pomegranate, which impart great contrasting flavors. Always try to incorporate the Six Essential Tastes of Ayurveda: salty, sweet, sour, astringent, pungent, and bitter (see page 22). Lastly, have fun with the choices you make!

Twelve-Day Cleanse

Start the Twelve-Day Cleanse on a Monday so that Days 6 and 7 (when only liquids are consumed) fall on a Saturday and Sunday (assuming these are your days of rest). Alternatively, if you find you get hungrier on weekends and/or eat less while you are working, ensure that Days 6 and 7 fall on light workdays.

Start each day with a cup of hot lemon tea (juice of ½ a lemon in hot water; you may add a little fresh ginger and/or a pinch of cayenne). Try not to eat before

10 am. Avoid caffeine and alcohol and other stimulants during this purifying time – instead of coffee, drink herbal tea or purified water. If you find you are having major hunger pangs, drink a glass of water mixed with hemp protein powder.

Day 1:   Eliminate eggs, seafood, chicken, and meat from diet.

Day 2:   Eliminate dairy products.

Day 3:   Eliminate grains, starches, and sugar.

Day 4:   Eat only raw fruits, raw vegetables, and raw nuts.

Day 5:   Same as Day 4.

Day 6:   Liquids only (see note on next page). Every two hours, drink 6–8 oz (180–240 ml) of warm water with lemon; you may add ginger, cayenne pepper, and turmeric. You may also drink lots of distilled or purified water, Parsley Tea (page 285) or sage tea throughout the day. If your energy feels low, rest – let your body do its work and eliminate its toxins.

Day 7:   Same as Day 6.

Day 8:   Eat as much fresh fruit as you like, and drink as much water and herbal tea as you need.

Day 9:   Eat raw fruits and raw vegetables; drizzle veggies with oil and lemon juice. Drink veggie juices, water, and herbal tea.

Day 10:   Reincorporate grains, starches, and cooked vegetables.

Day 11:   Reincorporate dairy (if not vegan).

Day 12:   Same as Day 11.

Day 13:   Reincorporate eggs, seafood, chicken, and meat (if not vegetarian).

Winter Cleanse

If the liquid-only days are too challenging, you may substitute Days 6 and 7 with Day 4.

This is a variation of the Twelve-Day Cleanse, but with more warming foods for cooler winter days. Follow the same guidelines as in the introduction to the Twelve-Day Cleanse (page 299), including starting each day with hot lemon tea.

Day 1:   Eliminate eggs, seafood, chicken, and meat from diet.

Day 2:   Eliminate dairy products.

Day 3:   Eliminate starches and sugar, except for Organic Brown Rice Kitchari (page 171).

Day 4:   Eliminate grains. Eat cooked soups and vegetable stews.

Day 5:   Same as Day 4.

Day 6:   Clear liquids only: e.g., Clear Vegetable Soup (page 112), Vata-calming teas (see tea section, pages 283–288), and Parsley Tea (page 285) (see note).

Day 7:   Same as Day 6.

Day 8:   Reincorporate cooked vegetables such as in soups and stews.

Day 9:   Same as Day 8.

Day 10:   Reincorporate grains such as Organic Brown Rice Kitchari (page 171) and starches.

Day 11:   Reincorporate dairy (if not vegan).

Day 12:   Reincorporate eggs, seafood, chicken, and meat (if not vegetarian).

Yoga Poses for the Doshas

Yoga is an integral part of Ayurveda and the holistic healing process. Yoga, which means union, helps to connect mind, body, and spirit. By practicing yoga regularly, you will notice an increase in flexibility, your movements will be more graceful, and you will feel more grounded and in the present moment. If you are a beginner, be gentle on yourself and only go slightly past the point where you feel your muscles stretching. Do not strain yourself; pay attention to your body and allow your flexibility to slowly improve over time. Avoid self-judgment and let your mind clear as the various postures replenish and relax you. It may also be helpful to try beginner yoga classes and/or watch instructional yoga DVDs, particularly to get a better understanding of body alignment principles and modifications for poses. For your own daily personal practice, start with 5–10 minute sessions; over time, you will notice an increase in your ability, endurance, and energy levels.

It is important to begin each yoga session by lying down or sitting comfortably and focusing on your breathing. As you become aware of your inhales and exhales, also become aware of your body, mind, and emotions. Replenish yourself with long inhales. When you exhale, try to release more oxygen than you think you have inhaled, and notice the length and depth of your inhales expand. Visualize what parts of your body your breath reaches, dissolving any areas that feel tight or obstructed.

Specific breathing exercises can benefit specific doshas. Breathing to and from the abdomen helps to ground Vata. Breathing in and out from the ribcage, will give you a sense of empowerment, and is especially beneficial for Pitta. "Complete breaths," as does The Fire Breath (see page 313), energize and enliven the entire body, especially for Kapha. For complete breaths, inhale to the lower abdomen and lower back first, then allow it to work its way up, filling the rib cage, then the mid- and upper-back, up to the collarbones and neck; your body should feel completely full of oxygen. Exhale slowly, allowing it to release from the upper body first, then the rib cage, followed by the mid- and lower back, and lastly the abdomen.

Breathing is a wonderful tool to bring us back into our bodies and nourish us at any time throughout the day. Take notice of how your breathing patterns may shift during the day and in what situations. According to Ayurvedic and yogic traditions, having control of (or being aware of) your breathing is the same thing as having control of your life. Use exhales to release old toxins, old beliefs, old attachments – anything that is not from the present moment – and use inhales to replenish every cell of your body with oxygen and light.

While practicing *asanas*, or yoga postures, continue to be aware of your body, and take note of where and how your breath travels through you. This will deepen your yoga practice and make it far more beneficial than if you only concentrate on alignment, strength, and flexibility.

Just as it is important to begin a yoga session with breath awareness, make sure you end each session in *savasana*, the "just be" pose, for 5–10 minutes. Savasana is an important cooling-down period when the body, mind, and spirit can integrate the benefits of the yoga session. (See page 310 for instructions.) You may also choose to do this in a Seated Meditation pose (page 312).

By following these suggestions, your body, mind, and spirit will, over time, radiate with light. Of course there will be ups and downs, but remember that the downs are crucial periods to continue practicing yoga as these are usually the times when we are transitioning from the past to a new period in life. It takes courage to practice yoga – by doing so, you are opening up your heart, body, and mind, becoming a fully functioning human being in the truest sense.

Sun Salutation

Yoga Poses

Sun Salutation is a beneficial way to begin the day for all doshas.

The Sun Salutation gives Kapha a wonderful kick start to the day as this is a dynamic set of poses. Take one inhale and exhale in each posture to get Kapha moving. Complete 6–10 repetitions of the series.

To reduce and calm excess Vata, take 3 long inhales and exhales in each pose while focusing on alignment, not perfection. Complete 4–6 repetitions of the series.

Sun Salutations are also a good way for Pitta to become calm and centered for the day. To reduce Pitta, take 1–2 inhales and exhales in each pose to expel excess fire and increase inner focus while building natural strength. Complete 6–10 repetitions of the series.

Standing Mountain   Forward Bend

Lunge

Plank

Chataranga

Standing Mountain: Stand tall, letting your shoulders drop and spine lift as you root downward, evenly distributing your weight through the legs and feet. Place your hands together in *namaste*, or prayer position, and notice how this helps to balance the right and left sides of your body and brain. On an inhale, raise the arms overhead. On an exhale, bend forward with a straight back into the Forward Bend.

Forward Bend: The secret to this pose is letting the weight of your head surrender to gravity. As you hang your head down, imagine the spaces between each vertebra increasing. On the exhale, imagine toxins, old beliefs, and old attachments flowing down the spine and releasing through the top of the head. Inhale up the spine and widen the sacrum. Step back with your right foot to transition to the Lunge.

Lunge: Feel your groin stretch, and lift your upper body out of the hip sockets. On the inhale, let your rib cage and heart expand in all directions. Step back with your left foot to transition to the Plank.

Plank: Ensure your hands are directly beneath the shoulders and use your arm strength. The insides of the elbows should face one another; avoid hyper-extending the elbows. Engage the abs and hips to protect the lower back (keep the hips from sagging) and inhale down to the heels. Transition down into Chataranga.

Chataranga: From Plank, keep the elbows next to the sides of the body and the abs strong; lower the knees, chest, and chin towards the floor. Build the strength in your arms and abs by keeping the chest and chin just above the floor before transitioning to Cobra.

Cobra

Downward Dog

Reverse Lunge

Supported Forward Bend

Cobra: From Chataranga, let the chest be pulled forward and off the floor. Untuck the toes while engaging the lower back muscles and abs to protect the back. Keeping the elbows at the sides of your body, press the shoulder blades down, and let the inhale and exhale travel from the chest all the way down the torso and back out again. Press the upper quads to the floor. Relax the neck and face as you lean back. Transition to Downward Dog by curling the toes under and pushing the sitting bones up and back.

Downward Dog: Press down through the palms of your hands, lengthening the arms and the spine as you point the sitting bones up and back. Stretch the calves and backs of the legs as the heels press toward the floor. Keep the abs engaged to support the back as it widens and lengthens in Downward Dog. Step forward with the right foot for Reverse Lunge.

Reverse Lunge: For this second lunge in the series, always ensure that the opposite leg from the first lunge is forward so you strengthen both sides of the body. Focus on lengthening through the back leg and stretching through the bent hip. Stay supported with the abs and breathe. Next, step forward with the back foot to Forward Bend (page 305), then transition to the Supported Forward Bend.

Supported Forward Bend: From Forward Bend, straighten back, and lift up through the abs, coming up halfway out of the fold. Let the fingers rest on the floor or shins. Stay strong through the quads, allowing the backs of the legs to stretch. Keep the collarbones long, the chest open, and the head in line with the spine. With a straight back, return to Standing Mountain (page 305) to complete the Sun Salutation.

Repeat the series according to your dosha (see page 304), ensuring that you alternate which foot steps back for the first Lunge.

Kapha Poses

Counteracting Kapha's slow-moving state requires stimulating, heat-building exercises that utilize Kapha's gift of stamina. Kaphas should take short rests between each asana, vary your yoga routine, and go slightly beyond your edge (limit). The poses performed by Jan Wallden (Kapha being her primary dosha) are especially good for a Kapha body type; however, all poses (including those for Vata and Pitta) in this section are beneficial for Kapha, especially if they are done in an invigorating way.

Forward Bend (page 305) is useful for reducing Kapha as it stimulates and tones the digestive system.

Cobra (page 306) stretches the abdomen and relieves constipation.

Downward Dog (page 306) warms the body while building strength and flexibility. Practice breathing awareness through the entire body while in Downward Dog, to energize Kapha. (Variation: Walk the Dog – bend alternate legs as you stretch the calves, or alternately raise each leg while maintaining support and alignment through the grounding arms and leg.)

Bridge

Bridge regulates the thyroid gland to balance metabolic rates, especially beneficial to Kapha. Lie on your back, bend the knees, and place the feet hip-width apart and parallel. Press the hips into the air and use the strength in the legs and buttocks to hold you up, pushing the hips higher while sending energy down to the feet. Press the shoulder blades toward each other and away from the neck and clasp the hands. To release the pose, slowly lower the spine.

Shoulder Stand

Shoulder Stand brings blood to the thyroid gland, helping to reduce Kapha by stimulating and balancing the metabolism. Note that this is an advanced pose. If you are a beginner, start with the spine lying flat on the floor and place your legs up a wall. Over time, work your way into full Shoulder Stand by lifting the hips from the floor and supporting your back by keeping the abs engaged and hands behind the lower back. Lift one leg at a time away from the wall. Keep elbows shoulder-width apart and ensure your head can easily move from side to side. (Note: avoid inverted poses – when head is below the heart – while menstruating.)

From Shoulder Stand, transition to Plough: keeping the back supported with engaged abs and hands at the lower back, bring the knees towards the ears and extend the legs out over your head, aiming the toes for the floor behind you. To come out of the pose, use the strength of the abs to gently uncurl, slowly lowering the spine, then the legs to the floor. Follow with Fish pose.

Fish

Fish increases circulation to the spine and brain and calms the mind, and is a good counter pose to Shoulder Stand. Lay flat on your back. Place the hands behind the back and then press them against the hips. Using your elbows for support, lift your upper body off the floor. Allow your neck and head to release back toward the floor. Let the chest, upper and mid-back widen as you inhale, allowing the shoulders to broaden. Follow with Bridge (page 307).

Sitting Twist

Advanced Fish: For a deeper backward bend, place the wrists under your sitting bones (beneficial for relieving carpal tunnel syndrome), lift your upper body off the floor, and tilt the head back until it touches the floor. Inhale into the chest.

Sitting Twist tones the abdominal muscles while stimulating metabolism and digestive fire, and helps to detoxify while increasing energy and flexibility. Sit tall and bend your left leg under the right knee. Stretch up the left arm and turn to the right, placing the left elbow outside of the right knee. Place the right hand on the floor at the tailbone. Press the sitting bones into the ground and gently twist to the right, gazing over your right shoulder. On each exhale, twist a little more. Repeat on the other side.

Pitta Poses

People who are born with predominantly Pitta characteristics generally have stamina, vitality, and muscular bodies, allowing them to engage in intense yoga sessions as long as they do cooling postures, like a Forward Bend (page 305) or Savasana (page 310), at the end.

To reduce Pitta, perform these poses in a calm, relaxed fashion while staying aware of the connections to mind, body, and spirit. The poses illustrated by James Nicholson (a predominantly Pitta body type) are good for reducing Pitta; however, all the poses are beneficial if they are done with a relaxed yet alert mind.

Side Triangle

Side Triangle is an excellent pose for lengthening and strengthening the sides of the body. Start standing with feet one leg-length apart, with weight evenly distributed on both feet. Stretch the arms out, parallel to the floor, on either side of you. Turn the left foot out, reach the left arm out to the left, and then stretch the left fingers down to the floor on the inside of the left foot. If your fingers cannot touch the floor, rest them on your shins. Ensure you do not feel compression on the left side of the body. Work towards looking up at your right thumb while maintaining strength and stretching through the legs and sides of the body. Focus on your breathing, imagine it opening the rib cage as you open the chest, twist the spine, and lengthen the arms and legs. Repeat on other side.

Dancer

Dancer requires balance and concentration. Standing on the left leg, take your right foot in your right hand and bend it back to the right buttock, allowing the right quadriceps to stretch. Once you have mastered standing on one leg, gradually extend your left arm above your head. To extend deeper in Dancer pose, press the right foot continually into the right hand, allowing the spine to curve, and reach forward through the left hand. Repeat on the other side.

Pigeon

Bow

Pigeon opens the front of the body and balances the digestive fire, especially useful for Pitta. Start on your hands and knees. Bend the right knee forward to place it under the chest, then extend the left leg back. With hands on either side of you for balance, lift the chest, allowing the weight of the body to stretch and open the hips. Repeat on other side.

Advanced Pigeon: Lean forward and rest your head on your fists or on the floor. Breathe deeply, allowing thoughts to slow down while the hips open. Repeat on other side, or walk hands back to starting Pigeon position with the chest lifted. Bend the left leg and reach the left hand back to hold the left foot. Gently pull the left foot toward the left sitting bone, stretching the quadriceps and groin while continually raising the upper body and opening the chest. Repeat on other side.

Bow massages the abdominal organs. Lie with your stomach down on a mat. Bend the knees, and take hold of the feet at the outsides. Pull the feet towards the sitting bones while pressing the feet back into the hands. Allow the shoulders to roll back and the head and chest to lift off the mat. Breathe as you relax the neck and face.

Reclining Bound-Angle lifts the diaphragm away from the stomach and liver, helping to relieve acid reflux and revitalize digestive organs. Ensure you are comfortable and able to fully relax in order to maximize the benefits of this pose. Lie back on a bolster (or a rolled-up blanket) placed along the spine from the neck to the waist or sacrum. Press the outsides of the soles of your feet together and allow the knees to open and fall to each side.

Savasana diffuses excess heat and relaxes the abdomen. Lie flat on your back (or on a bolster, see Reclining Bound-Angle above) with feet side by side and arms at your side with the palms of your hands facing up. Close your eyes and release your entire body, imagining it melting into the floor. Take long, calm breaths, drawing the inhales down to fill the belly, imagining the space your yoga practice has created in your body being filled with radiant light. Remain in savasana for 5–10 minutes.

Vata Poses

Slower meditative yoga that focuses on the breath is best for calming Vata. Standing poses which require concentration and focus quiet the typically active Vata mind. Hold each pose for 3–6 breaths, focusing on alignment and opening the body to breath. Concentrate on building stability and staying grounded. The Wind-Relieving (see below) poses and Forward Bend also help to balance Vata. The poses demonstrated by Sonoka Ehara (Vata being her primary dosha) are especially useful for a Vata body type, however, all yoga poses are beneficial when done slowly and steadily. Make sure to end your yoga session with a long savasana and meditation.

Wind-Releiving Pose

Wind-Relieving Pose: Lie on your back. With the left leg stretched out, pull the right knee in towards you, gently stretching the right quad and groin. Try to press your nose to the right knee to stretch the neck and use the abdominal muscles to support the back. Repeat with the other leg.

Cat: On your hands and knees, as you inhale, lift the head as you look up, and allow the spine to drop. As you exhale, drop the head, tuck the chin toward the chest, and arch the spine like an angry cat, pulling in the abdominal cavity. Repeat 4–6 times. Keep the movements connected to your inhales and exhales as you focus on opening the vertebrae of the spine, releasing Kundalini energy.

Side Twist

Side Twist is a balancing pose requiring concentration and focus, relieving the Vata wind and quieting the Vata's busy mind. While squatting with the knees together, twist your body to the right, drawing the left elbow over the right thigh. Press the palms of your hands together and look up towards your right elbow. Repeat on other side.

Forward Bend (page 305): Focus on lengthening the spine and bringing the head towards the knees, releasing old energy through the crown of the head.

Butterfly opens the first *chakra* (energy center in the body) at the tailbone, which reduces anxiety, an attribute of Vata. Sit with a tall spine, imagining a golden cord gently pulling the crown of your head upward. Hold the outsides of your feet and press the soles together. Press the knees towards the floor. Allow the inner thighs to stretch, and over time your hips and knees will release more and more.

Butterfly

Tridoshic Pose

This is a great pose for all doshas to practice at the end of a yoga session.

Seated Meditation: Yoga leads the way to meditation, as the poses open our bodies and quiet our minds, clearing way for connecting with our spirit – the ultimate goal of yoga. Sit with a tall spine and sacrum wide. Close your eyes. Imagine your body filling with light through the top of the head, down the spine, and through every cell. (I call this filling up at a free cosmic gas station!) Maintain pose for 2–5 minutes or longer.

Seated Meditation

Alternate Ayurvedic Therapies

This section includes Ayurvedic activities such as breathing techniques, aromatherapy and color therapy, a five-minute massage, and visualization that will help you to maintain a stress-free, healthy, and joyful lifestyle.

Pranayama: Breathing Techniques

Pra means "to live," or "to breathe"; *pranayama*, is the practice of yogic breathing. Pranayama techniques feed, stimulate, and regulate the vital life force in our bodies. As we say in yoga, when you have control over your breath, you have control over your life. *Pranayama* refers to the practice of breath awareness ("I am breathing in, I am breathing out"), which expands our capacity to breathe. It is also a method of clearing both the body and the mind in order to reveal our true nature. Breath awareness supplies our blood, organs, and brains with vital oxygen, which helps to increase mental clarity and our power of concentration (more information can be found on page 302). Below are two pranayama techniques:

The Fire Breath

Some people pay to go to oxygen chambers when there is a simple way to get the same benefits for free! This is an energizing breathing exercise that increases the "pure life force," sometimes called *chi* or *kundalini*. It is excellent for reducing Kapha, as it stimulates energy and diminishes feelings of lethargy.

Sit in a comfortable position with your spine straight, imagining the spaces between your vertebrae opening. Concentrate on breathing in and out from your abdomen. Inhale deeply through your nostrils into your abdomen, then pull your abdomen inward – aiming the belly button back to the spine – for a quick exhale through the nostrils. Repeat this 20 times, then take a break, letting the increased oxygen permeate your entire body. Repeat until you do 5 sets of 20. Over time, you can work towards doing this 100 times without a break.

Alternate Nostril Breathing

This breathing exercise is good for all doshas and balances the right and left sides of the body. We often have a dominant side of the brain, either the right brain (considered the female or yin side) or the left brain (considered the male or yang side). (In North America, many people are over stimulated in the left brain.) Alternate nostril breathing helps to then regulate, clear, and balance us, making ourselves much more capable and creative in addressing situations in our lives.

Try this breathing technique if you are having trouble sleeping at night or at any time you want to feel clear, centered, and balanced.

Begin by taking the index finger of the left hand, blocking your right nostril, and inhaling through the left nostril (if you wish to use your right hand simply switch to place the index finger on the left nostril and the thumb on the right). Now block the left nostril with your thumb as you exhale through the right. Inhale through the right nostril then block the right nostril as you exhale through the left. Keep alternating, but do not continue for more than 5 minutes. If you feel light-headed, concentrate on breathing into your low belly.

Aromatherapy

Aromatherapy is the application or inhalation of essential oils to positively affect one's mood or health. Many essential oils have medicinal properties than can calm and heal, and in Ayurveda, they balance and calm the doshas. Allow your own sense of smell to determine which essential oils your body responds to at different times of the day or year; don't be afraid to work intuitively. Essential oils are available at health food stores or shops that sell natural products.

Vata can be balanced with orange, rose, geranium, lavender, cinnamon, clove, and sandalwood as well as other warm, sweet, or sour essential oils.

Pitta can be balanced with mint, lavender, rose, jasmine, gardenia, clary sage, lemon, lemongrass, and vetiver as well as other cool or sweet essential oils.

Kapha can be balanced with eucalyptus, mint, clove, marjoram, camphor, juniper, lemon, orange, basil, bergamot, and sage as well as other uplifting essential oils.

A few drops of any essential oil can be added to water, burned in an essential oil burner, or sprinkled in a room. Add 10 drops of any essential oil to ½ oz (20 ml) of any carrier oil (see note on next page) to use for a massage or add to a warm bath.

In addition, orange peels and cloves can be simmered on a stove to balance Vata and Kapha. Lavender can be sprinkled on a pillow or placed in a bowl (fresh or dry) to balance both Vata and Pitta. Shells or rocks can be sprinkled with any oil and left in a room; these can be refreshed from time to time.

Carrier oils are generally cold-pressed vegetable oils that are used to dilute essential oils for aromatherapy, massages, or baths, and also can be used on their own to soothe your dosha: to reduce Vata, use sesame, castor, or flaxseed oil; to reduce Pitta, use coconut or olive oil; to reduce Kapha, use sweet almond or safflower oil. These oils should always be cold-pressed to retain their vitamins.

Color Therapy

Using the colors of the light spectrum to stimulate the body's own healing process, color therapy balances energy wherever our bodies may be lacking, be it physically, emotionally, spiritually, or mentally. With Ayurveda, you can use different colors according to your dosha.

If you are new to color therapy, have fun experimenting with how colors affect your moods and energy levels. Notice how different colors in nature make you feel: compare gazing on a bright blue ocean to a deep orange sunset; or a dark starry sky or a somber gray morning to a dark green forest. Looking at differently colored paint chips can be another effective way to become more conscious of how color affects you. Once attuned, you can increase your energy, serenity, and sense of well-being as a result of color choices in your clothing, home, or workplace.

Vata can be balanced with white, green, violet, magenta, turquoise, and red.

Pitta can be balanced with white, green, deep ocean blue, violet, magenta, pale pinks, and turquoise. (Avoid strong colors such as red and black.)

Kapha can be balanced with red, orange, and magenta. Turquoise and green are also beneficial.

Here is a list of some colors and their properties:

- Blue cools, soothes, and increases clarity. It calms Vata and Pitta and lifts Kapha.

- Green calms, refreshes, and gives a feeling of being in nature. It harmonizes all doshas and is valued for healing medical conditions such as tumors.

- Magenta helps us to let go of obsessive attachments and the past, and promotes happiness. It is balancing for all doshas.

- Orange is energizing and joyous, increases sexual energy, and strengthens the immune system. It is particularly uplifting for Kapha.

- Red is fiery, passionate, and powerful. It is assertive, courageous, and vital. It aids willpower. It warms Vata, energizes Kapha, and increases Pitta.

- Turquoise is cool, refreshing, and energizing, and is also an anti-inflammatory. It helps get rid of stagnation and reduces fevers. It can be used as a protection from unwanted energies. It benefits all the doshas.

- Violet promotes insight, intuition, and self-love. It is especially beneficial for Vata and Pitta.

Five-Minute Abhyanga Massage

This invigorating Ayurvedic massage strengthens your immune system and increases circulation, leaving you feeling refreshed. This massage takes only a few minutes and can be done anywhere, just ensure it is done at least half an hour before eating. If you have more time, you may add oil to this massage: sesame or almond oil for Vata; cold-pressed olive, coconut, or sunflower oil for Pitta; or corn, mustard, safflower, or almond oil for Kapha.

Start by standing or sitting. Briskly rub the palms of your hands together for 10–20 seconds. Place your left hand over your left ear and right hand over your right ear, then briskly run your hands back and forth over your ears for 10–20 seconds; this touches all the acupressure points, or *nadis*, on the ears that invigorate the entire body. Next, use both palms to lightly wipe or clean the aura around your head using downward movements. Shake your hands as one would flick water off to clear energy. Next, run your palms down the front and back of your body with downward strokes, using circular motions for all major joints (e.g., shoulders, elbows, knees); keep shaking the hands to get rid of old energy.

Grounding Visualization

This tridoshic grounding method will leave you feeling rooted and confident of your true self, rather than feeling under the influence of or bogged down by the world around you.

Stand with your feet parallel and close together with your weight evenly distributed. Push your feet firmly to the ground and imagine you are pulling up the energy of the earth through your feet. Keeping the leg muscles engaged, without locking the knees, stand tall. Let your tailbone drop and tuck under while pulling your belly button inwards to the spine, and feeling a lift in the pubic bone. Feel your upper body lift out of your hipbones, and the spine lengthening upwards, imagining the spaces between your vertebrae widen. Let your shoulders drop down. Continue the upward-lengthening of the spine: imagine the neck vertebrae lengthening upward and widening the base of your skull, then imagine the brain fluids that reside here flowing easily. Visualize any stiffness in the neck dissolving, allowing a clear passage for energy to flow between the mind and body.

Now, with this full body-awareness, imagine pulling in energy from the sun above, like a golden light, through the top of your head, running down through the spine and through the bones of your legs, rooting you deeply to the earth.

With practice, you will be able to do this visualization in a few seconds wherever you are, grounding yourself in who you are while centering yourself in the present moment.

Food Guidelines for Basic Constitutional Types

Reprinted with permission from *The Ayurvedic Cookbook* by Amadea Morningstar with Urmila Desai (Lotus Press, 1990).

NOTE: Fruit and fruit juices are best consumed by themselves for all doshas.

Fruit:

VATA		PITTA		KAPHA	
NO	**YES**	**NO**	**YES**	**NO**	**YES**
Dried Fruits	Sweet Fruits	Sour fruits	Sweet fruits	Sweet & sour	Apples
Apples	Apricots	Apples (sour)	Apples (sweet)	fruits	Apricots
Cranberries	Avocado	Apricots (sour)	Apricots (sweet)	Avocado	Berries
Pears	Bananas	Berries (sour)	Avocado	Bananas	Cherries
Persimmon	All berries	Bananas	Berries (sweet)	Coconut	Cranberries
Pomegranate	Cherries	Cherries (sour)	Coconut	Dates	Figs (dry)
Prunes	Coconut	Cranberries	Dates	Figs (fresh)	Mango
Quince	Dates	Grapefruit	Figs	Grapefruit	Peaches
Watermelon	Figs (fresh)	Grapes (green)	Grapes (sweet)	Grapes*	Pears
	Grapefruit	Kiwi#	Mango	Kiwi*	Persimmon
	Melons (sweet)	Lemons	Melons	Lemons	Pomegranate
	Oranges	Limes (in excess)	Oranges (sweet)	Limes	Prunes
	Papaya	Papaya	Pears	Melons	Quince
	Peaches	Peaches	Pineapples	Oranges	Raisins
	Pineapples	Pineapples	(sweet)	Papaya	Strawberries*
	Plums	(sour)	Plums (sweet)	Pineapples	
	Raisins (soaked)	Persimmon	Pomegranate	Plums	
	Rhubarb	Plums (sour)	Prunes	Rhubarb	
	Soursop	Rhubarb	Quince (sweet)	Soursop	
	Strawberries	Soursop	Raisins	Watermelon	
		Strawberries	Watermelon		

* These foods are OK in moderation.   # These foods are OK occasionally.

Vegetables

VATA		PITTA		KAPHA	
NO	**YES**	**NO**	**YES**	**NO**	**YES**
Frozen, dried, or raw vegetables	Cooked vegetables	Pungent vegetables	Sweet & bitter vegetables	Sweet & juicy vegetables	Raw, pungent & bitter vegetables
Beet greens*	Artichoke	Beets	Artichokes	Artichokes*	Asparagus
Bell peppers	Asparagus	Beet greens	Asparagus	Cucumber	Beets
Broccoli #	Beets	Carrots #	Bell peppers	Olives (black or green)	Beet greens
Brussels sprouts	Carrots	Chili peppers (hot)	Broccoli	Parsnip #	Bell peppers
Burdock root	Cucumber	Daikon #	Brussels sprouts	Potatoes (sweet)	Chili peppers
Cabbage	Daikon	Eggplant #	Burdock root	Pumpkin	Broccoli
Cauliflower	Fenugreek greens*	Fenugreek greens	Cabbage	Rutabagas	Brussel sprouts
Celery	Green beans (well-cooked)	Garlic	Corn (fresh)	Squash (Acorn, Butternut, Spaghetti,* Winter)	Burdock root
Corn (fresh) #	Horseradish #	Horseradish	Cauliflower	Tomatoes	Cabbage
Eggplant	Leeks (cooked)	Kohlrabi #	Chili peppers (mild)	Zucchini	Carrots
Jerusalem artichokes*	Mustard greens	Leeks (cooked) #	Cucumber		Cauliflower
Jicama*	Okra (cooked)	Mustard greens	Celery		Celery
Kohlrabi	Olives (black & green)	Olives (green)	Green beans		Corn (fresh)
Leafy greens*	Onion (cooked)	Onions (raw)	Jerusalem artichoke		Daikon
Lettuce*	Parsnip	Onions (cooked)*	Jicama		Eggplant
Mushrooms	Potato (sweet)	Pumpkin #	Leafy greens (esp. collards and dandelion)		Fenugreek greens
Onions (raw)	Pumpkin	Radish	Lettuce		Garlic
Parsley*	Radish	Spinach #	Mushrooms		Green beans
Peas	Rutabaga	Tomatoes	Okra		Horseradish
Potatoes (white)	Squash (Acorn, Butternut, Scallopini, Summer, Winter, Yellow Crookneck)	Turnip greens	Olives (black)*		Jerusalem artichoke
Spaghetti squash #	Watercress	Turnips	Parsley		Jicama
Spinach*	Zucchini		Parsnip		Kohlrabi
Sprouts*			Peas		Leafy greens
Tomatoes			Potatoes (sweet or white)		Leeks
Turnips			Rutabagas		Lettuce
Turnip greens*			Squash (Acorn, Butternut, Scallopini, Spaghetti, Summer, Winter, Yellow Crookneck)		Mushrooms
			Sprouts		Okra
			Watercress*		Onions
			Zucchini		Parsley
					Peas
					Potatoes (white)
					Radish
					Spinach
					Sprouts
					Squash (Scallopini, Summer, Yellow Crookneck)
					Turnip greens
					Turnips
					Watercress

* These foods are OK in moderation.   # These foods are OK occasionally.

Grains

VATA		PITTA		KAPHA	
NO	**YES**	**NO**	**YES**	**NO**	**YES**
Cold, dry, puffed cereals	Amaranth*	Amaranth#	Barley	Oats (cooked)	Amaranth*
Barley#	Oats (cooked)	Buckwheat	Oats (cooked)	Rice (brown or white)	Barley
Buckwheat	All Rice (including brown rice)	Corn	Rice (basmati or white)	Wheat	Buckwheat
Corn	Wheat	Millet	Rice cakes		Corn
Granola	Wild rice	Oat bran*	Wheat		Granola (low-fat)
Millet		Oat granola	Wheat bran		Millet
Oat bran		Oats (dry)	Wheat granola		Oat bran
Oats (dry)		Quinoa			Oats (dry)
Quinoa		Rice (brown)#			Quinoa
Rice cakes#		Rye			Rice (basmati, small amount with clove or peppercorn)
Rye					Rice cakes#
Wheat bran (in excess)					Rye
					Wheat bran#

Animal Foods

VATA		PITTA		KAPHA	
NO	**YES**	**NO**	**YES**	**NO**	**YES**
Lamb	Beef#	Beef	Chicken or turkey (white meat)	Beef	Chicken or turkey (dark meat)
Pork	Chicken or turkey (white meat)	Duck	Egg whites	Duck	Eggs (not fried or scrambled with fat)
Rabbit	Duck	Egg yolks	Fish (freshwater)*	Fish (freshwater)#	Rabbit
Venison	Duck eggs	Lamb	Rabbit	Lamb	
	Eggs	Pork	Shrimp*	Pork	
	Fish (freshwater)	Seafood		Seafood	
	Seafood	Venison		Shrimp	
	Shrimp			Venison#	

* These foods are OK in moderation.   # These foods are OK occasionally.

Legumes

VATA		PITTA		KAPHA	
NO	YES	NO	YES	NO	YES
Black beans	Aduki beans*	Black lentils	Aduki beans	Black lentils	Aduki beans
Black-eyed peas	Black lentils*	(Urad dal)	Black beans	(Urad dal)	Black beans
Brown or green	(Urad dal)	Red (Masoor)	Black-eyed peas	Brown or green	Black-eyed peas
lentils	Mung beans*	lentils	Brown or green	lentils	Channa dal
Channa dal	Red (Masoor)	Tur dal	lentils	Kidney beans	Chickpeas
Chickpeas	lentils*		Channa dal	Mung beans*	(Garbanzo
(Garbanzo	Soy cheese*		Chickpeas	Soy beans	beans)
beans)	Soy milk (liquid)*		(Garbanzo	Soy milk (cold)	Lima beans
Kala channa*	Tepery beans*		beans)	Soy cheese	Kala channa
Kidney beans	Tofu*		Kala channa	Soy flour	Navy beans
Lima beans	Tur dal*		Kidney beans	Soy powder	Pinto beans
Navy beans			Lima beans	Tempeh	Red (Masoor)
Pinto beans			Mung beans	Tofu (cold)	lentils
Soy beans			Navy beans		Soy milk (hot)*
Soy flour			Pinto beans		Split peas
Soy powder			Soy beans		Tepery beans
Split peas			Soy cheese		Tofu (hot)*
Tempeh			Soy flour*		Tur dal
White beans			Soy milk (liquid)		White beans
			Soy powder *		
			Split peas		
			Tempeh		
			Tepery beans		
			Tofu		
			White beans		

Nuts

VATA		PITTA		KAPHA	
NO	YES	NO	YES	NO	YES
	Almonds*	Almonds		Almonds	
	Brazil nuts*	Brazil nuts		Brazil nuts	
	Cashews*	Cashews		Cashews	
	Coconut*	Hazelnuts		Coconut	
	Hazelnuts*	Macadamia nuts		Hazelnuts	
	Macadamia nuts*	Peanuts		Macademia nuts	
	Peanuts#	Pecans		Peanuts	
	Pecans*	Pine Nuts		Pecans	
	Pine nuts*	Pistachios		Pine nuts	
	Pistachios*	Walnuts (Black		Pistachios	
	Walnuts (Black*	or English)		Walnuts (Black	
	or English*)			or English)	

* These foods are OK in moderation.   # These foods are OK occasionally.

Seeds

VATA				PITTA				KAPHA	
NO	YES			NO	YES			NO	YES
Psyllium#	Chia Flax Sesame Pumpkin Sunflower			Chia Flax Sesame	Psyllium Pumpkin* Sunflower			Psyllium Sesame	Chia Flax* Pumpkin* Sunflower*

Sweeteners

VATA		PITTA		KAPHA	
NO	YES	NO	YES	NO	YES
White sugar	Barley malt syrup Brown rice syrup Fructose Fruit juice concentrates Honey Jaggery (gur) Maple syrup Molasses Sucanat Sugar cane juice	Honey* Jaggery (gur) Molasses	Barley malt syrup Brown rice syrup Maple syrup Fruit juice concentrates Fructose Sucanat* Sugar cane juice White sugar*	Barley malt syrup Brown rice syrup Fructose Jaggery (gur) Maple syrup (in excess) Molasses Sucanat Sugar cane juice White sugar	Raw honey Fruit juice concentrates (esp. apple and pear)

* These foods are OK in moderation.   # These foods are OK occasionally.

Condiments

VATA		PITTA		KAPHA	
NO	YES	NO	YES	NO	YES
Chili peppers*	Black pepper*	Black sesame	Black pepper*	Black sesame	Black pepper
Ginger (dry)*	Black sesame	seeds	Cilantro leaves	seeds	Chili peppers
Ketchup	seeds	Cheese (grated)	(fresh)	Cheese (grated)	Cilantro leaves
Onion (raw)	Coconut	Chili peppers	Coconut	Coconut	(fresh)
Sprouts*	Cilantro leaves*	Daikon*	Cottage cheese	Cottage cheese*	Daikon
	(fresh)	Garlic	Dulse	Dulse	Garlic
	Cottage cheese	Ginger	(well-rinsed)	(well-rinsed)*	Ghee*
	Cheese (grated)	Gomasio	Ghee	Hijiki*	Ginger (esp. dry)
	Daikon	Horseradish	Hijiki (well-	Kelp	Horseradish
	Dulse	Kelp	rinsed)	Ketchup	Lettuce
	Garlic	Ketchup	Kombu	Kombu*	Mint leaves
	Ghee	Mustard	Lettuce	Lemon	Mustard
	Ginger (fresh)	Lemon	Mango chutney	Lime	Onions
	Gomasio	Lime	Mint leaves	Lime pickle	Radish
	Hijiki	Lime pickle	Sprouts	Mango chutney	Sprouts
	Horseradish	Mango pickle		Mango pickles	
	Kelp	Mayonnaise		Mayonnaise	
	Kombu	Onions		Papaya chutney	
	Lemon	(esp. raw)		Pickles	
	Lettuce*	Papaya chutney		Salt	
	Lime	Pickles		Seaweeds	
	Lime pickle	Radish		(well-rinsed)*	
	Mango chutney	Salt (in excess)		Sesame seeds	
	Mango pickle	Seaweed,		Soy sauce	
	Mayonnaise	unrinsed		Tamari	
	Mint leaves*	(in excess)		Yogurt	
	Mustard	Sesame seeds			
	Onion (cooked)	Soy sauce			
	Papaya chutney	Tamari*			
	Pickles	Yogurt			
	Radish	(undiluted)			
	Salt				
	Seaweeds				
	Sesame seeds				
	Soy sauce				
	Tamari				
	Yogurt				

* These foods are OK in moderation.   # These foods are OK occasionally.

Spices

VATA		PITTA		KAPHA	
NO	YES	NO	YES	NO	YES
Neem leaves*	Ajwan	Ajwan	Basil leaves	Almond extract*	Ajwan
	Allspice	Allspice	(fresh)*	Amchoor	Allspice
	Almond extract	Almond extract*	Black pepper*	Tamarind	Anise
	Amchoor	Amchoor	Cardamom*		Asafoetida (hing)
	Anise	Anise	Cinnamon*		Basil
	Asafoetida (hing)	Asafoetida (hing)	Coriander		Bay leaf
	Basil	Basil	Cumin		Black pepper
	Bay leaf	Bay leaf	Dill		Caraway
	Black pepper	Caraway*	Fennel		Cardamom
	Caraway	Cayenne	Mint		Cayenne
	Cardamom	Cloves	Neem leaves		Cinnamon
	Cayenne*	Fenugreek	Orange peel*		Cloves
	Cinnamon	Garlic (esp. raw)	Parsley*		Coriander
	Cloves	Ginger	Peppermint		Cumin
	Coriander	Horseradish	Rose water		Dill
	Cumin	Mace	Saffron		Fennel*
	Dill	Marjoram	Spearmint		Fenugreek
	Fennel	Mustard seeds	Turmeric		Garlic
	Fenugreek*	Nutmeg	Vanilla*		Ginger (esp. dry)
	Garlic	Onion (esp. raw)	Wintergreen		Horseradish
	Ginger	Oregano			Mace
	Horseradish*	Paprika			Marjoram
	Marjoram	Pippali			Mint
	Mint	Poppy seeds*			Mustard seeds
	Mustard seeds	Rosemary			Neem leaves
	Nutmeg	Sage			Nutmeg
	Onion (cooked)	Savory			Onion
	Orange peel	Star anise			Orange peel
	Oregano	Tarmarind			Oregano
	Paprika	Tarragon*			Paprika
	Parsley	Thyme			Parsley
	Peppermint				Peppermint
	Pippali				Pippali
	Poppy seeds				Poppy seeds
	Rosemary				Rosemary
	Rose water				Rose water
	Saffron				Saffron
	Sage				Sage
	Savory				Savory
	Spearmint				Spearmint
	Star anise				Star anise
	Tamarind				Tarragon
	Tarragon				Thyme
	Thyme				Turmeric
	Turmeric				Vanilla*
	Vanilla				Wintergreen
	Wintergreen				

Dairy

VATA		PITTA		KAPHA	
NO	**YES**	**NO**	**YES**	**NO**	**YES**
Goat's milk (powdered)	All dairy*	Butter (salted)	Butter (unsalted)	Butter	Ghee
		Buttermilk (commercial)	Cheese (mild and soft)	Cheese (all kinds)	Milk (goat's)
		Cheese (hard or Feta)	Cottage cheese	Buttermilk (commercial)	Yogurt (diluted, 1:4pts or more with water)
		Sour cream	Ghee	Ice cream	
		Yogurt	Ice cream	Milk (cow's)	
			Milk (cow's or goat's)	Sour cream	
			Yogurt (diluted, 1:2–3 pts water)	Yogurt (undiluted)	

Oils

VATA		PITTA		KAPHA	
NO	**YES**	**NO**	**YES**	**NO**	**YES**
	All oils (esp. sesame)	Almond	Avocado*	Apricot	In very small amounts:
		Apricot	Coconut*	Avocado	Almond
		Corn	Olive*	Coconut	Corn
		Safflower	Sesame*	Olive	Sunflower
		Sesame	Sunflower*	Safflower	
			Soy walnut*	Sesame	
				Soy	
				Walnut	

* These foods are OK in moderation.   # These foods are OK occasionally.

Index